ACRL Publications in Librarianship no. 46

Richard Garnett

The Scholar as Librarian

BARBARA McCRIMMON

American Library Association
Chicago and London 1989

*Association of College and Research Libraries
Publications in Librarianship Committee*

Arthur P. Young, Chair
James A. Benson
Jonathan Lindsay
Charles Osburn
Beth J. Shapiro
Julie A. Carroll Virgo
Richard H. Werking

The paper used in this publication meets the minimum requirements of American National Standard for Information Sciences--Permanence of Paper for Printed Library Materials, ANSI Z39.48-1984. ∞

Library of Congress Cataloging in Publication Data

McCrimmon, Barbara.
   Richard Garnett, the scholar as librarian / by Barbara McCrimmon.
     p. cm. — (ACRL publications in librarianship ; no. 46)
   Bibliography: p.
   ISBN: 0-8389-0508-0 (alk. paper)
   1. Garnett, Richard, 1835–1906. 2. Librarians—Great Britain—Biography. 3. Literary historians—Great Britain—Biography. 4. London (England)—Intellectual life—19th century. 5. British Library. Dept. of Printed Books—History. I. Title. II. Series.
   Z674.A75 no. 46
   [Z720.G25]
   020'.5 s—dc19
   [020'.92'4]   89-297
   [B]

Copyright © 1989 by the American Library Association. All rights reserved except those which may be granted by Sections 107 and 108 of the Copyright Revision Act of 1976.
Printed in the United States of America.

93 92 91 90 89 6 5 4 3 2 1

Richard Garnett

Dr. Richard Garnett, about 1890 (Hilton Hall Archive)

Contents

Preface	vii
Key to Abbreviations	xii
1. Richard Garnett the Elder, 1789–1850	1
2. Young Man in London, 1851–1854	13
3. Journalist, 1855–1857	18
4. Author and Editor, 1858–1859	26
5. Shelley Scholar, 1860–1861	35
6. Year of Fate, 1862	43
7. Married Life, 1863–1867	51
8. New Family, New Friends, 1868–1870	56
9. Much Ado about Shelley, 1871–1874	64
10. Portrait Interlude	72
11. Assistant Keeper of Printed Books, 1875–1878	78
12. Dr. Richard Garnett, 1879–1884	87
13. More Shelley, 1885–1887	98
14. The Twilight of the Gods, 1888–1889	106
15. Keeper of Printed Books, 1890–1892	115
16. Poems and Problems, 1893–1894	122
17. Richard Garnett, C.B., LL.D., 1895	128
18. The Old Order Changeth, 1896–1898	135
19. A New Century, 1899–1900	141
20. Journeys and Publications, 1901–1902	147
21. An Ending and a Beginning, 1903–1905	152
22. Finale, 1906	162
Notes	171
Appendix: Works of Richard Garnett	197
Index	201

Preface

The life of Richard Garnett spanned the entire Victorian period, and from mid-century he was a part of the British literary, as well as library, scene. He was a thorough Victorian in his attitudes and values, having been brought up with the classics and German imaginative literature. Like many other intelligent persons of the era, he was self-educated, and learned how to write from reading good books. He wrote poetry, epigrams, and short stories based on earlier models, yet with his own strongly individual stamp. He got a start in journalism through his Uncle Jeremiah Garnett, editor of the *Manchester Guardian*, and he contributed thousands of words of literary criticism during his lifetime. Of this oeuvre, the *Times*, in his obituary, said he had been able to "bring what is highest in literature to the understanding of common people without in any way impairing the dignity of his subject. Nor did he let dignity stand in the way of humanity—the sly wink of humour, or play on words, often enlivened his discourse unexpectedly."[1] His sense of comedy, along with a gentle kindliness inherited from his father, made him universally beloved. One of his friends commented, "The memory of him will warm me until my end."[2]

In addition to his own writing, Garnett was intensely interested in the writing of others. He was so conversant with world literature, and with the contents of the British Museum library, of which he was an integral part for nearly fifty years, that in his maturity he was one of the most influential persons in the world of letters. He was looked to throughout the British Empire, in Europe, and in the United States as a source of information and assistance for any literary project, and he gave freely of his time and expertise. He was acquainted with dozens of writers in Britain and abroad; indeed, his correspondence reads like a literary history of the Victorian period, from the Pre-Raphaelites to the Decadents.

He was also the earliest of Shelley scholars. He made friends with the son and daughter-in-law of Percy Bysshe Shelley, and thus secured the privilege of studying their family papers. He was responsible for most of the discoveries that were made amongst these manuscripts during the nineteenth century, and he helped restore Shelley's reputation, which was at its nadir when Garnett began to admire his poetry. Although he produced no major work on Shelley, he published a number of articles on the poet and edited selections from both his poetry and his prose.

A contributor of many essays to magazines and articles for two editions of the *Encyclopaedia Britannica*, Garnett also wrote over a hundred biographical sketches for the *Dictionary of National Biography* and other such compilations, and full-length biographies of Emerson, Carlyle, and Coleridge. He edited or wrote introductions for numerous literary works: his name appears on the title pages of more than sixty books, and he has been given twenty-seven entries in the *Cambridge Bibliography of English Literature*. He published seven volumes of poetry and translated other poets' verse from several languages. His stories in *The Twilight of the Gods* are recognized as classics of English satire.

Yet his greatest reputation was made in the library, where his contributions to the profession gained him world-wide fame. When Garnett's father entered the British Museum as an assistant keeper, the "library departments," as the departments of printed books and manuscripts were known, dominated the interest of the trustees, and the director of the entire institution was called the "principal librarian." The Department of Natural History harbored specimens of flora and fauna brought back by British explorers from around the world, while the Department of Antiquities contained the marbles from the Parthenon in Athens, procured from the Turks by Lord Elgin, along with other artifacts from excavations in Greece, Italy, and the Middle East, as well as the trilingual Rosetta Stone, which had unlocked the secret of Egyptian hieroglyphics. Priceless manuscripts that had been scattered when Henry VIII suppressed the monasteries of England were collected by Robert Cotton and the first and second earls of Oxford, and these were added to the books and curios of Sir Hans Sloane to be purchased by the government in 1753. Subsequently enlarged by the library of George III, the collections were stored in an old mansion on Great Russell Street. This building was replaced during the 1840s by a grand, classical structure which contained more space, yet within a few decades it was full to overflowing. The book stock was increased enormously in both size and quality during the tenure of the two Garnetts by the enterprise of the keeper of printed books, later principal librarian, Antonio Panizzi, whose far-sighted administration was seen as a model for all libraries in its stress on freely providing scholars with all they needed for research.

While striving to make the British Museum library the best in the world in the breadth of its collections, Panizzi directed an equal effort toward compiling a new, more thorough, and more correct catalogue of the books than then existed. It was done in manuscript, for use only in the Reading Room, a place restricted to respectable readers with admission tickets. The books did not circulate outside the building.

Both Garnetts participated in the work on the catalogue, but Richard the younger, after his first years at the Museum, was assigned to classify the newly acquired books for arrangement on the shelves, and after that he was given charge of the distribution of books to readers in the Reading Room, a task at which he excelled. He became famous for his wide literary knowledge, stored in a remarkable memory and generously recalled and shared with others. As he rose through the ranks he was given more and more responsibility, and as assistant keeper of printed books he was instrumental in initiating the program of printing the entries for the catalogue in order to save much of the room taken up by the hundreds of volumes of the manuscript catalogue. Once they were in print, the catalogue entries could be distributed wherever they were wanted, and they soon constituted an invaluable bibliographical tool for librarians everywhere.

Garnett also wrote many essays and addresses on librarianship which were helpful to his colleagues. As keeper of printed books from 1890 to 1899 he was one of the leaders of his profession, and when he retired, it was written of him, "In the year 1899, by the unanimous judgment alike of his fellow-librarians and of the literary public to whose needs they minister, Dr. Garnett stands out as the most prominent representative of the library world."[3]

It was a combination of qualities that made Garnett such a paragon. His keen interest in the power of verbal expression and his ability to use the English language with force and grace were complemented by the energy and inventiveness in regard to his daily occupation that made him stand out among his peers. At the same time, in these ways he exemplified a generation of librarians who had these qualities in varying degrees and who were dedicated to the enlightenment and mental enrichment of their contemporaries through books. Their efforts to increase the accessibility of printed matter resulted in the creation of the profession of librarianship, where there had been only sinecures and protectiveness before.

These individuals, widely read and with highly developed literary tastes, who chose librarianship as a career, were part of a much larger movement toward integrating groups into which society had always been divided. A common literary heritage was one of the most important parts of this objective; another was the broadening of the literary horizon to include notable works by authors from every part of the world, and in this the library played a crucial role. Garnett devoted his strong mind to promoting these efforts, with the result that he was able to contribute significantly to the progress of both literature and librarianship.

Such a man's professional life holds much of interest, but many of the details of his work at the British Museum have been treated elsewhere,[4] and since his literary life is less well-known today, an account of it here can fill out what has previously been published about him. This aspect of his career is abundantly documented in the archives maintained by his descendants; in the British Library, Department of Manuscripts, and Department of Printed Books Archives; and in the Richard Garnett Papers in the Harry Ransom Humanities Research Center at the University of Texas at Austin. This material has been the chief source for the facts in this biography, and it has been used with the permission and the help of the persons in charge of the repositories.

My work could not have been accomplished without the interest and assistance of three members of the Garnett family: Patrick Garnett and Richard Garnett, great-grandsons, and the late Mrs. Anne Lee Michell, granddaughter of Dr. Garnett. All have been generous with time, advice, and hospitality, and Richard Garnett has given expert editorial comment on the typescript. Mrs. Lee Michell's unpublished edition of a large portion of her aunt Olive Garnett's diary, a copy of which is available to scholars in the Harry Ransom Humanities Research Center, has been a most revealing source, while the original diary, written in several small notebooks, has been quoted throughout this text.[5] My investigations in the archive maintained by Richard Garnett at Hilton Hall, Cambridgeshire, were facilitated by the expert arrangement of the papers by Oliver Garnett. Other relatives of Dr. Garnett who aided my study were Anthony, Michael, Robert, John, and Ted Garnett; the late Helen Garnett; the late Rev. Garnett Jones and Mrs. Jones; Veronica Syme Condon; Harriette Tennant and the late Celia Tennant Luck; Enid Goodall; and Elwy Horsfall. Important information has come to me through many persons, chiefly Paul Wood and Christine Dean of the Otley Museum and Mr. and Mrs. Donald Knight in Yorkshire; the late Prof. Owen Ashmore, Mary Brigg, and the Holliday sisters in Lancashire; Shirley Edrich, J. A. Edwards, Timothy Egan, Mr. and Mrs. W. Forster, Edwin Hawkins, Barry C. Johnson, Gordon Phillips, C. H. H. Owen, R. J. Roberts, and His Honour Judge Eric Stockdale in southern England; in Canada, George Brandak and Prof. William E. Fredeman; in Australia, Claude Prance; and in the United States, Herbert Cahoon, P. W. Filby, Prof. and Mrs. George M. Harper, Prof. William V. Jackson, Dr. Sherry Levy-Reiner, Robert McCown, F. O. Mattson, R. Russell Maylone, Prof. Thomas C. Moser, and Robert Yampolsky.

The libraries that have given access, service, and permission to quote from their holdings, in addition to those previously mentioned, are the Henry W. and Albert A. Berg Collection of the New York Public Library, Astor, Lenox, and Tilden Foundations; the Carl H. Pforzheimer Library; the University of British Columbia Library; and the University of Reading Library. At the Robert Manning Strozier Library of the Florida State University, Director Charles Miller and his staff have provided constant support for my undertaking.

Permission to quote from published and unpublished writings of the Garnett family has been given by Patrick and Richard Garnett and Anne Lee Michell; from those of Sir Percy and Lady Shelley and Florence Scarlett by Lord

Abinger; from those of William Michael Rossetti by Mrs. Imogen Dennis; from those of Sir Edmund Gosse by Miss Jennifer Gosse; from one of Coventry Patmore by Michael Patmore; from one of E. W. B. Nicholson by Edmund Akenhead; and from his doctoral dissertation on the letters about Shelley in the Richard Garnett Papers at the University of Texas at Austin, by Prof. William R. Thurman, Jr. F. J. Hill, formerly of the British Library, has permitted me to use his notes for a projected biography of Richard Garnett, which are now among the Garnett Papers in Austin.

Key to Abbreviations

ALM   In the possession of Anne Lee Michell
BL   In the British Library, Department of Manuscripts
HH   In the Hilton Hall archive
HRHRC In the Richard Garnett Papers at the Harry Ransom Humanities Research Center, the University of Texas at Austin
PG   In the possession of Patrick Garnett
UBC   In the Angeli-Dennis Papers at the University of British Columbia Library

* An asterisk by a footnote number in the text indicates a substantive, rather than a merely referential, note.

Chapter 1

Richard Garnett the Elder, 1789–1850

The surname Garnett is common in the North of England; the presumption is that it came with William the Conqueror as *de Gernet* and that an early bearer of it acquired land in Westmoreland, his descendants moving into surrounding areas.[1]* The family with which we are concerned can be traced to Bingley and Otley in West Yorkshire from the sixteenth century. Through records and wills a solid line can be drawn from a first Richard of Bingley, who married Margaret Chippindale, through their son, John, who leased rights to dig coal and smelt iron on Baildon Moor in 1653, and his son, Richard, to a third Richard, who married Lydia Hudson of Eldwick Hall and bought property around Baildon in 1691. His son Richard (1691–1757) married Sarah Butler, daughter of Jeremiah Butler, an emigrant from Kilkenny in Ireland, and this lady brought to the family a lasting men's name, for there have been Jeremiahs among the Garnetts ever since.

The first of these Jeremiah Garnetts lived from 1731 to 1815. He was a tallow chandler of Otley, and in 1757 he married Martha Flesher. In 1770 he bought a share in a mill on the river Wharfe where paper was made, and by 1786 he was in sole control of the papermaking operation, turning out pasteboard, press paper, and wrapping paper. Over time the mill advanced to fancy glazed papers, and it provided a comfortable living for the family for generations.

Jeremiah and Martha's second daughter, Sarah, born in 1762, married a member of a wealthy industrial family of Yorkshire, Timothy Horsfall, who had a woollen mill at a place called Goitstock, not far from Otley. In 1798 he heard of a cotton-spinning mill for sale in Lancashire, and he sent his nephew, William Horsfall, and Sarah's brother Jeremiah, born in 1775, to investigate the mill, which lay on the bank of the river Ribble at a village named Low Moor, about a mile north of Clitheroe. The purchase was recommended and soon the mill began operation as Garnett and Horsfalls, with the two young men in charge and several of the Horsfall family, along with old Jeremiah

1

Garnett of Otley, as partners. By 1861 the enterprise was profitable enough to allow the Garnetts to buy out the Horsfalls and, eventually, to acquire a fine house facing the river, called Waddow Hall, which was the site of several grand reunions of the clan.

In 1795 Jeremiah of Otley had a stroke and his eldest son, William (1760–1832), took over management of the paper mill. William and his wife, Mary Rhodes, were both considered to be unusually intelligent, and of their eleven children, four had outstanding careers. Their fifth son, Thomas, born in 1799, became manager of the Low Moor mill in 1824, and his sons, William and James, succeeded him, with James's sons, Tom, Newstead, and William, following into the twentieth century. The fourth son of William and Mary was Peter, born in 1795, and he took over the Otley mill, renaming it P. Garnett & Son, the name it bears today, although no Garnett now has any connection with it. His son, Jeremiah, and grandson, Harry, ran the mill after Peter, and it was sold in 1935. All these men were community leaders as well as benevolent entrepreneurs. The first and third sons of William and Mary had literary careers—Jeremiah, born in 1793, became editor and part-proprietor of the *Manchester Guardian*; the eldest son, Richard, born in 1789, became a distinguished scholar and assistant keeper of printed books at the British Museum.

This Richard was a precocious child with a flair for languages, leading his parents to think he might have a future in international trade. Therefore, they sent him to Leeds, thirteen miles from Otley, to study French and Italian with a Swiss instructor. In 1803, however, when England declared war on Napoleonic France, the opportunity for foreign travel vanished, and fourteen-year-old Richard returned to Otley and went to work at the paper mill with his father. There he remained for eight years, wasting his best talents. He spent his spare time studying languages, and in 1811 he secured a position as second-master of a school in Southwell, Nottinghamshire. This humble entry into the white-collar world was the first for the Otley Garnetts, and Richard was not insensible to the rise in his estate. Yet his acquaintances in Southwell at first were few, and his satisfaction with his work decreased as time went on. He found relief for some of his loneliness and frustration in writing poems, mostly about love and based on classical examples. Finally, he began to study theology, Greek, and Hebrew, with the intention of seeking a career in the church.

It was necessary for a candidate for ordination to obtain the promise of a curacy before taking the examination, and Richard was able to secure such a "title" to a church in Hutton Rudby, Cleveland. He was examined in York by the archbishop's chaplain, who pronounced him outstanding in scholarship. He was appointed deacon and went directly to assume his duties. After two years, during which he continued his leisure-time studies, he returned to York and was ordained a priest. This advance in his profession allowed him to move to Blackburn, Lancashire, as a curate in charge of a church in the hamlet of Tockholes, about three miles south of the city. At the same time he was made second-master of the Blackburn grammar school, thus combining his two vocations most agreeably. He was also situated near to his Uncle Jeremiah and brother Thomas in Low Moor, Clitheroe, and to his brother Jeremiah in Manchester. In the neighboring town of Whalley lived a young man about to take orders who became one of Richard's best friends—S. J. Allen, an amanuensis and research assistant to the intellectual vicar of Whalley.

In 1822 Garnett felt financially able to take a wife. He returned to Southwell to marry Margaret Heathcote, daughter of the Reverend Godfrey Heathcote of the cathedral there. Soon afterward he became acquainted with Robert Southey, the poet laureate, with whom he had some common interests, one of them the threat seemingly posed by the removal of the disabilities of the Catholics in Britain. With Southey's encouragement, Garnett wrote several letters on the subject which were published in the *Protestant Guardian*, their chief thrust being the fragility of the evidence for the miracles attributed to Catholic saints.

On 10 April 1826 Southey gave Garnett an introduction to a friend in London, in which he said:

> ... Mr. Garnett ... is ... a very remarkable person. He did not begin to learn Greek till he was twenty, and he is now, I believe, acquainted with all the European languages of Latin or Teutonic origin, and with sundry Oriental ones. I do not know any man who has read so much which you would not expect him to have read. ... The Bishop of Chester knows him, and I hope will give him some small preferment, on which he may have leisure for turning his rare acquirements to good use.[2*]

Garxnett *did* receive a favor from the bishop of Chester, Charles Blomfield, who examined him and proclaimed him worthy of advancement to a living. He was presented to the incumbency of Tockholes, and in July of 1826 he and Margaret moved there. His many friends in Blackburn presented him with farewell messages in which they praised him highly.

On 7 November 1827 a little girl was born to the Garnetts, but by this time Margaret had advanced tuberculosis and within a year she was dead. The child followed her to the grave in January of 1829. Garnett was devastated. He felt he must leave the Blackburn area, and the Heathcotes came to his rescue through one of their relatives, Dr. Woodhouse, dean of Lichfield, who helped him secure an appointment as priest-vicar in the cathedral there. Garnett resigned from Tockholes and was installed at Lichfield on 30 May 1829 as a minor canon. In that year he began to contribute articles for the *Encyclopaedia Metropolitana*, which was being edited in London. One of these was on the fourth-century church, early Christianity being one of his specialties. Other articles were on subjects in natural history and in education.

To further occupy his mind, he turned from the Catholic controversy to philology, which his talent for languages made particularly congenial to him, and he took occasion to write to authors whose work he admired—for example, John Mitchell Kemble and Hensleigh Wedgwood, who were investigating English philology—and also to foreign scholars to whom they introduced him. In this way he built up an international correspondence with philologists, while his own opinions and judgments grew in assurance.

In 1832 or 1833 he met Jane Rayne Wreaks. Her father, John Wreaks, was a former master cutler of Sheffield, whose financial reverses had forced him to retire to Bingley, where his three daughters kept a school. Rayne was friendly with the wife of Thomas Horsfall, the sixth son of Timothy and Sarah Garnett Horsfall, who lived in nearby Burley-in-Wharfedale, and it was probably there that she and Richard met. A common interest in education was only one of the attractions the widower and the spinster had for each other, and on 15 May 1834 they were married. Their first son, Richard, was born on 27 February 1835 in a substantial brick house at the corner of Beacon Street and Gaia Lane in Lichfield, a short distance from the cathedral.

In late March there came a letter from John Gibson Lockhart, editor of the *Quarterly Review*, to acknowledge the receipt, through the agency of Bishop Blomfield, of a proposal by Garnett for a series of articles on English philology. This was a fairly new field, in which little had been published. The first of the articles appeared in the September 1835 issue of the *Quarterly*. It was entitled "English Lexicography" and it compared three dictionaries: Dr. Johnson's, as revised by H. J. Todd and published in 1818; Noah Webster's, published in New York in 1828 and in England in 1832; and Charles Richardson's *New Dictionary* of 1835. Garnett, who had contemplated revising Johnson's work, was critical of all three dictionaries and gave numerous examples of ill-considered statements and attributions, according to his view. Of this article his son Richard later wrote: "The sensation it occasioned in learned circles was very great, and he was not long without gratifying proof of the attention it excited on the Continent."[3] Another of Garnett's new epistolary acquaintances was Sir Frederic Madden of the Department of Manuscripts at the British Museum, who was editing ancient British literature and was interested in the historical development of the English language.

On 30 January 1836 Garnett wrote to his sister, Anne Beanlands, that his eleven-month-old son Richard was "a fine stout boy" (probably meaning *sturdy*), but was not yet walking or talking [HRHRC]. On 28 July Rayne was delivered of a second son, William John, who was declared to be "stouter than Richard," though as he grew up he was never so strong in health as his older brother. In announcing the birth to Anne, the Reverend Richard also told of a new development in his career: on 25 June the dean and chapter of Lichfield had presented him to the vicarage of Chebsey, a village between

Lichfield and Stafford. The living carried £250 a year, which was a comfortable amount, but the place was comparatively isolated, and he soon began to wish for more intellectual company.

During 1835 and 1836 a select committee of the House of Commons, in response to complaints, had held hearings on the administration of the British Museum, and on 14 June 1836 it issued a report. One of its recommendations was that staff be required to give up any outside positions which might conflict in any way with their Museum duties. This meant that the clergymen among them who had livings would have to choose between their two incomes. The Reverend H. H. Baber, keeper of printed books, decided that if the plan were implemented by the trustees, he would retire to his church in Cambridgeshire. Hearing of this possibility, Garnett considered his own chances of filling Baber's post, or a subordinate one, if Baber were succeeded by another member of the department. He went to London at the beginning of June and called at the Museum to talk about Old English with Madden and to consult the catalogues. He received encouragement to apply for Baber's position from some of his acquaintances; indeed, it has been said that his name was "freely canvassed" for three months.[4] A letter of 25 August 1836 confirms that this was the case. Writing to his wife, who was visiting relatives, he said:

> I have heard nothing direct from the Museum yet, but I have seen the regulations lately entered into which seem to render the inferior situations much less desirable than they formerly were. In future the second librarians are only to have £400 a year, *without any allowance for a house*, so that considering the expense of living in London, Chebsey would be the better place of the two. If I had known this sooner I might have saved myself and my friends a good deal of trouble. [HH]

Nevertheless, the attractions of London were brought home to him by the letters he received from Madden, who was generous in sharing the latest information about literary and philological matters. The two men agreed that a popular history of English poetry would be a valuable contribution to literature, and Garnett considered ways of compiling one.

The second of his *Quarterly Review* articles had appeared in the issue for February 1836. Entitled "English Dialects," it was based on a consideration of some regional glossaries recently published, and Madden asked if he might identify the author in print, since *Quarterly Review* articles were unsigned. The third article, which came out in September 1836, was a review of a work dealing with the derivation of the Celtic languages from Sanskrit. The erudition displayed in these articles was as extraordinary as that of the first.

In March of 1837 the suggestion of the parliamentary investigating committee, banning the holding of two offices concurrently, was adopted by the trustees of the British Museum. Baber resigned and a contest began for his place. The man in line for it was the assistant keeper, Henry Francis Cary, but Garnett had heard, in January, that Cary was thinking of resigning, and he wrote to Madden on 4 February, "If there should thus happen to be a vacancy in your body—I shall feel much obliged by your giving me early intimation of it—as I might be induced to offer myself as a candidate. I have a little interest with several of the Trustees—and should be glad on many accounts to spend ten or a dozen years among the literary stores of the Museum" [HH].

Madden replied on 4 April that Baber would be retiring at mid-summer, and that even if Cary should succeed him, there would be at least one vacancy to be filled. Garnett lost no time in soliciting support from Lockhart of the *Quarterly*, from the bishop of Lichfield, and from John Parker, a Yorkshire Whig of Lincoln's Inn, later to become the member of Parliament for Sheffield.

Nothing further was heard on the matter, however, for several months. When Antonio Panizzi, the most energetic of the assistants in the Department of Printed Books, was chosen to succeed Baber as keeper, Cary decided that he wanted the position and made a hue and cry about being slighted, while there was resentment among the other people at the Museum at the appointment of an Italian, however well qualified, to preside over a large section of a British national institution. Madden, who had been promoted to the keepership of the Department of Manuscripts, was furious over Panizzi's promotion and became his most bitter enemy within the Museum. Garnett had almost given up hope of attaining the assistant keepership when, in mid-January 1838, he received from the archbishop of Canterbury, the chief of the three principal trustees, a notice of the resignation of Cary and an offer of his place. Garnett quickly returned his acceptance. The archbishop then reminded him of the regulation that "no church preferment can be held with an office at the Museum" [HH]. Garnett requested that he be allowed to hold his living until Michaelmas (29 September), and this favor was granted.

Early in March 1838 Garnett was notified that his appointment was official, and he went to London to make arrangements. He found a house for his family at 22 Mabledon Place, Burton Crescent, a pleasant neighborhood just off the Euston Road in the parish of St. Pancras. The family moved there early in April, and on 16 April Garnett appeared at the British Museum without Panizzi's having been told to expect him. To the new keeper, the presence and personality of his chief assistant were very important, and he might well have resented the appointment of a stranger without his knowledge. Yet Garnett proved to be more congenial than Cary had been, and the two men worked together harmoniously throughout their relationship.

During Garnett's first year in the Museum, however, he played a part in a confrontation between his superior and the trustees, when a minor incident in the daily routine was exaggerated by Panizzi's opponents into an occasion for suspicion and censure. The main occupation of the department was the revision of the general catalogue of printed books, on order of the trustees, and the entire staff was involved in the project. Panizzi had directed all the cataloguers to consult him if they had a question about a form of entry. Garnett came upon an anonymous work with a title in which no word stood out as the best one to place first in the catalogue. He went to Panizzi and was told to enter the work under the first significant word in the title. This was the practice of the noted Italian cataloguer Audiffredi, but was not that of the Museum previously. When Panizzi's dictum reached those who feared he intended to revolutionize standard procedures, the library subcommittee of the trustees was induced to investigate. Garnett had to testify, Panizzi had to defend both himself and Garnett, and the whole affair was troublesome.[5]* Panizzi defended Garnett again in 1849, when John Payne Collier, in testimony before the Royal Commission on the British Museum, accused Garnett of not being "competent to his duty," in mistaking an edition of a work by the obscure Renaissance poet Richard Barnfield. Panizzi replied that Garnett knew "of English literature as much as Mr. Collier, and a great deal more on other subjects."[6]

Indeed, Garnett became an efficient cataloguer. On 9 May 1839 he reported to the trustees that in his first year on the job he had written or revised 8664 titles of new books, 918 serial titles, and 208 proceedings of academies, a total of 9790 entries.[7] As time went on he was asked to help arrange the entries under the heading *Bible* and to arrange a large collection of Spanish plays for the binder. He was content with his departmental role, which his elder son attested had been "in entire harmony with his desires," providing him with a life of "calm, uneventful happiness."[8] The only stress came from Panizzi's absences on vacation or on business, when the assistant keeper had to act in his place. Panizzi composed long lists of duties to be performed and acts to be avoided—for example, no binder's bills to be signed—and in at least one case (July through October of 1845) the responsibility was of unexpected duration, when Panizzi extended his stay on the Continent. However, Garnett was too indulgent to make a strong leader. One of the cataloguers recorded that when Panizzi was away it was easy to get a leave of absence from Garnett, and characterized him as "of the gentlest disposition, his shyness being only equalled by his amiability."[9]

On 13 March 1840 a daughter, Ellen Rayne, was born to Rayne and the Reverend Richard, completing their household. They had established a London branch of the Garnett family that would come to be known in Otley and Low Moor as "the British Museum Garnetts." They were visited occasionally by relatives coming south on business or pleasure, while Benjamin Beanlands, Anne's second son, was at Lincoln's Inn as an attorney-at-law and could be called on for legal advice.

Garnett's research in philology resulted in several more publications: in *Archaeologia*, the journal of the Society of Antiquaries; in the *Quarterly*; and in the *Edinburgh Review*. As one of the founding members of the Philological Society in 1842, he delivered several papers that were printed in its *Proceedings*. The quality of his thought on language was praised by two of his compeers, Robert Gordon Latham, who called these papers "by far the best works in comparative grammar and ethnology of the century,"[10] and John William Donaldson, who in his *New Cratylus* praised Garnett's "comprehensive and truly philosophical analysis of the constituent elements of Language."[11]

In a letter of 28 February 1842 to S. J. Allen, Garnett reported on his family: "Our oldest boy has just commenced his studies in Latin and begins to have a tolerable idea of the nature and contents of the accidence. I suppose he will have to be placed at one of the metropolitan schools in a while, but I have not yet decided which, whether St. Paul's, Merchant Taylor's, or King's College. Something will depend on his probable destination in life, which is not yet fixed, even in part. He has decent abilities, but is rather of a desultory turn at present" [HH].

Young Richard's "desultory" attitude, noted on the day after he had turned seven, may have been the result of his lack of mental stimulation during the day, for his intelligence was well above average: he was able to read at the age of three and had started on Latin at six. A story that has been recorded by his daughter Olive is revealing in this connection. In one of these early years, when he was "left alone in the study, he noticed, lying down on the top shelf of the tall book case two large handsomely bound volumes stamped 'History of Greece,' and, longing to get them, began to clamber up it. But just as his hand was stretched out to the goal, down he fell, the shelves, books, and all on top of him. At the noise this made his mother rushed in, dragged him up, and shook him violently, smacking him, 'and I sat,' he told me when he was Keeper of Printed Books, 'thrust into the corner watching her pick up the books, scolding me, while I cried bitterly. It was the first disappointment in my life.' That History of Greece had fallen open on the floor. It was a backgammon board!"[12]

Another story from the same source tells that a lady caller who was "shown into a room she supposed empty, to wait, heard a voice enquire, 'Pray, ma'am, what do you think of the political situation in Europe?' It came from little Richard hidden behind the 'Times,' reading the leading article. 'I thought the cat had spoken,' said this visitor."

Richard and William John sought lighter reading matter in the windows of book shops, where books lay open on display. The boys would check every day to see whether the pages which they had already read might have been turned to expose another part of the text. Richard also possessed at least one book—a novel by his mother's cousin, Barbara Hofland, who lived in London. It was her *Son of a Genius*, and it was inscribed: "From the author to her dear little friend, master Richard Garnett." The book was first published in 1816, but this copy was dated 1841, which was probably the time of the gift. The boys also had access to the *Penny Magazine*, the uplifting journal for children published by the Society for the Diffusion of Useful Knowledge, and they read it faithfully. But their time was not entirely devoted to intellectual pursuits, for they later confessed to having rung neighborhood doorbells and then dashed away. William John was an incurable prankster.

Just after William John's eighth birthday, in August of 1844, he and Richard began to attend a day school kept by the Reverend C. M. Marcus at Number 16 Caroline Street, a street which then ran south from Bedford Square, just west of the British Museum. Although the boys were dressed in Eton jackets and tall hats, the school little resembled the famous public school, for Mr. Marcus regularly evaded his creditors: often, as soon as the students had been admitted through the front door, he would disappear out the back. His teen-age son, Edward, was told to keep order on these days, but it may be imagined that Edward's efforts could easily be flouted by a band of energetic youths. Sometimes Mrs. Marcus and her daughter emerged from the kitchen to restore order to the loud and unruly students, who were sailing paper darts, blowing pea-shooters, and playing marbles or leap-frog. It is hard to conceive of much learning taking place in such an environment, yet Garnett was indulgent toward Mr. Marcus, for whom he felt sorry, and he took care to be prompt with payment for his sons' schooling. He also tutored them himself in the evenings.

According to the younger Richard, the budding artist John Everett Millais attended the Marcus school for a short time and painted a portrait of the master which soon disappeared from the boys' sight.[13] Millais was then sent to a more appropriate school to learn drawing, but, partly owing to this brief acquaintance, he was one of Richard's favorite painters. Several other boys, who stayed on longer, became lifelong friends to Richard: W. J. Brodribb, Frederick Farrar, John Padmore Noble, Frederick and Julius Pollock, and Linley Sambourne.[14*]

On 20 September 1845 the Reverend Richard reported to S. J. Allen: "My two boys continue busy with their studies. They have just begun the Aeneid, with which they seem to get on pretty well. Indeed I flatter myself that they have altogether made a fair progress in Greek and Latin in the thirteen months they have been at school" [HH]. By the time he was fourteen years old, Richard is said to have read "for his own amusement the whole of the 'Poetae Scenici Graeci,' Diodorus Siculus's History, the works of Boiardo, Ariosto, and Tasso, and the stories of Tieck and Hoffmann."[15] These works formed the basis of his literary taste for the rest of his life.

During 1848 the Reverend Richard contracted what was called catarrh, or chronic bronchitis, a condition that grew steadily worse during the ensuing year. He told Allen on 8 February 1850:

I can easily understand your anxiety respecting your rising family, my own position being such as to cause many serious thoughts for the future. I have scarcely ventured to entertain the thought of sending my two boys to Oxford or Cambridge, indeed I am less felicitous about it as King's College is capable of supplying an education sufficient for an assistant at the Museum or an employee in a government office, which is the most likely to be their destination. Their further advancement in the social ladder must depend upon themselves. [HH]

By the following June, Garnett's weakness was so pronounced that Panizzi urged him to apply for a leave of absence from the Museum. He did so, it was granted, and he returned to Otley with his family. He sketched out a petition to John Parker, now a member of Parliament, for a pension for Rayne and the children, in case he became unable to work or were to die: "After discharging my duties at the British Museum more than twelve years, without the smallest interruption from sickness or any other cause, my health has all at once become very precarious, and is now, I fear, in a state which renders it doubtful whether I may not, ere long, be disabled from active service" [HH]. He thought the Queen might be disposed to allow his name to be placed on her list for favors, on the basis of his service at the Museum and also of his literary achievements. The petition may never have been sent. At any rate, no pension was received.

In July Garnett managed to take his sons to Low Moor to visit the relatives there, and he enrolled them in a grammar school at Whalley, a few miles away. This was a gloomy time for the boys. They were lonely and worried about their father; their fellow-students were of a rougher sort than they were used to; and Richard was not pleased with the subjects of study that were offered, as he wanted to learn foreign languages rather than bookkeeping and penmanship. Ellen had been taken in by the Thomas Horsfalls, to be reared with their daughters, Sophie and Emmeline, and the Reverend Richard and Rayne returned to London, where he continued to decline.

On 6 August he wrote a letter of advice to young Richard in which he commented: "Should you ever have a situation in the Museum, or any other public office, which is by no means improbable, you will find that slovenly work is looked on very unfavourably, and that blundering work is worse than none" [HH]. He hoped that Richard would develop a clear handwriting, which was essential for a clerk or librarian, and this Richard did.

On 27 September 1850 the Reverend Richard Garnett died in London and was buried in Highgate Cemetery, in what is now the Old, or West, Section. He had signed a will drawn up by Benjamin Beanlands on 7 June, making his brothers Jeremiah and Thomas his executors and the guardians of his children. He left Rayne her clothes and the household goods, the money in the bank, some money "out on security," and an inherited £200 which was in the hands of his brother Peter in Otley. She would also have £200 from his father's will upon the death of his step-mother. He directed that the rest of the property (such as books) be sold and that what remained after payment of debts be invested so that Rayne, and after her death the children, should receive the dividends. Rayne sold the furniture and books, and paid the debts, and on 22 February 1851 the total remaining was £750 [HRHRC]. This was a respectable sum, but a further source of income for the survivors was imperative.

Just who first approached Panizzi about securing a place for young Richard in the British Museum library is not known, but it is likely to have been the Reverend Richard himself, since he had had ample warning of his approaching death. In any case, Rayne was advised of Panizzi's favorable reception of the idea, and she informed her son to that effect. He and William John were staying at Whalley until the Christmas recess, and he wrote to his mother on 21 October:

> My dear Mamma, I received your letter last Wednesday and feel exceedingly glad and thankful to hear that you are now better. The serious loss we have all lately sustained will no doubt have been a severe trial to you; but you must endeavour to bear up against the affliction, both for your own sake and for ours. It has always been my wish, as it was that of my dear father, to enter into the British Museum, and I shall be very glad if an opportunity of doing so occur. I cannot say how obliged I am to Mr. Panizzi for his kindness. . . . [HH]

At the end of the school term William John was transferred to a school near Otley for a few months. After that he would go to his Uncle Jeremiah in Manchester to find employment in the cotton industry. Now it was up to Richard to help support his mother and Ellen, as well as himself. At fifteen, he was head of a family.

On 24 February 1851 Jeremiah of Manchester went to London and met with Panizzi and the principal librarian of the British Museum, Sir Henry Ellis, about Richard. He told Rayne, by post, that he was "happy to say that everything seems going on satisfactorily. They had jointly spoken to the Archbishop [of Canterbury] and the Bishop of London, both of whom they found favourably inclined. They had also prepared a formal application to the Trustees . . . which . . . is, no doubt, already sent in; and Sir Henry and Mr. Panizzi both appear very sanguine as to the result" [HH]. He indicated that application had also been made on Richard's behalf to two other institutions, but they are not named. Richard is said to have declined to prepare for Oxford or Cambridge, even though some of his relatives had offered to help finance his education, for he was as independent as his father had been, and meant to make his own way. Indeed, he considered himself quite able to assume a responsible position without the advantage of attendance at a university, important though he knew that to be for advancement in London. At the British Museum, fortunately, a university degree was not a requirement; and for the sake of his father's memory and the deep affection between them, Richard was proud to follow the Reverend Richard's wishes for his career.

It was most unusual for a fifteen-year-old to be proposed for a regular staff appointment at the Museum, but when Richard turned sixteen, on 27 February 1851, a better case could be made. Panizzi has always been given credit for making the appointment possible by his remarkable persuasive powers, which were often inspired by his characteristic sympathy for those in financial need; but no doubt the Reverend Richard's reputation and popularity made the task easier. On 8 March the formalities were concluded and Richard joined the assistants in the Department of Printed Books at what was then an excellent salary of £130 a year. Rayne had gone to stay with her sister, Emily Pearson, in Norton, near Sheffield, until she was somewhat recovered from her bereavement, and Richard was alone in the great city to make his fortune.

Chapter 2

Young Man in London, 1851–1854

Richard went to work at the British Museum on 17 March 1851, copying entries for the catalogue of printed books in his smooth and readable hand. The next-youngest assistant in the department was at least ten years older than he, but Richard was well accepted, partly out of respect for his father and partly for his winning personality and businesslike attitude.

He took a room in a house not far from Mabledon Place, in a new development called Myddelton Square, on the heights above Clerkenwell, near the North London waterworks. Then designated Pentonville, the area is now part of Islington. The row houses stand around three sides of a square, with the church of St. Mark's at the open end. Richard lived at Number 36. He was said to have walked to the Museum in the mornings, carrying in one hand a sack lunch and an umbrella and, in the other, a newspaper, which he read as he went along. The paper would have been the *Manchester Guardian*, to which his Uncle Jeremiah had given him a subscription. On his way home at four o'clock, he would stop in a coffee house to read the other newspapers. He was "always reading, and reputed to possess the gift of eating his lunch, going on with his work, and skimming the 'Athenaeum' all at the same time."[1] He kept an account book for his expenses, his only discernible extravagance being books.

One of his spare-time projects was studying foreign languages, perfecting those he knew and learning others. His method was to read poetry in the languages concerned, for he was even more smitten by the muse than his father had been. His brother William John wrote of him that he "devoted much of his leisure time . . . to an exhaustive analysis of [poetry's] great masters. Shelley, Keats, and Tennyson were the chiefest objects of his adoration, but he rendered himself master, of not only every British poet worthy of the name, from Milton downwards, but was conversant with every great [poet] the world has produced, his inherited powers of acquiring foreign languages enabling him to read and appreciate Aeschylus and Virgil, Dante, and Goethe in the original."[2]

He also studied world events with constant concern, and indulged in all he could afford of London's spectacle. He tried to write to William John at least once a month, both to bridge the distance between them and to help educate his brother by stimulating his mind and influencing his taste and opinions. Never hesitant about stating what he thought on any topic, Richard, albeit usually charitable and polite, disliked hypocrisy or dissembling. His opinions, based on wide reading and on application of the Garnett family virtue, common sense, were firmly held and hard to change. To William John he could be quite frank, so that his letters, carefully preserved almost from the start, convey a clear picture of the development of a young intellectual with a strong literary bent in mid-nineteenth-century London.[3*]

Another of his interests was fine art. He encouraged William John, who had some talent for drawing, and Ellen, who had very little, to make good use of what ability they possessed. In May of 1850 a private exhibition of paintings had been held where three young members of the Pre-Raphaelite Brotherhood—Millais, Holman Hunt, and Dante Gabriel Rossetti—had caused a sensation with their pictures and their philosophy, which involved realistic treatment of romantic subjects. Richard was of a temperament to be enchanted by such a style; but he regularly made the rounds of all the shows and galleries, and he reported in detail on what had impressed him among the works on display. Of the Royal Academy show of May of 1857, he said that there were two classes of pictures: those by, and not by, Millais. He was so intrigued by Millais' "Sir Isumbras at the Ford" that he tried to write a long narrative poem based on it, but he only succeeded in making a small start, as his talent was for short verse.

When the Great Exhibition opened in the Crystal Palace in Hyde Park in May of 1851, Richard went through it several times, writing to William John lengthy descriptions of the sights. "The Portuguese," he said on 4 June, "have with the most praiseworthy liberality, put out a quantity of snuff for the public to partake of, it is very good." In July Rayne's sister, Mrs. Pearson, came with her children to London and called at the British Museum, hoping to see Richard, but somehow missed him. They may have expected him to be at a public desk, and failed to ask that he be brought from the staff quarters. Subsequently, a number of relatives and friends visited the Museum and Richard was allowed to show them around the library. Other family members were givers, rather than receivers, of favors. When the men came to town on business, they invited him to dine at their hotel; and when wealthy Miss Henrietta Garnett of Low Moor brought her nieces to London, she would take him to a play or a concert.

There were some relatives living near the city with whom he was able to spend Sundays and holidays. Chief among them were Jeremiah of Manchester's eldest daughter, Eliza, and her husband, Charles Cumberland, who lived at King's Langley and were very hospitable to their young cousin. Charles's sisters, Mrs. Monach and Mrs. Part, and their husbands, also welcomed him, as did Benjamin Beanlands, who lived in pleasant bachelor quarters in the city.

Richard's closest friends were two of his former schoolmates at Mr. Marcus's—Padmore Noble and Julius Pollock. Richard dined at the Pollock home several times, and on 24 January 1858 he told William John that he had "tasted caviare and olives at Julius's. Caviare eats like bloaters, looks like black currants jam, is very good in moderation. Olives are altogether detestable, like horsebeans soaked in vinegar and brine." Julius already smoked cigars and was an amateur photographer. It was he who first took Richard's portrait, in 1852.

At the end of 1851, Richard felicitated William John on having "at length got a fixed salary," for though it might be small, many others had "risen to wealth from just as small beginnings, as I hope you may do some day." William John had gone into a cotton wholesaling firm in Manchester, and was now an accounting clerk. He was to remain in cotton for twenty-five years, and he became very knowledgeable about the industry, but he was never successful in his own finances and never came close to being wealthy—quite the reverse. In adulthood, he was constantly in debt and became known in the family as a ne'er-do-well. However, as a youth he tried to maintain himself. Richard kept a bank account for him and one for Ellen, and, with Benjamin Beanlands's advice, helped them to invest their inheritance. Jeremiah had given each of them some stock in the *Guardian*.

Ellen was attending the Clergy Orphans' School in St. John's Wood in Northwest London, and Richard was the overseer of her life there. He visited her as often as possible, commiserated with her when she got "hooping cough," and paid for the extraction of three of her teeth. Ellen hated the school, suffered from chilblains, and never afterward would eat bread and butter; but she stood at the top of her class and received several prizes, one of £2 for virtue at Christmas 1855. Richard arranged his summer holiday to coincide with hers so that he could take her with him to visit their mother. Ellen became a typical Victorian spinster governess. She was plain and, as she grew older, her tall frame carried a goodly weight, so that she earned the respect of her pupils with her commanding presence and extreme devotion to duty. Yet she also evoked true affection in some of them. The parents appreciated her ability; the elder Sitwells, for example, remained her friends long after her professional days were over and she had retired to Scarborough, where she was invited to share their Christmas luncheon each year.[4*]

Richard finished his two-year apprenticeship in cataloguing in 1853 and was then given more demanding tasks, such as correcting old entries against the books themselves. Still, he continued to write entries for newly acquired books, especially those in the Romance languages. He was reading French novels— chiefly George Sand and Balzac—along with Kingsley's *Hypatia* and Disraeli's works, while his affinity for German grew until he was translating the poetry of Heine and Goethe. Rayne had been given permission to stay in a house in Lichfield Cathedral close, one of those reserved for widows of clergymen, and Richard went in July to spend his vacations with her. He was proud to have been born in the same town as Samuel Johnson, and he enjoyed his time there, fishing in the river with William John, who often managed to join the family party. Yet he never ceased to study and read, for those were always his chief pleasures.

He was also composing verses of his own, keeping them in a notebook [HRHRC] and revising them frequently. He wrote some love poems for Padmore Noble, although love was not one of his favorite themes. In a letter of 1 March 1854 he remarked to William John, "I am told that there is to be a new edition of Tennyson illustrated by Millais; this should be good. Few poets supply finer subjects for a painter than Tennyson. What a glorious thing an illustrated Shelley would be—but I think you are not acquainted with his works." This was his first mention in correspondence of Shelley, who was to become the center of his intellectual life.

Poetry was the foundation of the enduring friendship Richard was making with the poet Coventry Patmore, who was earning his living in the Department of Printed Books at the British Museum. Patmore had seemed a somewhat remote figure to Richard, who recalled much later that, upon coming to the Museum, "I was introduced to all my colleagues, with one, doubtless, accidental exception. I was some time before finding who the tall, spare, silent man was, who alone of the assistants, sat in the King's Library; who, though perfectly urbane when he did converse, seemed rather among than of the rest of the staff, and who appeared to be usually entrusted with some exceptional task."[5] Patmore did, indeed, stand apart from the general industry of the department. He had entered it under the patronage of the socialite politician and writer Richard Monckton Milnes, and he commanded respect as a published poet. His superiors even tolerated his writing verse during his hours of duty. He had been courted by the Pre-Raphaelites after Millais had painted an interpretation of his "Woodman's Daughter," and he gave them poems for their publication, *The Germ.*

In a letter of 2 December 1854 to William John, Richard mentioned Patmore's "new book of poems, called The Angel in the House, i. e., Mrs Patmore. It is anonymous and much superior to anything he has done before, being very gracefully and pleasingly written, though his versification is often rough and he has little fancy or imagination." This rather contrary evaluation of Patmore's talent was to be repeated in Richard's later reviews of his works and in his biographical sketch for the *Dictionary of National Biography,*[6]* yet the Patmores were among his kindest friends, and they encouraged his poetic ambitions. He was very fond of them both, although he thought it indiscreet to write poetry for publication about one's wife. Patmore gave Richard copies of his *Angel in the House* and of his *Poems* of 1844, as well as of his unpublished "Odes."

When William John sent Richard some sketches he had made, Richard sent him money for drawing materials, and expounded his own theory of art, in a letter of 19 January 1855:

Poetry, Painting, Sculpture, and I believe I may add Music [of which I am unfortunately ignorant] . . . seem to me to be one and the same thing at bottom; one and the same Spirit speaking in different ways. . . . The artist, then, may be described as a man inspired by the Spirit of Nature, the Power which, in the words of Shelley,

> "Wields the world with never wearied love,
> Sustains it from beneath, and kindles it above."

[Art is essentially divine and cannot derive from evil.] *A great artist never is a bad man.* Milton, Raphael, Mozart, Shelley, Canova, for instance, were ornaments to their species. And when the reverse appears to be the case, we are sure to find on inquiry that the seeming delinquent was in truth more sinned against than sinning. Lord Byron is a striking proof of this.

The concept of the link between art and morality came from Shelley's *Defence of Poetry,* written in 1821, and it was promoted by the great critic Ruskin as well. Despite its manifest exaggeration, it was Richard's credo throughout life. He excused the libertine Byron on the grounds of pernicious early influences.

Chapter 3

Journalist, 1855–1857

Richard was hoping to have some book reviews published in the *Manchester Guardian* or, at the very least, to have some comment from his Uncle Jeremiah, whose writing style he admired, on the copy he had been sending there from time to time. He was, however, timid about approaching the noted editor, and carried on a campaign for attention through William John, who was in close touch with his uncle's household.

Early in June of 1855 William John wrote that the *Guardian* was going to become a daily, in imitation of its rivals in Manchester, now that the stamp duty had been abolished by Parliament. Jeremiah had presumed that, with more copy being needed to fill more issues of the paper, Richard might help by sending book reviews regularly and in some quantity. Richard replied to William John on 24 June, "I suppose that I am expected to send an article as soon as any book appears worth reviewing? At all events I shall do so if I hear nothing to the contrary." On 9 July he was pleased to note that one of his articles had been published, but another that he had sent, on Leigh Hunt's *Old Court Suburb*, had not, and he asked William John to try to find out, without letting on that Richard was anxious, whether the article was unsatisfactory or space was short. This information William John was to transmit "immediately," so that Richard might know how to proceed with "the composition of new articles."

Thus it was with alternate elation and disappointment that Richard began his writing career in the pages of the *Guardian*. He was proud to be able to provide the latest bookish information from London, and he no doubt looked forward to a supplement to his income; but Jeremiah was only one member of the staff of the paper, and his interest was mainly in politics. "The vexation I could not help entertaining," Richard wrote to William John on 24 July, "at seeing my article postponed to a review of Flourens on Longevity,[1]* which had been previously noticed by every paper in London, has been to a great extent dissipated by the insertion of the notice of 'Whom Shall we Hang?' and this time without annoying alterations, except in the matter of punctuation, in which point the people of the *Guardian* seem incorrigible. I must confess I felt rather dubious as to its being inserted, owing to the extreme freedom with which I had expressed my opinions, but I suppose the boldest measures are the safest. I suspect, however, that a similar freedom of disapprobation has put the stopper on my notice of Leigh Hunt."

On 25 January 1856 was published Richard's article comparing the first issues of the new *National Review*[2*] with those of other quarterlies. Five days later Jeremiah had to retract his well-meant suggestion for a continuing relationship with the *Guardian*. It seems that his partner, J. E. Taylor,[3*] had promised another person the privilege of reviewing books for the newspaper, and Jeremiah had no control over that department. So were dashed Richard's hopes for steady employment by the *Guardian*; but he continued to send reviews on the strength of the possibility of their being accepted.

During the previous August he had visited his Yorkshire relatives, his vacation time now coinciding with the weeks during which the British Museum was closed for cleaning, and upon his return in September he had found that Padmore Noble had been in Ireland and now professed "his intention of marrying out of County Cork. *I* only know one Irish lady," said Richard on the thirteenth to William John, "Mrs. McCaul, who certainly gives me a very favourable idea of the generation." This good woman was the wife of the Reverend Joseph B. McCaul, who had joined the staff of the British Museum library in March of 1851, along with Richard. The McCauls gave parties, at one of which Richard would find an Irish bride for himself.

At the end of 1855 the Lichfield bank in which Rayne had at least part of her funds failed, and William John wrote to Richard offering to sell some of his stock in order to help her out. Richard replied on 7 January 1856 that the offer "does you great credit. But you must permit me to remark, that in the first place it would be quite unreasonable that you and I, having such dissimilar incomes, should contribute in the same proportion; secondly that... Mamma... declines to receive anything at present, hoping to do without any assistance.... It has always been quite understood that I provide for any emergencies that may arise either from loss of money or unforeseen claims upon what is in hand—thus, for instance I am at present paying for Ellen's German and music and shall probably have to disburse a good deal more before her education is completed." So Richard's financial burdens were increasing, rather than diminishing, with the years.

In his spare time he had continued to read extensively, and on 22 January 1856 he told William John that he had found Goethe's *Wilhelm Meister* "a most lifelike book [with a] strong impression of subdued power about the whole." On 12 February he added that, to him, "Mignon is by far the most beautiful and interesting character." He retained his admiration for Mignon to the end of his days, but he thought Goethe's inner meanings would only be perceptible to the German mind and that his writing would lose much by translation. Such reservations did not prevent him from translating some of Goethe's poems; but when the resulting verses were published, the reviewers agreed that it was impossible to translate Goethe well.

Early 1856 was a time of excitement at the British Museum, when Sir Henry Ellis's sudden resignation as principal librarian "took everyone by surprise," and discussion ensued among the staff about his possible successor. Richard wrote on 27 February (his twenty-first birthday) to William John, "It is generally believed among us that when the *Athenaeum* says it is *probable* that the Museum will in future be governed by a board, the wish is father to the thought. In that case, Mr. Panizzi will in all probability be the new librarian. There can be no doubt that he is the best qualified individual for the post, and his intimacy with Lord Palmerston will probably make his election sure. The office is in fact virtually in Lord Palmerston's gift." Panizzi received the appointment on 4 March and gave credit to Lord and Lady Palmerston for their help.[4] However, the idea of a ruling board under the trustees was not implemented.

The following letter of 6 March to Panizzi displays Richard's elegant command of the language and also indicates something of his situation in the department in his fifth year there:

> My dear Sir, The outlying position of my seat, and, it may be my own lack of inquisitiveness, render me usually about the last to hear of anything that may be going on in the Museum. I am not, therefore, much surprised that I should not have been aware of my colleagues' intention of waiting upon you to congratulate you on your recent appointment till too late to accompany them. But I should certainly feel exceedingly annoyed had I no opportunity of atoning for the omission in writing. Averse as I am to occupying your time without necessity, I had rather appear intrusive than ungrateful. And assuredly, my dear Sir, no one in this department can feel more indebted to you than I do—alike for the kindly warmth with which you promoted my appointment, and the extreme courtesy and forbearance I have invariably experienced at your hands—a condescension which I beg you will believe has been by no means lost upon me.
>
> That you may long continue to discharge the functions of Principal Librarian with the same credit to yourself and advantage to the Museum that have signalled your administration of the Printed Books Department, is, my dear Sir, the sincere wish of
>
> Yours most truly,
>
> Richard Garnett[5]

Richard had been engaged in "preparing a hand-catalogue of the [books] in the long-room," or the Arch Room, the most remote of the staff rooms on the main floor. His next task would be correcting the catalogue entries for the Spanish poet Pedro Calderon, whose poems fascinated him: he even translated some of them into English verse. He had also been given a list of Spanish pamphlets to mark for possible acquisition, and the catalogue entries for some

French newspapers to correct with the aid of a special bibliography.[6] These duties indicate that he had been successful in mastering the Romance languages by independent study, and that he enjoyed the confidence of his superiors.

Panizzi, in advancing to the top, was distanced from the daily affairs of the Department of Printed Books; but he continued to control the promotions among his former staff there. It was a privilege he so cherished that he laid himself open to a charge of favoritism in his administration of it, and Richard was to feel its bitter results in future years. Still, he and his colleagues evinced "great contentment" from Panizzi's choice of his successor as keeper—John Winter Jones, who had followed Richard's father as assistant keeper and who was gentle and accommodating, in contrast to the strong and stern Panizzi.

Richard now obtained an entrée to the *Literary Gazette*, to which he would contribute fifty-five reviews in the next four years. His first article to appear was a review of Alphonse de Lamartine's *Vie de César*, in the issue for 15 March 1856, and is typical of Richard's critical writing. After remarking on Lamartine's "studied absence of study" and hasty generalizations, he points out several instances of "carelessness in facts," such as that Caesar's "Veni, vidi, vici" was said in Spain, whereas it was really said in Pontus. On 9 April he told William John that the review "appears to have given great satisfaction." It was followed quickly by two more reviews, and in June by one of the *Works of Adam Mickiewicz*, the Polish poet, in a French translation. This article was a real challenge, and to aid his criticism Richard made English translations of seven of the sonnets, which, he admitted, "subjected to a double rendering... can hardly have escaped a fate analogous to that of Sir John Cutler's silk stockings, converted by reiterated darnings into a pair of worsted ones."[7]*

Late in May of 1856 there was a great fireworks display in London to celebrate the end of the Crimean War, and Richard was invited to join a party got up by Padmore Noble to watch from one of the parks. He told William John on 26 May, "I do not know whether we shall have a day's holiday at the Museum, which edifice you see is to be illuminated. It is said [jokingly among the staff] that the catalogue is to be brought out and brilliantly lighted up, that its beauties may for the first time become perceptible to the general public." The manuscript catalogue of printed books had been a target of complaints ever since the Reverend Richard's day, but it was still available only to scholars with readers' tickets. On this occasion the many catalogue volumes remained on their shelves in the Reading Room while Richard and his young friends toured Hyde Park, Green Park, and other places to watch the fireworks. They went to Noble's for refreshments, then to Regent's Park to see the sunrise. Richard "got home at seven in the morning, so fatigued that I had been very glad to turn into the Euston Square station and sleep for half an hour on a bench," he reported on 14 June.

In July William John wrote that Mr. Taylor of the *Guardian* had gone to Italy for two months and that Richard's chances of getting an article published might thus be improved. Richard promptly sent off a review, one of several that were apparently awaiting publication, for he said on 22 November that he had in his desk "articles on a novel called *The Mildmayes* and on three recent books of poetry and am going to propose four German books for review. So I think I have been tolerably active." These were in addition to the reviews of four novels that were in the *Literary Gazette* editor's hands, along with some minor paragraphs that had already been printed. All the reviews he had mentioned were published, and his steady assignments continued. He also "made overtures to the conductors of the Illustrated [London] News and the new Biographia Britannica and received civil if not decisive answers," as he reported on 23 July. This is the first evidence of his enduring interest in biography.

The summer of 1856 was a time of change for Ellen, now sixteen and ready to leave school and make her own living. She had few choices of career and needed someone to speak for her. Her best chance was to be a governess, an open field for respectable and intelligent young women, and her Yorkshire relatives now came to her aid. One of them arranged with a Mrs. Heathcote, of the family of the lamented Margaret, to employ Ellen to help care for a backward child. This, however, was a charge for which Ellen was not prepared, and before long she had to be rescued and settled into a teaching position. Richard's duty of escorting Ellen to Southwell in August had given him an opportunity of visiting all his relatives in the North of England, and he went from Sheffield to Low Moor and then Otley. He also called on an old couple who were friends of his father's in Blackburn, went to Whalley to see his old school, and to Manchester to see William John and their Uncle Jeremiah. He returned to London by way of York, where the cathedral astonished him with its grandeur.

On 13 March 1857 Richard reported on a favorite diversion, chess, which he must have learned to play early in life. He said he had "only once played with a really scientific chess player . . . and he soon reduced me to a state of smash. The only person I play with now is Mr. Monach; we are about equal, he making the best moves, and I the fewest mistakes." There is in this comparison a bit of character delineation, for Richard's bent of mind was less creative than critical and organizational. The game of chess was one of his few recreations in his later busy years. Another hobby was betting on horse races. He joined a half-crown sweepstake on the Derby and won at least once, when his way of celebrating was to buy flowers for the other members of the pool.

In March 1857 he also had to swallow the first harsh criticism of his writing. A reader of the *Literary Gazette* reacted negatively to his comments on the posthumous publication of the correspondence of J. G. von Herder. This reader mailed to the editor the first column of the review, "with such marginal annotations as Nonsense! Trumpery! Rubbish! Execrable stuff! scrawled liberally on the margin. I think I shall survive it," said Richard in his letter of 13 March to William John, "indeed I suppose I ought to be thankful that he condescended to stop where he did."

This was the time when Jeremiah Garnett and the *Guardian* were in the thick of an emotional election campaign for the representation of Manchester in the House of Commons, and the paper was credited with defeating the incumbents, John Bright and Milner Gibson. These men had voted against the Corn Laws, or tariffs on imported grain, which had been instituted in the interest of free trade for British manufactures, the life's blood of Manchester. They had also opposed the Crimean War and all foreign intervention, which Jeremiah and the prime minister, Lord Palmerston, favored. Jeremiah had once supported Bright, but had turned against him and found two "Palmerstonian Liberals"[8] whom he helped win the contested seats. Richard, agog with excitement, wrote to William John on 21 March:

> You cannot think how much interest I take in the election, it is easy to see that Uncle is the life and soul of his party, and I regard it as quite a family matter. Nothing could well do us more credit than that a Garnett should upset such an organisation as the [anti-Corn Law] League, and such men as Bright and Gibson. ... I only wish I were there and able to help as a canvasser, as a lecturer, as a secretary, as anything. If you should find any opportunity of making yourself useful in any such way, I hope you will take it; besides the goodness of the cause, it would be extremely useful as an introduction to public business, in which I hope you will one day take a conspicuous share. I have done what I could by sending a letter to the Guardian signed A Voice from the South. Considered as a composition it is, I think, about the best thing I ever wrote [but it arrived at Manchester when Uncle was away], and may consequently be regarded as *non avenue*.

Richard was not unmindful of John Bright's many excellent qualities, and hoped that he would not retire from public life after losing to the man backed by the *Guardian*. In fact, Bright and Gibson immediately got other seats for Parliament. Even Jeremiah recognized their ability, but he thought Manchester would be better represented by men of a different political philosophy.

On 2 May 1857 there was a great event in the British Museum—the opening of the new circular Reading Room that had been constructed, over the past three years, in the open quadrangle around which the main building had been formed. This huge room had been planned and supervised by Panizzi, and was one of his most popular achievements. Richard had helped to choose and arrange a collection of reference books which decorated the two levels of the circumferential walls. He had to stay until seven o'clock on several evenings to prepare for the gala opening ceremonies, which were attended by the cream of London society. The room was then on display to the general public for a week.

A significant happening in Richard's life was described rather casually in a letter of 1 June to William John: "I saw the proof-sheets of Tennyson's new poems the other day, but was not permitted to inspect them." The incident must have occurred at Edward Moxon's shop in Dover Street. He was the publisher who specialized in poetry, not only of the best poets, such as Tennyson, but also that of young and untried persons. He had published Patmore's *Poems* in 1844, and it may have been Patmore who encouraged Richard to visit the office. The "new poems" of Tennyson must have been "Enid and Nimue: The True and the False," a trial edition (in 1857) of some of the *Idylls of the King* (1859). Richard's presence in Moxon's shop as the proofs were coming off the press marks his acquaintance with the proprietor of the firm that was to publish his *Relics of Shelley* in 1862, though not his own verse. Moxon had begun a series of one-volume editions of famous poets in 1839 with a volume of Shelley, which was probably the one Richard owned.

Meanwhile, the *Literary Gazette* was giving Richard "an overpress of work," and he was also finding it awkward to make plans for his holiday because, as he wrote on 7 July, "there are several others to be consulted besides myself, and I was fairly 'crushed in the clash of jarring claims,' as Tennyson has it. Since the recent changes at the Museum, I have depended more on the arrangements of others than was formerly the case, like the Emperor of Germany's mutton, which could not be carved at all without seven chamberlains."

The changes mentioned were occasioned by the death of James Cates, who had been superintendent of the Reading Room since 1825. They consisted of the re-assignment of Thomas Watts, the senior assistant keeper, to that position, which he made into one of distinction, and the promotion of William Brenchley Rye to be an assistant keeper, carrying on Watts's former duties. Watts had been in charge of the "placing," or designation by subject, of the newly acquired books for arrangement on the shelves, and when Rye undertook this task, he got Richard to help him. Richard's rank had been raised from assistant second class to assistant first class on 25 April, and his work was so exemplary that, before the end of the year, Rye had turned over to him almost the entire burden of the placing. Since there were over seven hundred divisions and subdivisions in the classification scheme devised by Watts, the procedure was an intricate one; but Richard had found his real calling.

Nothing could have suited his tastes and talents more than the inspection of hundreds of books to ascertain their subjects, thus keeping an intimate association with the latest literature, as well as becoming acquainted with the older works being added to the collections. In this way he discovered all sorts of topics for his own writings. His facility with foreign languages, of which a knowledge of at least twelve was required for accurate placing, had become noteworthy, and he was deputed to read the trade lists from Germany, Italy, and Spain, as well as America, and to select titles for possible purchase.

In October he took part in another privileged activity at the Museum: "The MS. Room and King's Library will soon be open to the public [for the first time], and we have been engaged in putting out the most curious books, etc. for exhibition," he said on the eleventh. This was the beginning of the superb display of manuscripts, documents, and rare books which has attracted thousands of visitors to the British Museum over the years.

Now it was discovered that the two-penny *Guardian* was losing circulation to its rival, the *Manchester Examiner*, which sold for a penny; so it was decided to lower the price to try to regain the advantage. Upon receiving this news from William John, Richard said that there was no reason for anyone to prefer the *Examiner* over the far superior *Guardian*, with its foreign correspondents and excellent political reporting, though he himself was enough interested in politics to want to read several newspapers. He continued on 11 October: "This battle of quality v. cheapness confirms my old idea of there being a fine opening for a cheap literary journal in London—not only is the Athenaeum's price high, but it contains a good deal for which many readers do not care. I should like, then, to start a journal of half the size and price, conducted with the greatest regard to economy, and containing only such reviews of books and other literary and artistic matter as the public at large would be likely to care for—in a word, an Athenaeum for the Million. If, *par impossible*, I should ever meet with anyone possessing the requisite capital and enterprise, this may become something more than an idea." No backer for this dream journal ever turned up, and the *Athenaeum* continued to hold sway over the literary and artistic world of London.

On 22 October he rejoiced to say that "at last I have succeeded in getting [a leading] article into the Guardian. You will find [it] in yesterday's paper, it is the third leader." Two weeks later he wrote in vexation, "As yet the world has not seen much of the fruits [of my efforts to write for the *Guardian*], two articles sent not having been inserted." Since the leading articles were on world affairs, Jeremiah Garnett may well have been the one to accept or reject them, and he was ill and thinking of retiring. This made Richard fear that his gift subscription would end. The British cotton industry was feeling the effects of unsettled times across the Atlantic, where, Richard commented on 8 December, "a second Toussaint l'Ouverture in the States might with slight assistance from fortune ruin America and Lancashire together." He was constantly torn between his basic humanism, for he despised slavery, and his loyalty to the family enterprise at Low Moor, which depended on raw cotton from the United States, and which would suffer from any interruption of the supply. He kept abreast of developments with apprehension.

As a farewell to a productive year, he announced his latest project: "I am studying Danish—a very nice language—a sort of ladylike German."

Chapter 4

Author and Editor, 1858–1859

Richard Garnett's literary, as opposed to a purely journalistic, career began with the publication of three books by him. Although the writing of political essays and reviews was by no means a trivial occupation in an age of high-quality journalism aimed at an educated and critical elite, it could not satisfy the ambition of a budding author and poet, nor were its financial rewards as great as might be hoped for from larger works. It was a good proving ground, but Richard was ready to undertake larger projects.

All these years he had been writing and perfecting poems, and he now selected the best of them and gave them to a printer, Robert Hardwicke, to be published anonymously at the author's expense. The result was *Primula: A Book of Lyrics,* a thin octavo in paper covers containing twenty-nine poems and priced at one shilling. It was a collection of rather stilted verses about a misty country inhabited by fairies, a sea inhabited by sirens, and a distant world of Oriental sages and harems. Three sonnets from Mickiewicz were included and one called "Imitation of Leopardi," the Italian pessimistic poet. Richard's first interest was in form, his second was in imagination, and his models were romantic.

The reviews were on the whole complimentary, but with significant reservations. Patmore, in the *Literary Gazette*, gave the most common criticism of Richard's lifelong output of poetry: that although "the versification [often] is faultless" and "the phraseology thoroughly good . . . the total impression conveyed is not one . . . of expansive admiration."[1] He disliked the largely artificial subject matter, for he preferred poems about real people. The *Times*, however, said, "The polish is extraordinary for a first book"[2]—gratifying praise, but not enough to spur the sales, which were barely enough to recoup most of Richard's investment in it.

As soon as *Primula* was well launched, his second volume got underway. On 25 April 1858 he wrote to William John:

I have some news which will assuredly afford you much pleasure. Some little time since, Messrs. Williams and Norgate, of their own accord, offered to publish an edition of Papa's philological writings at their own expense; there could be no doubt as to the satisfaction with which we must all receive such a proposal, and I have latterly been very busy preparing the work for the press. Last Wednesday I had the satisfaction of placing the whole in their hands, and I hope it is by this time in Germany, where, for economical reasons, it will be printed. My editing, if editing it can be called, consists in the addition of a few not over valuable notes, and a memoir based upon that drawn up by Uncle,[3*] of which I think I have told you. I *hope* I have done this well, but assuredly of all kinds of composition, biography is the most difficult and delicate.... We are (i. e. Mamma is) to have half the profits, if any. I have had some correspondence with Mr. Wedgwood and Drs. Donaldson and Latham on the subject and have inserted some of the letters Papa received in the Memoir, which is shorter than could have been wished, but I felt it a point of honour not to put the publishers to any more expense than was absolutely necessary. The same reason precluded any objection to the book being printed in Germany, which will not conduce to its typographical elegance.

If not exactly elegant, *The Philological Essays of the Late Rev. Richard Garnett of the British Museum*, edited by his son, was well printed, and the paper was good enough to survive to the present day in excellent condition. It was ready in February of 1859, and Richard sent two copies to William John, one of them surely for his Uncle Jeremiah, one copy to Ellen, one to his mother, and copies to the uncles in Low Moor and Otley, as well as to the three philologists whose help he had solicited. These were "duly acknowledged, and in general very satisfactorily," but the reviews were not as favorable as he had hoped they would be, for philology had progressed since the articles had been written.

Meanwhile Richard was advancing in his library career. He was enjoying the friendship of Thomas Watts, who, in May, took him to a meeting of the Philological Society, upon whose program Richard made sardonic comments to William John. The evening was redeemed by a reunion with William Brodribb, his former schoolmate at Mr. Marcus's, now a fellow of St. John's College, Cambridge, who promised to visit him at the Museum. On 3 June he "had the honour of conducting the Marchioness of Huntley and her daughters over the Library." He had also begun to substitute for Watts at the desk in the center of the new circular Reading Room, when occasion required, although the keeper, Winter Jones, was concerned lest the task of placing the books should suffer from Richard's moving to the Reading Room for as long as a week. It is significant that Watts chose Richard, of all the assistants, to take his place in the demanding role of supervising the circulation of books in the library. The experience would be valuable to Richard when he took the position officially in 1875.

His social life was expanding also. He asked William John not to tell their mother that he was going to Brighton for a weekend with friends, as she deplored long journeys on account of the expense. "I think, however," he confessed on 3 June, "that a trip to the seaside now and then is well worth the money." A walk to Barnet, about ten miles north of London, through beautiful countryside, would have been more acceptable to Rayne, as would his accompanying Miss Henrietta Garnett of Low Moor and her nieces to a reading by Dickens. Then he was invited to a large party given by Professor David Masson of University College, London, who was to become one of his benefactors. The invitation came through Mrs. Patmore's older sister, who was the mother of Mrs. Masson, and with whom the Massons lived. Among the guests were two of Tennyson's sisters and Hepworth Dixon, editor of the *Athenaeum*.

At this time a change of management at the *Literary Gazette* put in jeopardy Richard's steady employment there as reviewer. He had contributed twenty-one reviews in the first seven months of 1858, but it was not until the second volume of the new series of the magazine that another appeared. In the meantime he turned to other publications as outlets for his urge to write. The proprietor of the *Critic*, Edward William Cox, "honoured" Richard, along with some of his confreres at the British Museum, with an invitation to his house at Russell Square and Montague Place, near the Museum, on 3 December. Cox published two reviews by Richard, one on 4 December and another on 12 February 1859, but no more.

It was during the first half of 1859 that Richard's literary career took wing. On Saturday, 12 February, he apologized to William John for his failure to write since their Christmas reunion in the North:

> You excuse yourself on the grounds of pleasure and occupation. I cannot say much for myself on the former head, but on the latter my claims are irrefragable. I am preparing a new edition of my poems for the press with considerable additions—a long and all-engrossing labour. Bell and Daldy have taken the book in hand, on terms so far favourable that I shall not be called upon to pay anything for a twelvemonth . . . [it] will this time appear with my name. . . .

This was *Io in Egypt and Other Poems,* another small book, cloth-bound and attractively printed at the Chiswick Press of Charles Whittingham, the master printer. It contained sixty-two original poems, forty-one of them new, the rest from *Primula*. There were twelve translations at the end: four from Mickiewicz; four from Goethe, including "Mignon's Song"; and four from other poets—a German, a Hungarian, and a Portuguese. There were also "Sir Isumbras: A Fragment," thirty-six lines of the narrative Richard had begun upon viewing Millais' painting of that name in 1857; "The Pope's Daughter," derived from Dante Gabriel Rossetti's "drawing of Lucretia Borgia washing her hands after poisoning her husband," as Richard described it, which he had seen at a private exhibition; "To the Crimea," a patriotic poem; and two humorous poems that have been much quoted and anthologized, "Our Crocodile" and "The Fair

Circassian." One of the sea poems, "Where Corals Lie," would later be set to music by Edward Elgar.

The reviewers were generally lukewarm, but the *Critic* said that *Io* and Owen Meredith's *The Wanderer* were the best poetry books of the season, adding that "reading one of [Garnett's] best poems and gazing on a splendid piece of sculpture is almost a similar act."[4] An individual who commented favorably on *Io* was William Michael Rossetti, who was, like Richard, a government employee, but who wrote art criticism and edited the Pre-Raphaelite magazine, the *Germ*, for his brother Gabriel's group of artists and poets. Richard was on the fringe of the Pre-Raphaelites, and William Rossetti became a good friend in the future.

Although Richard's relatives in Yorkshire argued over whether the first word in the title *Io in Egypt* meant "Jo" for "Joseph in Egypt" or "10" for the ten plagues, and the sale of the book was so small that the remainder was eventually destroyed by the publishers, there was one poem that attracted immediate attention and was to set Richard off on a new kind of scholarship. It was "To the Memory of Shelley," a tribute to his favorite poet, whose writings had signally enriched his life:

> ... Thy spirit's hunger is my soul's repast,
>   Thy aching toil my treasury of gold.
> That I might soar in speculation free
>   Thou wert Calamity's most iron'd thrall;
> Thou gatheredst light with woe and misery,
>   I look into a book and have it all. ...

Richard took the bold step of sending a copy of *Io in Egypt* to the son of the poet by Mary Wollstonecraft Shelley, Sir Percy Florence Shelley, and his wife, who lived at Boscombe Manor, Hampshire, on the Channel coast between Bournemouth and Christchurch.[5]* For some time there was no response. Then there came a gracious letter from Lady Shelley and with it a copy of *Shelley Memorials from Authentic Sources*, edited by her, a biographical work containing the texts of letters written by Percy Bysshe Shelley and extracts from Mary Shelley's journal, as well as an unfinished "Essay on Christianity" which expressed some of Shelley's least controversial meditations on religion. The book was fresh from the press of Edward Moxon—Lady Shelley had postponed her reply to Richard until she could repay his gift in kind.

The *Shelley Memorials* had its genesis in an abortive project of Sir Percy and Lady Shelley to sponsor the publication of a fair and accurate biography of Percy Bysshe Shelley derived largely from the family papers Mary Shelley had left to them. They entrusted this task to the poet's early and dear friend, Thomas Jefferson Hogg, who seemed the ideal person for it. He had used the papers lent him, but had declined to let the Shelleys see his manuscript before publication. The first two volumes were issued by Moxon in April of 1858, and the Shelleys were horrified to discover that Hogg had distorted the record to compliment himself at the poet's expense. They feared that in the last two volumes Hogg would be equally unscrupulous in discussing Shelley's relationship with Sir Percy's mother, who had eloped with Shelley when he was still married to another woman. So they retrieved the papers and asked for the privilege of reading in advance, and censoring, the rest of the manuscript.[6*] Their letters went unanswered, to their distress,[7*] but the remainder of the biography was never published. Hogg simply abandoned the project in silence.

At almost the same time, Moxon had brought out a book of reminiscences, *Recollections of the Last Days of Shelley and Byron*, by another friend of Shelley's, Edward Trelawny. Although this book was more sympathetic to Shelley, it was not so to Mary, whom Lady Shelley idolized. Then a third friend of the poet, Thomas Love Peacock, published an essay-review of Hogg's and Trelawny's volumes, along with a minor work on Shelley;[8] and Lady Shelley thought Hogg had been let off too lightly. Therefore she proceeded to compile almost three hundred pages of material from the Shelley archive and saw it through the press.

Percy Bysshe Shelley was a complex character who still defies easy understanding. He was generous, kind-hearted, and loving, yet rebellious and prone to wildly unorthodox behavior and the proclamation of contrary opinions that outraged his parents and his schoolmasters. He was expelled from Oxford for publishing and presenting to the college administrators a pamphlet arguing "The Necessity of Atheism," and was banished from his father's house as a result. He eloped with two young women, the second while still married to the first, a fact that the heirs of his second wife, Mary, wanted to gloss over. The first wife, Harriet Westbrook Shelley, was carrying her second child when Percy and Mary Wollstonecraft Godwin ran away to Europe, and two years later she drowned herself in the Serpentine in Hyde Park, London. Shelley and Mary were distressed by this event, but they were bound by their mutual love and were convinced by the doctrines of Mary's father, William Godwin,[9*] that love was the only important consideration.

In the twentieth century, documents have come to light that have established beyond doubt many of the details of Shelley's life; but in 1858, just thirty-six years after he drowned off the coast of Italy, and just seven years after the death of Mary, who had endeavored to minimize Harriet's influence on Shelley, the facts were not so clear. Old Sir Timothy Shelley, who never forgave his wayward son, had reluctantly supported Mary and little Percy after the poet's death, but he had allowed no biography to be written during his lifetime, and he had lived until 1844. Thereafter Mary failed to complete her own biographical writing, although she did publish an edition of the poems with Moxon in 1839 and included in it extracts from her journals, giving details of the composition of the various works. Only in 1857 did Sir Percy and Lady Shelley, probably after a conversation with Hogg, decide that it was time for a proper biography to be written and choose Hogg to write it. He took advantage of their trust to slant his account against Shelley and Mary, and even Harriet, and it was this ungrateful deed that started the turmoil of charge and counter-charge that sullied Shelley scholarship for the next fifty years.

Sir Percy Shelley was an easy-going, amiable man who resembled his father only in his clear blue eyes and "indescribably sweet expression," as Richard put it to William John on 21 November 1859. He was intelligent, but unambitious, and was disinterested in politics. His taste was for the sea, which had also fascinated his father (Sir Percy owned a succession of yachts and sailed around Britain and the Mediterranean in them), and for the drama—when he was at home he wrote and directed amateur plays and musicals for a theater he had had built on the Boscombe grounds. His attitude toward the controversy that swirled around the facts of his parents' lives was generally rational and sensible, and he participated with Lady Shelley in matters dealing with their memories, perhaps more out of a sense of duty than one of commitment.

Lady Shelley was a strong-minded, vivacious woman who was forthright in expressing her opinions and could be a good hater. Nevertheless, she was generous and kind to those she favored, and had a winning personality. She was well liked in society as a stimulating companion.[10*] She and Sir Percy had taken in an orphaned infant niece of hers, Bessie Florence Gibson, and were rearing her as their own. Theirs was a warm and happy household, and it was suffused with the spirits of Percy Bysshe and Mary Shelley. In a small area off her boudoir Lady Shelley maintained a shrine to the poet and his wife and their friends. She called it the "sanctum" and only a favored few were allowed into its precincts. As a young widow, she had fallen under the spell of the mature Mary Shelley, and to her she owed her successful marriage to Sir Percy; therefore she was unable to countenance any disparagement of either Mary or Percy Bysshe Shelley in print.

This protective attitude of Lady Shelley was abetted by Charles Ollier, Shelley's early publisher, and by his son, Edmund. Shelley's letters to Charles Ollier were included in the *Shelley Memorials,* which was in press when Ollier died in June of 1859. Richard later suggested that Edmund Ollier, who succeeded his father as Lady Shelley's adviser, was the editor of the book.[11*] It was assumed that Lady Shelley could not have written the editorial matter, although it bore her style and her sentiments, and speculation on the true author has sometimes pointed to Richard, who did not know the Shelleys at the time of the book's preparation, and sometimes to the Shelleys' friend, John Touchet.

All these persons, nevertheless, subscribed to the "Shelley legend" that Lady Shelley fostered: Shelley and Mary had merely been misunderstood by those who criticized them, whereas Harriet Shelley had forfeited her husband's love by bad behavior. *Shelley Memorials* was meant to promote this view, and it was immediately condemned by the press as dedicated to obscuring the deplorable, but commonly known, parts of Shelley's life. Leigh Hunt, another dear friend of the poet, in a note in the *Spectator* attempting to counteract the unfavorable impression left by the reviewer of the *Memorials* in the previous issue, concluded with a comment appropriate to the situation: "Great men of advanced and unworldly natures need the growth of time to do them a justice equal to their greatness. It is sufficient meanwhile . . . if credit for good intentions be given them by good hearts."[12] Richard, Ollier, and the Shelleys had such good hearts.

When Richard wrote to thank Lady Shelley for her gift of the *Memorials*, he mentioned that he had noticed some typographical errors in it, and he offered to send a list of them for her use in a second printing. She replied that these would be welcome, and on 17 August 1859 he sent her the promised list, adding twelve suggestions for emendations to the text of Shelley's poems, as published by Mary in 1839, the only complete edition. Richard had studied it and had discerned what he believed to be faulty readings of Shelley's difficult handwriting, or else printer's errors. He noted that the letters of Shelley to Charles Ollier in the *Memorials* made clear that the poet had often complained of errors in the publication of his verse, and Richard had noticed several that he had pointed out to Edward Moxon, and which Moxon considered valid. Since Moxon's death, there seemed to be no one in the firm who could judge such things, so Richard was sending them to the Shelleys for their information.[13]

On 17 September he wrote to William John, "I forget whether I told you that Lady Shelley had sent me a copy of the Shelley Memorials and that I had been able to render her some assistance towards the second edition. I have since discovered some very curious letters of and relating to Shelley in an old newspaper of the *Satirist* stamp—I believe quite unknown to her and all biographers. I shall copy them for her as soon as I have time, but it will probably require a good deal." In those days of tedious hand-copying with a quill pen, Richard was to make countless transcriptions of library materials for others. This particular assignment, however, to copy from *Stockdale's Budget,* a compilation of sensational gossip and trivia published in 1827 by John Joseph Stockdale, gave him an opportunity to announce the title and date of a hitherto unknown early publication by Shelley which was hinted at in a letter of Shelley's to John Stockdale the elder, father of John Joseph, in 1810, and was substantiated by Richard's further research. The Stockdales were book dealers in Pall Mall who had agreed to distribute the volume of poems, which had been printed at Worthing at the expense of Shelley's grandfather, Sir Bysshe Shelley. John Stockdale the elder found one of the poems to be a plagiarism from Matthew Gregory "Monk" Lewis, the writer of horror stories, and notified Shelley, who then asked him to suppress the book. The title, *Original Poetry by Victor and Cazire*, indicated joint authorship, and Shelley himself was not responsible for the false attribution of originality, which had been made by his co-author. This person, Richard discovered some years later, was Shelley's sister Elizabeth.

Lady Shelley responded, on 24 August, that she had been seeking material for a second edition of the *Memorials* and had sent word of the discovery of the Stockdale letters to "the friend in town who is kind enough to look over the proof sheets for me & hope by this means to rectify many errors."[14]* She said Sir Percy would attend to the suggestions for correcting the poems when he had finished yachting for the summer and settled down at home; and the next time they came up to London they would try to arrange a meeting with Richard. This they must have done in September, for on 6 October Lady Shelley wrote that she and Sir Percy appreciated all Richard was doing for them and for the memory of Percy Bysshe Shelley, and that they only wished they had met him sooner. She also hoped that within six weeks they would be able to receive him at Boscombe Manor.

As Richard phrased it many years later, Lady Shelley told him that she felt something should be done to counteract what she considered false ideas and libellous statements about the poet, and she wanted to enlist Richard's help by letting him see the mementoes and papers at Boscombe. "I went," he recalled, and "I think I angered someone else who might have thought himself better qualified to do such a work."[15] That person was, no doubt, Richard Holt Hutton, literary editor of the *Spectator*. Hutton had at one time requested permission of the Shelleys to write from their family papers, and they had refused. This was reason enough for him to be resentful of a younger man's receiving the honor; but though he did write critically of Richard's work on Shelley, he also wrote reasonably and well, and showed no sign of having taken offense.

Richard went to Boscombe in mid-November and was allowed to visit the sanctum. Its most sacred relic was a silver urn containing Shelley's heart, which had been snatched from his funeral pyre on the beach near Lerici, Italy, by Trelawny. There were also locks of hair, a glove, and other personal items; the remains of a book Shelley was said to have had in his pocket when he drowned; portraits of Mary, her mother, Shelley, and some of their friends; and manuscripts in profusion, mostly bound into volumes and kept in a glass case. In a niche that led off the sanctum was a model of the monument to Shelley and Mary that Lady Shelley had had erected in 1854 in Christchurch Priory.

After a preliminary viewing of these treasures, Richard had a long conversation with Sir Percy, who gave him Shelley's own copy of his *Refutation of Deism* (1814). Lady Shelley then came down with influenza and had to retire to her room, barring any further study of the relics, so Richard walked over to Christchurch, about five miles to the east, to see the monument. It had been sculpted by Henry Weekes and it showed a lifeless Shelley lying across Mary's lap and arms, while she looked down on his face in a Madonna-like pose. In the afternoon Richard walked to Bournemouth, which he thought very attractive. He also admired the Boscombe estate and the surrounding area, which was then quite isolated, as he described it to William John on 21 November: "The house . . . stands close by the sea, from which it is separated by a thick plantation of firs. The neighbouring country is wild, heathy, and barren, largely planted with pine and Scotch fir, which grow to the very edge of the cliff, at the bottom of which a narrow strip of sand extends along the sea for miles. . . . Boscombe is a new house . . . with large rooms and plenty of them, and most comfortable in every respect."[16]

Richard spent another night at the manor and then had to rise at five-thirty in the morning to be driven to the railway station, ten miles away, for his return journey to London. This, he told William John, gave him "an opportunity of witnessing [a brilliant] dawn. . . . In the East, the intensest crimson—in the West a full moon of purest silver—every leaf and twig and blade of grass sheathed in sparkling white frost." Lady Shelley later expressed dismay that he had done so much "walking during your short day here—& then the early cold journey next day!"[17] But Richard had no regrets. He had been walking on air, full of excitement and anticipation.

Chapter 5

Shelley Scholar, 1860–1861

Richard's literary relationship with Lady Shelley has been frowned upon from the first by critics who were dedicated to the unvarnished truth about famous people and who considered him unduly influenced by Shelley's daughter-in-law. These persons were unimpressed by the circumstances that caused him to fall so completely under her sway. In 1859 he was twenty-four years old, a budding poet, enamored of Shelley, and trying to establish a reputation in the British world of letters without the great advantage of a university education or an influential mentor. He was just beginning to break into the tight commercial community of writers; he had confidence in his command of the English language, in his understanding of the bounds of good taste, and in his Garnett common sense. Added to this was his unusually wide reading in several languages. To such a person, self-assured yet ingenuous, and anxious not to promote himself in any way that might be called vulgar, the opportunity of meeting Shelley's son, of seeing Shelley's personal possessions and his manuscripts, of being a guest in the fine home of a baronet, and of developing a personal accord with the Shelley family was overwhelming. Richard was always reluctant to reveal the details of his early acquaintance with the Shelleys, partly from modesty and the awe with which he approached their friendship, but partly because of his admiration for Lady Shelley and respect for her protective hoarding of the Shelley relics. His conviction of the sanctity of genius made it easy for him to join in her attempts to rescue Shelley's reputation from the gossips and moralizers.

On 12 January 1860 he told William John that he had "had a very kind letter from Lady Shelley the other day saying that Sir Percy and she were about to pass through London, and hoped to call upon me, but they have not yet appeared." He added that he had found the article in the last *Fraser's Magazine* interesting, but not in keeping with the information he had had from Lady Shelley. This article was the second part of the "Memoirs of Percy Bysshe Shelley" by T. L. Peacock,[1] an answer to the *Shelley Memorials*, and in it

Peacock rose to the defense of Harriet Shelley by implying that she had done nothing to justify Shelley's leaving her, but had been wronged by Shelley and Mary. Lady Shelley immediately took steps to counter this reflection on Shelley's honor, for she was determined to make his desertion of Harriet seem a natural outcome of Harriet's behavior—indeed, she obviously believed this to be true. The result for Richard, as he told his brother on 28 February, was

> [a] visit to the South, which was occasioned by a summons from the Shelleys, who desired my assistance in preparing a reply to Mr. Peacock's paper in Fraser . . . or at least such part of it as refers to Shelley's separation from his first wife. I went down accordingly, read the documents they showed me, took copies of these back to town, and have since been engaged in preparing a pamphlet, rebuking Peacock, asking him where he expects to go to, etc., and, which is more to the purpose, confuting his statements. I think I have done this pretty effectually, at the same time I wish to persuade the Shelleys not to publish any production at present, but to let me prefix a *general* contradiction of his assertions to a paper on some other Shelleyan subject to be contributed by me to Macmillan's Magazine, my notion being that if he does not answer this the victory will be ours without the annoyance of a formal controversy, and that if he does we can then publish my pamphlet with the advantage of the last word. If the Shelleys do not see the matter in this light, or if Macmillan will not take my article, we shall probably be driven to publish a series of separate papers, and I may become involved in [an unpleasant] personal controversy. . . . If I do not wish this, it is certainly no compensation as regards Peacock, who is a mean, spiteful, and cantankerous beast. *Au reste* a first-rate classical scholar and a very clever man; if you can get the collected edition of his novels (more properly extravaganzas) out of any of your libraries, you will find no end of amusement from them. . . .

The new *Macmillan's Magazine* was being edited by David Masson, who had already accepted a poem of Richard's for publication, and *Macmillan's* was to be Richard's chief publishing medium during the sixties.

The Shelleys believed that Peacock had seduced Harriet and thus made forfeit her right to Shelley's love, as well as Peacock's right to criticize Shelley for his infidelity. However, they were reluctant to make a formal accusation, or to publish what evidence they had of Harriet's alleged fall into prostitution,[2*] which had led to pregnancy and suicide, because Shelley's daughter by Harriet, Ianthe Shelley Esdaile, was likely to be hurt by such a revelation. Still, after the death of Mrs. Esdaile in 1878, no new information on the subject was forthcoming from the Shelleys. Richard preferred to believe that Harriet had taken to drink, and was thus unworthy of her talented spouse. This idea had come from Hogg, with the added reason that Harriet's father had kept a coffee house, or tavern, so that she must have been exposed early to "free living" and was hardly of a lineage appropriate for Shelley's wife. However, Richard covered his dark suspicions with discretion, as he wrote to Lady Shelley, "convinced it is most important that nothing in disparagement of Harriet's character should appear at present. Throughout the whole business, the indiscretion of friends has done ten times more harm than the malice of enemies."[3] In this he was quite accurate.

The article that Richard produced under his elaborate plan to avoid open confrontation with Peacock was "Shelley in Pall Mall," which Masson accepted for the June 1860 issue of *Macmillan's Magazine*. It consisted of the letters that Richard had found at the British Museum in *Stockdale's Budget* of 1827: fourteen letters written to John Stockdale the elder, eleven of them from Shelley, two from Sir Timothy Shelley, and one from the publisher John Ballantine of Edinburgh, who had rejected Shelley's Gothic novel *St. Irvine, or the Rosicrucian* as atheistic. In 1811 Stockdale had issued *St. Irvine* and also *The Necessity of Atheism*, and this had generated a file of communications from the poet. Years later the son, John Joseph Stockdale, had published a scandalous account of a courtesan, entitled "Memoirs of Harriet Wilson," for which he had been prosecuted. As a kind of justification, he then published twenty-six issues of the *Budget*, containing more scandals, to try to prove that such things were both real and common, and he included the letters from Shelley in the first nine issues[4*] to capitalize on Shelley's notoriety at the time. Richard realized that, despite their unsavory environment, the letters would be of interest to Shelley scholars in establishing dates, such as Shelley's first acquaintance with Harriet Westbrook and the publication of the poems of "Victor and Cazire," and for his own article he interspersed the texts of the letters with editorial comment.

His introduction began, however, with a disclaimer of the contentions in Peacock's recent publications on Shelley's life, and stated that before long this verdict on Shelley's treatment of Harriet "must be refuted by the publication of documents hitherto withheld," which would provide evidence that "most decidedly contradicts the allegations of Mr. Peacock." These promised documents were the subject of speculation for years, yet they never came to light. In all the various caches of letters of the Shelley circle that have turned up in the twentieth century, there have been none that could be said to justify Shelley's desertion of Harriet, and none that have reflected on Peacock's honor. Richard's credulity on these points can only be attributed to his belief that great poets had to have been good men, and to the heady atmosphere at Boscombe; he had no reason to doubt Lady Shelley's interpretation of the papers in her possession.

The introductory paragraphs of "Shelley in Pall Mall" had at first been written as if they came from Lady Shelley, but this was changed at her request[5] and Richard took full responsibility for the work. Richard also asked Masson to edit out anything in the article that he thought would look like "*intentional* misrepresentation against Mr. Peacock,"[6] for he preferred to imply that any error on Peacock's part was due to the faulty memory of old age or the lack of documentary evidence such as Richard was privy to. Masson removed one phrase, but left the article otherwise as Richard had written it. Most readers, nevertheless, found the references to Peacock in the introduction offensive, and Richard's reputation suffered accordingly. It was fortunate for him that his relationship with *Macmillan's* was in no way jeopardized by what amounted to the greatest mistake of his life.

He was now polishing a number of translations of German poetry he had made, as he told William John on 18 May: "I have scarcely a hope of getting them published at present, but shall at all events try [Alexander] Macmillan, who is well-disposed to me. . . . I really think my versions are the best hitherto made, and their publication would probably give a fillip to the sale of the Io, which is sorely in need of one." In June he gave the translations to Masson and soon after received payment for a biographical article on Jonathan Swift he had written for the *Encyclopaedia Britannica* as the result of an introduction provided by Frederick Farrar.

His social circle was becoming a fairly distinguished one, he told William John on 10 June:

> I have been nowhere except to the great annual party of the Ormes, Mr. Masson's parents-in-law, with whom he lives.[7]* The gathering is generally made up in about equal proportions between respectable old gentlemen of professorial mien and young authors, artists, etc., who amalgamate like oil and water. I need not say in which division I range myself. Among those [usually present] are Rossetti, the painter's brother, a first-rate critic on books and pictures, [and several minor artists]. . . . Among greater guns were Holman Hunt, whom I have met at Patmore's, "Tom Brown," and Professor Maurice,[8]* but these only descend to bestow a portion of their evening upon mortals, and I missed the two latter.

That summer, Richard went on a vacation tour in southwest England, ending at Boscombe. He promised William John a full account of his travels, but as he knew it would be shared with other members of the family, he took the occasion of an earlier letter, of 28 July, to relate his "most memorable adventure," with the request that William John keep it from their mother, for

> she would be alarmed and uneasy when I make my next excursion. It is the remarkable circumstance of my having spent a night and the greater part of a day on the cliffs between Teignmouth and Torquay [Devonshire], for which I have to thank the spirit of adventure, as I thought it then, or reckless folly, as it seems to me now, which led me to try to make my way from the former to the latter of these places by the beach, when the tide was coming in. This beach, smooth enough at Teignmouth, soon becomes a wild chaos of rocks, which it is no easy matter to traverse even at low water. I ought to have turned back the instant I found there was no road, but, persevering, was cut off by the tide about 6:30 p.m. in a pretty bay at the foot of the lofty cliffs. . . . These cliffs are composed of red earth of the most slippery and crumbling character; I fought my way up for about forty feet, but then found further progress impossible, and not only so, but that I had got,

Heaven knows how, into a place from which it seemed impossible to get away. There was nothing for it but to sit down on a small and insecure projection of earth, and there I remained for nine mortal hours, behaving, I hope, with reasonable fortitude, but still the prey of considerable anxiety, enormous ennui, and some apprehensions that the earth would give way or that I should fall off from sleep or giddiness. No one, I am sure, who has never been in my position, can form an idea of the strangeness of the sensations produced by the sight of the slow, remorseless advance and ceaseless agitation of the waves; the weird, vague forms assumed by neighbouring objects as the night gradually closed in, the wail of the wind and the clamour of the sea, continually modified in aspect by the rocks it struck against in its advance or retreat, the thousand and one unaccountable sounds which frequently, with startling distinctness, mimicked familiar noises, as the roll of carriages, the call of distant voices, etc. At midnight the tide began to retire, and by half past three, it was sufficiently light for me to attempt to descend. After an infinity of unsuccessful efforts, which frequently involved me in great danger, I contrived to scramble across the almost perpendicular face of the cliff to a sort of boss of earth covered with a straggling plant unknown to me, and wild roses, which tore my hands grievously, but afforded me a firm hold. Here I was more at ease, and after several failures in impracticable directions, managed at last to get down to the rocks, just eluding a deep chasm communicating with the sea, into which I must have fallen if the bunch of grass to which I clung had proved less tenacious. By this time the tide was up again, and effectually stopped me by the time I had scrambled half a mile on my way back to Teignmouth; this time, however, I could take up my quarters on a smooth ledge of rock, where I awaited its retreat with what patience I might. At noon it began to fall, by one I judged the rocks practicable, and had not gone far before I met an old coastguardsman who had been in quest of me, and who, observing my abandoned umbrella stuck in a precipitous part of the cliff, naturally inferred a catastrophe, and had descended to the beach in search of the body. I had, it appeared, been observed going along the rocks the previous day, and my destiny had been the subject of no little speculation among the Teignmouthians. Not wishing to run the gauntlet of these good folks' curiosity, I got the worthy coastguardsman . . . to guide me to the top of the cliffs by the first practicable path, and immediately proceeded to Torquay without waiting for refreshment. Consequently I was twenty-seven hours without breaking my fast except by a glass of ginger-beer, yet felt no hunger, and only a very slight sensation of faintness. After all, my adventure was not unproductive of good, for it prevented my going to Jersey from Torquay, in which case I should have missed the Shelleys.

Richard said later that he had recited Percy Bysshe Shelley's poems to help endure the long hours of darkness on the cliff. If any evidence were needed of his rugged constitution and strength of mind and will, this story should provide it. Sir Percy Shelley, the first to hear what had occurred, cruised along the shore of Devon in 1878, past the spot where Richard had been marooned, and wrote to him, "There was a heavy thunderstorm over the land—and I remembered your thrilling tale."[9]*

In the fall Patmore published the second part of *The Angel in the House*, and Richard got the assignment to review it for *Macmillan's*, a rather uncongenial task, he discovered, as he said to William John on 13 November. "I never wrote more reluctantly or to less purpose; in fact, when I sent the article it was with the full expectation of having it returned upon my hands.... My dissatisfaction rather concerns the form than the substance of the essay, for I think it a much fairer criticism of the book than has yet appeared.... Patmore has certainly done everything to give his adversaries an appearance of right, and I believe would now admit that my predictions and admonitions while his poem was in progress have been in every respect justified by the result." Patmore had consulted Richard throughout the composition of the poem, from an early reading to a group of friends through revisions; and in August, while on vacation, Richard had written a mature and measured critique which Patmore should have found useful.[10*]

Richard's association with the firm of Macmillan was of great advantage to him. In addition to accepting his work for publication in its magazine, it provided a stimulating social milieu, for every Thursday Alexander Macmillan would come from Cambridge to London to spend the night and to be "at home to all and sundry, when tea and stronger fluids, with occasional tobacco, were going on."[11] These "Tobacco Parliaments," held in the magazine offices at a specially made round table, attracted such prominent men as Holman Hunt, Thomas Henry Huxley, Charles Kingsley, F. D. Maurice, Francis Turner Palgrave, Coventry Patmore, and Alfred Tennyson, whose autographs may still be discerned on the edge of the table. Richard was privileged to be among them. He announced to William John on 13 December 1860, "I have just returned from one of Macmillan's Thursday evening gatherings, the second I have attended. He assembles his authors and their acquaintances together and feeds them with coffee and beer. I have met some interesting people there, among them Mr. [Henry] Fawcett, the blind candidate for Southwark, and 'Tom Brown' Hughes."

His other social engagements were also increasing. He had been at the Ormes' twice, to a soiree at University College, London, and to the inauguration of Charles Edward Mudie's grand new quarters for his lending library. Then he was invited to spend Christmas day with Mr. and Mrs. Westland Marston,[12*] friends who were, before long, to become relatives. One of the guests at this Christmas dinner was Dinah Maria Mulock, a very pretty woman who wrote novels and whose company enchanted Richard.

On 13 November he had told William John that "the spirit moved me to write a sonnet about Garibaldi, and send it to the Guardian. If inserted (and I shall be much disappointed if it is not, it being decidedly one of the best things I have done) it will probably have appeared before this reaches you." But Jeremiah was decidedly unwell, and "Garibaldi's Retirement" was not accepted for the *Guardian*. Instead, it was published in *Macmillan's* for December and Jeremiah retired in January of 1861.

In December 1860 had appeared Farrar's book *On the Origin of Language*, which Richard had obligingly read through in July and August. He told William John on 13 December, "It is duly dedicated to me, and he has adopted most of my suggestions, sometimes with special acknowledgement and sometimes without. I had rather he had not mentioned my name. Papa's occurs frequently ...."

At the beginning of 1861 Richard listed his recent writings to Ellen: a short poetic drama about Michelangelo, a dramatic poem, "Iphigenia in Delphi," and a translation of a Moldavian ballad, "Miora." Three poems were published in *Macmillan's* during the summer, while the new monthly *Temple Bar* published his short story "A Real German Mystery" in August and a similar tale, "The Autobiography of an Evil Spirit," in January of 1862. Both were derived from factual accounts that Richard had apparently come across in connection with his duties at the British Museum. He doubted the authenticity of the first account because of what he considered faulty use of Hungarian words by one witness. The second account provoked his disdain for the vogue of trying to communicate with spirits.

At the British Museum a change was made that was to cause friction and jealousy among the staff: Panizzi persuaded the trustees to agree to the division of the first class of assistants into an upper and a lower section. Advancement to the upper level was to be a reward for men who had given twelve years of service and who exhibited special merit, but it was not to be based on seniority. The salary was to begin at £320 and to rise by £20 increments to a £400 maximum. The number of places was set at sixteen. Richard had served only ten years, so he would remain in the lower section and would be paid from £210 to £315 by £15 increments.

It may have been this turn of events, communicated by Richard to William John, and by him to the Lancashire relatives, that impelled Thomas Garnett of Low Moor to try to help his librarian nephew. On 21 August Richard wrote to Ellen:

> ... some little time since I had a letter from my uncle Thomas informing me that, seeing in the Times how the librarianship of the House of Lords was vacant, he had written to Col. Wilson Patten, M. P. for North Lancashire, requesting him to employ his interests in my favour. I felt certain, of course, that the appointment was much too dignified and valuable for me to stand any chance of obtaining it. At the same time, I considered it would not do to have it said that I had missed a chance from having failed to exert myself, that I might possibly obtain a sub-librarianship if, as I thought probable, the sub-librarian were promoted, and that at any rate it could do no harm to remind great people of my existence. I sat down, accordingly, and wrote to the chief clerk of Parliament, in whose gift the appointment is, to the Duke of Newcastle, Lord Eversley,[13]* Col. Wilson Patten, and my Uncle Jeremiah. As you may imagine, the appointment has been filled up in the way I expected, and I have got nothing but civil letters from the personages

applied to and the satisfaction of having done my best, as aforesaid. I am not at all sorry, for if there were no one dependent upon me in any way but myself, I should be reluctant to accept any appointment, however valuable, that should remove me from the Museum.... [HH]

Richard's reluctance decreased over the ensuing years, until, on his own initiative, he sought a different position. However, there is no doubt that he was content with his work in the British Museum and that only unusual circumstances would impel him to seek a change.

He was again contemplating a short visit to the Continent, and hoped that William John could join him. A round trip to Paris via Dieppe would cost only thirty-six shillings, and he thought they would not have to spend more than ten or twelve shillings in France. Then a crisis in Ellen's fortunes interfered with this plan. She needed to find a new situation, and Richard wrote to his cousin, John Horsfall, in Berlin, to ask if he could find her a place in Germany. John had been conducting the acquisition of wool for his brothers' mill at Bradford, and had married Alexandrine Mendelssohn, a first cousin, once removed, of the composer Felix Mendelssohn. It was found that a relative of Alexandrine in Königsberg would be happy to employ Ellen, and thus Richard's coaching of his sister in foreign languages would bear fruit. He decided to accompany her to Germany, returning by way of Brussels and Antwerp to Hull, and going from there to visit his Yorkshire family before proceeding to London again. He went first to Lichfield, left for Germany on 7 October, and was gone for six weeks.

The year 1861 ended with news of the Shelleys, who had toured the Mediterranean on their yacht, visiting Lerici, near where Percy Bysshe Shelley had spent his last days, and bringing back for Richard a walking-stick made from an olive tree on the property Shelley had occupied there. They were now in London for the winter. "They live six stories high in Victoria Street, Westminster, where the houses might pass for towers if they stood alone," wrote Richard to Ellen on 12 December. "In fact, I am reminded of Manfred and Shelley's Pisan residence[14]* whenever I call, which I do sometimes, enjoying myself amazingly in looking over old letters and papers, and planning new work about Shelley" [HRHRC].

Now Richard's life was about to assume a different aspect.

Chapter 6

Year of Fate, 1862

The new year began with the publication, not by Macmillan, but by Bell and Daldy, of Richard's third book, *Poems from the German*. It was in the same format as *Io in Egypt* and had an advertisement for *Io*, quoting from reviews, at the front. There were fifty-five poems, taken from Goethe, Heine, Ferdinand Freiligrath, Friedrich Hölderlin, and others. The translations were immediately reviewed, rather harshly, by the *Spectator*. Richard's adherence to proper form was praised, but it was regretted that "all the motion, all the light is vanished, and it is Goethe no more."[1] The reviewer thought that one simply should not try to translate a poet so ethereal as Goethe.

Richard had recently undertaken to learn astrology, which, along with other manifestations of the occult, was becoming popular, but which was frowned on by the Church of England. He was careful not to let his Yorkshire and Lancashire relatives know about this hobby, but would ask William John to inquire casually as to the hour of birth of any new arrival in the family so he could cast its horoscope. He made hundreds of astrological charts during his lifetime, many of which have been preserved [HRHRC]. They include charts for all the members of his extended family and for every prominent figure of the time for whom he could secure natal information.

A strange impulse led him to send a letter to the editor of the hostile *Spectator*, signed "G.," propounding evidence for the fates of some of the French monarchs, deduced from the times of their births as recorded in documents in the British Museum. The editor, who printed extracts from the letter for the edition of 22 February under the title "The Nativities of the Bourbons," expressed amazement at the credulity of those, like Richard, who accepted astrology, despite its unorthodox reliance upon "faith in blind destiny."[2] Many other acquaintances of Richard's were equally baffled by this quirk of his; but when challenged about it, he was never ashamed to admit his conviction that the position of the sun, moon, and planets at birth affected one throughout life, and that these effects could be predicted by study of the subject. His predictions, however, were often faulty.

His concern over the American Civil War, which was causing disruption in the cotton industry in Lancashire, sent him looking for planetary influences that might relate to its events. On 29 March he told William John that the omens were unfavorable for the Confederate States: "The next six weeks will be fertile in great events, one of which I suppose will be the disappearance of the cotton plant from the fields of the South; if so, God knows what will become of our [cotton factory employees] next winter . . . England and America have both grown rich by the labour of the slave, and will both have to learn the insecurity of a prosperity based upon robbery and injustice. The recent disasters of the Confederates are a curious exemplification of astrological notions."

Richard's own star signs must have been propitious at this time, for he had at last found a mate. While William John was acting as best man for one of his Otley cousins, on 13 May 1862, Richard was getting engaged to be married. He announced the event to his brother on the fifteenth. The young lady was

> Miss Singleton, only daughter of Edward Singleton, Esq., late of Carrigeen house, county Cork. The family—originally from Lancashire—is a very good one, you will find full particulars in Burke's Landed Gentry. . . . Mr. E. Singleton, who has for some years been the victim of a mental affliction, of which I do not yet know the exact nature, lives at his brother's; Mrs. Singleton and her two children have of late years alternately resided in Ireland, London, and on the Continent; they are at present temporarily located with Mrs. S's brother-in-law, Mr. Westland Marston, whom I have often mentioned in my letters. It is now about three years since I made their acquaintance at one of Mr. McCaul's musical parties, an intimacy gradually arose which was interrupted for a year and a quarter, but resumed when, upon my return to town last autumn, I found them staying at Mr. Marston's. . . .
>
> Olivia Narney Singleton is just twenty. She is rather tall and slender, with a corresponding contour of face, delicate complexion, brown eyes and hair, prominent forehead, and an elegant profile approaching the retroussée. . . . Though not regularly handsome, she would, I think, be generally considered graceful and pleasing, but of course you will allow for a lover's partiality. Her manners are in general quiet and somewhat reserved, but she can summon up a good deal of Irish vivacity on occasion. . . . She is clever and well-educated, fond of reading and music; having been so much on the Continent she speaks and writes French very well, and has more or less acquaintance with several other languages. On more important particulars I will only say at present that I am convinced that ours is a union of affection on both sides, and I certainly would never have contracted one from any other motive.

Olivia's mother was Olivia Potts, one of the three beautiful daughters of J. D. and Elizabeth Narney Potts. A second daughter married a clergyman named John Bourke and lived in Ireland; the third ran away with Westland Marston, of whom her parents so disapproved that her wealthy father "cut her off with a shilling."³ Olivia found that her husband, Edward Singleton, was totally unlike his cousin John Singleton Copley, the noted jurist who became Baron Lyndhurst. Although trained in law, Edward was irresponsible, and when he began to behave erratically, Olivia left him and went to live with the Bourkes. Then, upon receipt of a generous inheritance from her father, she took her two children, Olivia Narney and Edward James, to London to be educated. She rented a house next door to the McCauls and saw a good deal of the Marstons.

Richard is said to have spent the time of his first meeting with Narney, as she was called in the family, in talking to her rapidly in a low voice about poetry. Since he admitted to little feeling for music and an inability to dance, he had to find a girl who would be willing to sit at the side of the dance floor and listen to a discourse on his favorite subject, liberally illustrated with quotations. He proposed to her on 11 April 1860, by asking her cat, which lay on the hearth rug before them, if its mistress loved him. Narney replied to the cat that she did. A love of cats was essential for anyone marrying into the Garnett family. However, Mrs. Singleton considered her daughter too young, at seventeen, for marriage, and in order to avoid complications, took Narney and Edward to Geneva for eighteen months. There Narney was pursued by a dashing Swede, but, fortunately, his suit was denied as well. When the three Singletons drew up before the Marstons' house on their return from Switzerland, they found Richard on the doorstep, calling to ask if they were back. This convinced Mrs. Singleton of the seriousness of his devotion to Narney, and upon receipt of a second letter of proposal on 13 May 1862, she gave her consent to the engagement.

Now Richard could introduce his betrothed to his friends and relatives in the London area, and she was immediately accepted and loved among them. He also procured a trophy for her when he went alone for a reunion with Horsfall relations at the home of Timothy and Sarah's third daughter, Anne, and her second husband, William Moxon, a barrister, in Wimbledon. Mr. Moxon proved to be brother to the publisher Edward Moxon, and he gave Richard some autographs of the poets Edward had published—"Campbell, Rogers, Leigh Hunt, and Tennyson, now the pride of Olivia's album, of course," Richard told William John on 2 June.

For some time Richard had been collecting fragments of verse by Shelley that he had found in notebooks at Boscombe or Victoria Street, with a view to publishing them under the aegis of Sir Percy and Lady Shelley. One poem, entitled by Richard, and still known as, "Lines Written in the Bay of Lerici," was printed in *Macmillan's Magazine* for June to test its reception. Richard had supplied an introductory note in which he said that the rest of the contents of one notebook "of unprinted poems and other pieces" were "about to be published by Messrs. Moxon and Co."⁴ This remark elicited a reaction from Thomas Love Peacock, who, Richard said in his letter of 2 June, wrote to Sir Percy and Lady Shelley, stating that, as the poet's literary executor, "he wished to inspect the volume before publication, and should stop it if he found anything he did not like. He was answered that the book was being printed under Sir Percy's sanction and inspection, and this seems to have quieted him, as we have heard no more. There is no doubt that he could obtain an injunction, but probably the court would dissolve it upon a representation of the case." All the same, the Shelleys, and more especially Richard, had had "a great fright." And deservedly so, for Richard had decided to attack Peacock head-on in the projected book.

This was *Relics of Shelley*, which Moxon brought out later in June. It consisted of fragments of poetry and letters, a translation from Homer, and a fable written by Shelley in Italian and translated into English by Richard, both versions being included. There were also eight pages "On the Text of Shelley's Poems," setting forth Richard's emendations of versions in previously printed collections of Shelley's works. At the end were Richard's "Lines at Boscombe," written in 1860. They begin:

> So, Florence, you have shown to me
> All your wild regions by the sea . . .

"Florence" was the youngster who was being reared by the Shelleys, and was then about eight years old.[5]* She and Richard had become good friends during his visits to Boscombe.

In his poem he describes the forest of conifers that then shielded the manor house from the Channel, and through which little Florence had escorted him; surveys the seascape that at last lay before them; and makes a rather fanciful comparison with the scenery of Italy. The link between the two places is the presence of Percy Bysshe Shelley—real in regard to Italy, spiritual for Boscombe, where the relics of his life hallowed the house and the neighborhood:

> Yes, Shelley loved the forests dim
> By Pisa's coast—here they love him!

The "Pisan woods" had loomed over Casa Magni, the villa rented in 1822 by Shelley and Mary with their friends Edward and Jane Williams,[6]* on the edge of the Bay of Lerici, about thirty miles north of Pisa. Richard ended the poem by predicting that Florence would some day appreciate Shelley's poetry and so would understand Richard's pensiveness as they sat together on the English shore.

Unfortunately, before this attractive ending to the book, Richard had inserted his essay "Shelley, Harriet Shelley, and Mr. T. L. Peacock," with the quotation under the title: " 'Words that make a man feel strong in speaking the truth.'—Tennyson." There is no doubt that Richard *did* feel strong and righteous in defending Shelley against the slurs of Peacock. The latter had published his fourth article on Shelley, called a "Supplementary Notice," in *Fraser's* for March. It included a denial that the Shelley family could possibly have evidence, as they claimed they did, that would refute his defense of Harriet Shelley in his previous article. Richard retorted with a discourse of twenty-seven pages, using illustrations from the Shelley archive at Boscombe to press his point of view. His only worry in publishing this attempt to exculpate Shelley, he told William John on 29 March, was that Peacock would be so indignant as to cause an unpleasant public altercation. Then he added, "However the matter may end, it will be a sincere satisfaction to me to have helped the Shelleys, for whom I entertain the sincerest esteem and affection."

Nevertheless, he was prepared for a strong reaction from admirers of Peacock's writings, and he got it. He tried to reassure himself by telling his brother on 30 June:

> Perhaps I may be thought to have been too severe on Peacock. I wish, of course, to make it evident that I consider myself to be giving him a most complete and well-deserved castigation; if I have gone beyond this I am sorry, it is no easy matter to hit the mean. Of course I am prepared for a good deal of sharp criticism, for I imagine the sympathies of the reviewers will usually be on his side, and I suspect some of them will be immensely disgusted at the work having been performed by a young and almost unknown man, not connected with any of their cliques. I shall not, if I can possibly avoid it, notice anything that may be written, until I can publish the documents referred to in my papers.... The only rules that can be laid down in Shelley's affairs are that everything happens that nobody would have expected, and that everybody concerned gets into more or less of a scrape. So I must not expect to escape the common destiny.

The last two sentences were prophetic, for Richard's reputation among Shelley scholars has remained that of Lady Shelley's champion and the promoter of her unfavorable view of Harriet. He was apparently at this time confident of being able to publish the evidence that he had hinted about, but he was eventually forced to the realization that no such documents were to be revealed, which put his chief arguments in question and made his entire position awkward. In adopting so wholeheartedly and uncritically Lady Shelley's interpretation of the poet's life, Richard lost the mark of impartiality that would have given him higher rank among those who studied and wrote on Shelley.

The reviews of *Relics of Shelley* were uniformly hostile. The *Cornhill* reviewer thought that such trivia as the early versions of poems or unconnected snatches of verse by such a great poet as Shelley should not be published, because they did nothing to enhance his reputation and would doubtless have been withheld by the poet himself. "The few letters . . . are pleasant enough. . . . The rest of the volume is a mistake."[7] The *Spectator*, in a cogent review, also regretted the publication of the book:

> It is evident that Shelley's most attached friends and relatives, while from delicate and honourable motives they refrain as yet from telling all they know of Shelley's (in some respects) unhappy life, lest it should give pain to surviving relatives of

the persons involved, yet cannot help hovering round the subject of his more questionable actions, as the moth hovers round the candle, neither willing as yet to explain fully what might rebut the worst reflections upon his conduct, nor able to let the subject sleep till the time arrives when they could do so. The literary worth of the fragments . . . is not such as to have demanded separate publication. . . . There is in fact, scarcely any *motive* for the book, except Mr. Garnett's rejoinder to Mr. T. L. Peacock, in reference to the conduct of Shelley towards his first wife; and this it would have been far more dignified to defer till it was possible to produce all the particulars to which many mysterious references are made. Except a beautiful poem of Shelley's which was published a few months ago in *Macmillan's Magazine*, and one of some merit of Mr. Garnett's own, on the poet . . . there is nothing in this book that has any literary unity or finish.

After several quotations from the work and an insightful discussion of Shelley's ethics, the writer, presumably Hutton, concluded:

[Mr. Garnett] is not unfit to write, whenever the time shall come, a complete and harmonious life of the poet, embodying all that has yet appeared, and laying no undue stress on controverted points,—and till he does so, we hope he will not again publish on the subject.[8]

Thus, despite Richard's bringing to light the "Prologue to *Hellas*" and other materials which were welcomed by later Shelleyans, his stature was little enhanced by the book. Yet he was from then on known as a Shelley scholar, the one privileged to speak with and for the Shelleys. Most of the people who wrote on the poet during Richard's lifetime consulted him, and later critics have taken a more temperate view of the *Relics*. One of these, George Edward Woodberry, the American editor of the Centenary Edition of Shelley's poetry in 1892, said: "The labors of Dr. Garnett upon the chaotic manuscripts at Boscombe stand in the next place [to Mary Shelley's work in her edition of 1839] because of the invaluable additions thus made to the poems."[9] Thomas Hutchinson, in his Oxford edition of Shelley's poetry, called the *Relics* a "precious sheaf" and "a salvage second only in value to the *Posthumous Poems* of 1824,"[10] which had been edited by Mary. Arthur Symons, as a poet and an appreciator of other poets, praised Richard's "invaluable labour on the text of Shelley, for which all students of poetry owe him gratitude."[11] A more recent scholar, Neville Rogers, also has acknowledged Richard's efforts: "Working on visits to Boscombe in such time as could be spared from his arduous labour at the British Museum, he could do no more than take soundings and periodical dives into the then uncharted depths of the Notebooks. Modern divers, better provided, can fault missed points and mistakes of deciphering; nevertheless the wonder is that he managed to fish up so much."[12] All the same, Richard's essential contributions to Shelley studies have been clouded by the distaste with which his diatribe against Peacock was received and the scorn with which his association with Lady Shelley was condemned.

On 5 July 1862 occurred a doleful event—the death of Emily Patmore. Richard had told William John as early as 28 July 1860 that "Mrs. Patmore is very ill and I fear will not recover," yet the good lady had managed to keep going for another two years, during which she had helped her husband collect an anthology of poetry for children that had been published by Macmillan at the end of 1861 and that contained two of Richard's poems. Patmore was desolated by his loss, and Richard shared his grief. The two men spent the entire night of 5 July walking on Hampstead Heath, talking, and Richard was indisposed the next day as a result. His loyalty to Patmore and Patmore's reliance on him at such a time are proof of their mutual esteem.

Mrs. Singleton had taken Narney to Ireland for two months, and the young lovers were keeping in constant touch by mail. Richard's plans for an August vacation in Clitheroe and perhaps Wales or the Lake Country were well in hand when Ellen announced that she was going to return from Germany, as her position there was coming to an end. She could travel alone as far as Cologne, but then Richard would have to meet her and escort her home. Therefore he arranged a tour via Holland to Cologne, down the Rhine to Mainz, possibly to Frankfurt, Heidelberg and Strasbourg, and then to Paris, all by rail. Early in October William John came down to London to attend the industrial exhibition then in progress and to meet Narney and her mother and brother. Afterward, he and Richard proceeded to Cologne to meet Ellen on the fifteenth. Their projected itinerary was almost a duplicate of the route Richard had taken the year before, and he was to visit the same areas once more with Narney in 1898. It was the only part of the Continent he ever saw.

In his last letter of the year to William John, on 22 December, Richard spoke out against the British press's support of the Confederate States of America:

> ... the blindness of the English people and press [is] utterly incomprehensible to me. They go on drawing bills on the Devil at mighty short dates, putting their trust now in the valour of a Jackson, now in the incapacity of a Pope,[13*] now in a New York election, now in foreign intervention, now in the premium on gold, and as fast as it is demonstrated that none of these things avail to bring the war one day nearer its termination, some new pretext is discovered for crying peace when there is no peace. If everybody had thought as I did, we should a year ago have taken some decided step such as that suggested by Mr. Bright for opening up a new cotton field. If Lancashire even now at all comprehended the imminence of her danger, there would be meetings in every town, and an agitation with which this generation has seen nothing to compare. But if we prefer to link our fortunes to those of the slaveholders, what can we expect but to share their perdition? Surely this infatuation cannot last.

Richard promised to send a check for the subscription being raised for the Manchester poor and asked William John to ascertain whether money would also be needed for those in Low Moor. It was, indeed, for his cousins at the mill were hard pressed to cope with the distress of their workers. They were distributing food and clothing and had opened a school which "nearly 200 young men and women had attended."[14] Of almost three thousand people usually employed in cotton factories in Clitheroe and Low Moor, only five hundred were still fully employed in the fall of 1862. There ensued a bitter winter that added to the general misery. Nearly half a million people were out of work in the North of England, and this situation lasted, with minor variations, until the end of the War Between the States in late 1865. Charitable contributions would be needed during all that time.

Chapter 7

Married Life, 1863–1867

In January of 1863 Richard, Narney, and Mrs. Singleton began to hunt for a house. It had been decided that Mrs. Singleton and Edward would share the home and the rent, and they were looking in the area north of Regent's Park, around Primrose Hill, where some new houses had been built. In March they found one that suited them. It was on a short street called St. Edmund's Terrace, at the northwest corner of the park, across from the zoo and parallel with Prince Albert Road. The row of brick homes faced toward the Middlesex Water Works, a view that some visitors thought ugly, but that did not displease the Garnetts and Singletons. Their house was Number 4 (later to be re-numbered 3), and after a pleasant residence there, they would pass it on to the William Rossettis.[1]*

March brought a big celebration in London for the wedding of the Prince of Wales and Princess Alexandra of Denmark. Richard, in an access of romantic feeling, composed three stanzas entitled "A Welcome" to greet the spring bride, and they were printed in the March issue of *Macmillan's*. On the day of the ceremony Richard watched the procession from Bell and Daldy's in Fleet Street, and then, with Narney and a party got up by Mr. Noble and Padmore, viewed the general illumination after dark.

The wedding date for Richard and Narney had been set for the first part of June and in the midst of the preparations, Richard's literary career had been expanding. David Masson had assumed the editorship of a new journal, the *Reader*, that had begun in January, and Richard had immediately become a contributor to it, along with such writers as F. J. Furnivall, Francis Galton, Mrs. Gaskell, Philip Hamerton, Thomas Hughes, William Rossetti, and the Reverend Leslie Stephen. Richard's first article was a review of a biography of the German philosopher Moses Mendelssohn, great-grandfather of Alexandrine Horsfall, and it appeared in the April issue. His next article reviewed the second edition of Patmore's *Angel in the House* with *Faithful for Ever* as the second volume. Richard praised the book as "destined to occupy an honourable place among British classics," and the poet as one whose mind "had dwelt for an instant with Shelley's Muse in her lucid pavilions."[2]

Besides these reviews, Richard had written for the *Illustrated London News* a section reviewing the contents of the latest issues of magazines. Covering a dozen or more publications in each article, it gave a minimal report on each; but, as one commentator said, "It was so pointed, so vivacious, so well informed, that it stood out clearly even in the excellent literary journalism of its period."[3] Richard continued to conduct this feature of the newspaper from 11 April 1863 until January of 1886. He also contributed longer reviews throughout those years.

The wedding took place on 13 June 1863 in St. Mark's Church, Regent's Park, and the newlyweds went north for their honeymoon, accompanied by Mrs. Singleton's little Irish maid, Chapple, who was now to be Narney's for life. They stayed first at Leamington, went on to Manchester to let William John show them the city, to Bowness in the Lake District, where they spent a week making excursions, and thence to Morecambe on the coast of Lancashire. Next they went to Low Moor to stay with the Garnett cousins, and at the beginning of July they proceeded to Bingley to stay with the John Horsfalls, who had a home there. They also visited Richard's recently widowed Aunt Beanlands, who promised to let Richard and William John have their father's letters to her. Last of all, they went to Otley and the house by the mill, where Richard found the family Bible with the hours of birth of all old William Garnett's children, so that he could draw their horoscopes. "They certainly confirm the truth of astrology in a surprising manner," he reported to William John on 26 July. Of Narney, he added that she "became a great favourite everywhere, and was pronounced by Uncle Peter in a farewell oration 'an excellent sample of womanhood.' "

Back in London on 23 July, they found their house in St. Edmund's Terrace much to their liking. Mrs. Singleton and Edward had taken possession of it on 14 July and had prepared it for them very nicely. Among the wedding gifts were two paintings, and Richard bought a representation of Titian's "Divine and Earthly Love," which he thought "one of the most beautiful pictures in the world." It was of importance to him to the end of his life.

Soon there was a succession of callers, among them Lady Shelley, and Richard and Narney paid calls on their new neighbors. The Hepworth Dixons lived nearby, on St. James's Terrace; the Marstons, the Monachs, the Russell Martineaus, the Augustus De Morgans, the Ormes, and the Massons (now in their own home) all lived not far away. The Rossettis—Mrs. Gabriele Rossetti and her children, William, Christina, and Maria—lived across the park on Albany Street, and Dante Gabriel, who lived in Chelsea, visited them often. Narney became a special friend of Christina.

Richard was writing "a good deal" for the *Reader*, and he had discovered at the Shelleys' some letters of the poet Samuel Taylor Coleridge to William

Godwin, father of Mary Shelley, for which he had composed an introduction. Then he had written to Ernest Hartley Coleridge, whom he knew, to ask permission to publish them. One of the Coleridge family had objections, so Richard dined with "Mr. J. D. Coleridge and his father, the Judge,"[4]* to discuss the matter, and a solution was worked out. The letters appeared in *Macmillan's* in April of 1864.

William John's position in the Manchester firm had become precarious, and he was now rescued by an offer from a relative to help establish a cotton-ginning factory in Egypt. Robert Corkling was a merchant who was trying to find a source of raw cotton to replace the vanished American supply, and he had found that Egypt offered not only the crop, but cheap labor to process it. Corkling had married the daughter of the Reverend Richard Garnett's youngest sister, Mary Booth, and he was willing to give William John a responsible role in the venture. Unfortunately, profits were slow in coming and there was trouble with the Manchester banks that had lent the capital; but William John stayed in Egypt for five years, working at the factory as financial manager all winter and returning to England in the summer. He stabilized his position in 1866 by securing the title of British consular agent in Mansoura (El Mansura), in the Nile Delta, the top rank of his checkered career. He remained, however, a constant care to Richard, who faithfully wrote news and advice from London, where his own responsibilities were steadily increasing.

For the London Garnetts, 1864 began auspiciously with Richard's discovery of an unpublished letter of Shelley's bound into a book in the British Museum library, and this was followed by an invitation to Richard and Narney to visit Boscombe. Lady Shelley offered to invite Mrs. T. J. Hogg, the former Jane Williams, so that Richard could meet her and inquire about Hogg's papers; but the visit was delayed for an entire year, for various reasons, and the meeting with Mrs. Hogg apparently never took place.

In April Richard received a charming gift from Patmore, who had taken leave from the British Museum for his health and was traveling in Italy. He wrote from Rome, "I went to the Protestant Burial Ground to see if I could find some violets for you on the graves of Shelley and Keats. I have got one from Shelley's and three from Keats's. It was a little too late. A week before, I was told, the two graves were a mass of violets."[5]* When Patmore returned from Italy he remarried, his wife bringing him a comfortable income that allowed him to retire from the British Museum and conserve his health by living in the country. He bought an estate in Sussex called Heron's Ghyll, which he set about improving.

Another good friend of Richard's also left London when David Masson was appointed professor of rhetoric at Edinburgh University. About eighty of his friends gave him a farewell dinner at the Freemasons' Tavern on 28 October. These two losses were partly offset by the birth of a daughter to Richard and Narney on 17 May. She was named for that month.

Patmore's retirement left a place to be filled in the Department of Printed Books, and Winter Jones submitted Richard's name for promotion to the upper section of the first-class assistants. But Panizzi claimed that rank for one of his favorites, E. A. Roy, who had been tending the music collections and was now to work on the catalogue of books. Jones did not consider Roy's work outstanding, but Panizzi thought him long overdue for advancement and ignored the fact that he was two places below Richard in the staff roll. Richard was hurt at being passed over, but when Jones explained Panizzi's reasoning, he accepted the situation.

The year 1866 brought the addition of a new life to Richard's family and the loss of an old one. Robert Singleton Garnett was born on 27 March and was christened on 10 May in the presence of his godfather, Frederick Farrar, and also the Marstons, the Cumberlands, and the Nobles. On 4 April, Rayne Garnett died in Bournemouth, where she had gone for the sea air to relieve a chronic cough. She had played almost no part in Richard's life for some time. Another ending had come with the death of Thomas Love Peacock on 23 January, and his library was put up for auction in June. Upon Richard's recommendation, and through an agent he secured for them, the Shelleys bid successfully on three lots.

On 19 May was published the first of Richard's long series of monthly articles devoted to "Contemporary German Literature" for the *Saturday Review*, which he continued until the beginning of 1882. These reviews have been called "bright and lively,"[6] even though each was very brief, as he had to cover ten or twelve books in about two printed pages. In later years Richard found this task "an obstinate bore,"[7] yet with some redeeming effects: "The advantage of the German summary is that it enables one to be impertinent with impunity to eminent men, and to instruct others on subjects of which one knows nothing oneself. Still the employment is one in which I contrive in a humble way to do a little good, and in which an illiberal or cantankerous person might easily do much harm. Lastly and principally, it contributes to the boiling of the pot."[8] The paperbound books he received under this contract were said to have been stored in the bathtub off Richard's dressing room, where they collected dust and once astonished eight-year-old Arthur Rossetti, William's son, causing him to think the Garnetts never bathed.[9]*

In June there was a great movement in the British Museum when Panizzi resigned as principal librarian. He had wanted to be relieved a year before, but had been asked to stay on for a while and had agreed to do so. At last his health forbade his remaining in office any longer, and he turned over the reins to John Winter Jones. This did not mean the end of his influence at the Museum, however, for he retained his interest in all that went on there and proffered his advice, especially about the Department of Printed Books. The successor to Jones as keeper of the department was Thomas Watts, and the new assistant keeper in charge of the reading room was George Bullen, a "genial

Irishman,"[10] who got along well with everyone. Bullen took to his new position with more aplomb than had Watts, and he started the tradition of friendly service to readers that Richard was to continue brilliantly in the future.

At the January 1867 meeting of the trustees it was decided to establish a separate Department of Maps, Plans, and Charts, under the direction of the map specialist, R. H. Major, whose place in the upper section of first-class assistants thus became open. Richard had every expectation of achieving the rank this time, but again he was disappointed. Panizzi's influence secured the advance for W. R. S. Ralston, who was two years and two places below Richard in seniority, and Richard was highly indignant. He threatened to resign, and again had to be soothed by Jones; but he was a long time getting over this second slight, suffered within a few months of the first. Panizzi had, of course, specified that length of service was not to be the basis of selection for the higher rank, and besides that, Ralston had been working on the catalogue of printed books, which was so important to Panizzi, while Richard had been absorbed in classifying new acquisitions. Ralston had made himself the department's Russian-language expert by assiduous study, and his expectations were certainly as high as Richard's, but as it turned out, they were a little too high, and he was to leave the Museum in disgrace eight years later.[11]*

Richard, on the other hand, may well have made up his mind at this time that he would become keeper of printed books some day, by staying on and working for advancement at the next opportunity. Yet his otherwise perfect contentment with his work had been irremediably marred. This could be part of the reason for the few family letters for 1866 and 1867 that have been preserved.

Chapter 8

New Family, New Friends, 1868–1870

On 5 January 1868 Edward Garnett was born, named for his maternal grandfather and uncle, and destined to develop into more of a Singleton than either May or Robert, who inherited the Garnett facial features and general orthodoxy. Edward resembled his mother in features and his Irish forebears in personality, becoming less willing to be bound by convention than his siblings. He would be the most distinguished of all Richard's children, but he cost his mother some of her health. She had a setback in March, causing Richard to be absent from the Museum. He wrote to Alexander Macmillan on Tuesday, 31 March, "I am sorry to tell you that Mrs. Garnett has been very ill since Sunday, and I may be unable to leave her [for a projected appointment] if her indisposition should increase, but I hope and think that the reverse is more likely to be the case."[1] Her improvement was slow, however, for in September, although she was better, she was not yet strong.

In the *Saturday Review* for 18 January 1868 Richard had reviewed the first volume of *Das Kapital*, which had been published in England by Williams and Norgate, and he displayed a wary appreciation of its power:

> Herr Marx is a political economist of the most advanced democratic school. In his eyes the capitalist is the enemy of the human species, and the wealth of the individual involves the misery of the mass. These opinions are obtaining some currency in certain orders of society, and, as it is desirable that they should be thoroughly studied and comprehended, Herr Marx's work may repay attention. The author's views may be as pernicious as we conceive them to be, but there can be no question as to the plausibility of his logic, the vigour of his rhetoric, and the charm with which he invests the driest problems of political economy. His facts and illustrations, moreover, are chiefly derived from the social circumstances of England, where he appears to have resided for some years.[2]

Marx had been reading at the British Museum, but there was no reason for Richard to be aware of his presence there. In later life the men met and their daughters became friends.

Richard's friendship with William Michael Rossetti began to deepen when Rossetti decided to write on Shelley. In November of 1868 he went to call on J. Bertrand Payne, of Moxon's, to consult about the firm's new series of volumes of popular poetry, which Rossetti was to edit. The copyright on Mary Shelley's edition of Shelley's poems having expired, he wanted to begin the series with Shelley. He told William Allingham, the Irish poet, who was acquainted with Sir Percy and Lady Shelley, that in his elation over the possibility of the assignment, "willingly would I not only be doing it for pay, but do it for nothing, or pay to do it."[3] Payne had advised him that Richard had been collecting materials for a biography of Shelley, but that his project was "in abeyance and may probably not be done,"[4]* because Sir Percy objected to the accounting of Shelley's first marriage. This was surely a misunderstanding of the relationship of Richard with the Shelleys on the question of Harriet Shelley, yet even Richard may have had some difficulty in finding a discreet way to explain the events of Shelley's youth. In any case, Rossetti felt free to go ahead with an edition of the poems which would contain a biographical memoir.

However, word of his endeavor leaked out and was printed in the *Athenaeum* on 30 January 1869, whereupon Rossetti wrote to Richard, lest he think his friend was "poaching on his preserves."[5] Richard, habitually generous, offered to help him, and they dined together at the Garnetts' on 8 March, when Richard turned over some materials to him. They probably discussed a proposal, whether their own or Payne's, that they cooperate in writing a full-length biography of Shelley; but both men were too independent to accommodate easily to such a plan. Furthermore, Rossetti wanted to avoid any contact with Sir Percy and Lady Shelley, and he insisted, over Richard's importuning, on including in his memoir all the known and published facts of Shelley's life that he deemed necessary to understanding. He said frankly that he "should find it equally painful to resist or to yield to" pressure from either Richard or the Shelleys.[6]* This attempt at neutrality was not enough, however, to save him from some of the opprobrium that was bestowed on nearly all Shelley scholars in the late nineteenth century.

In July, Rossetti returned Richard's dinner invitation, and during the evening Edward Trelawny called. Rossetti was somewhat nervous about the encounter, since he knew Trelawny was on bad terms with the Shelleys but was quite aware of Richard's friendship with them. Happily, the meeting turned out well, and Richard made a "good impression" on the older man.[7] Rossetti was extremely grateful for Richard's unselfish assistance in sharing information and opinions, and in reading the entire manuscript of the memoir of Shelley.

Richard published another book in 1869—*Idylls and Epigrams, Chiefly from the Greek Anthology*. This one had a Macmillan imprint. It came out in March and was reviewed favorably in the *Saturday* and *Westminster* reviews. It contained 171 pieces (Richard always used Roman numerals: CLXXI), twenty-nine of which were entirely his own, the rest, translations from classical writers. Two of the latter were verses by his father, slightly revised. All were gracefully expressed and full of the penetrating insight into human nature that marked Richard's later creative writing.

The book started a vogue for epigrams that flourished in England for a number of years. Richard presented a copy to Frederick Locker, who had given Richard his own *London Lyrics* (1857) the year before. Then, in January of 1871, Richard sent a copy of the *Idylls* to Dante Gabriel Rossetti, after chatting with him at Marstons' and learning that the poet-painter "would accept" one.[8] In July of that year Tennyson acknowledged receipt of a copy, calling it a "graceful" work.[9]

On 9 September 1869 Richard's friend Thomas Watts, the keeper of printed books at the British Museum, died as the result of an accident. Richard wrote the obituary for the *Illustrated London News* and would later memorialize Watts in the *Dictionary of National Biography*. The keeper's sudden demise required another round of promotions at the Museum, and there was competition for the vacant position. Ralston felt that he was entitled to it and wrote to Panizzi asking for his recommendation. Despite his earlier favoring of Ralston for advancement, Panizzi responded with a letter that was characterized as "rather harsh and unforgiving."[10] Just what Ralston needed to be forgiven for is not revealed, but he did not receive the appointment. Panizzi and Jones agreed that the new keeper should be W. B. Rye, and Ralston took grave offense at the decision. Rye was the senior assistant keeper, so was in the traditional line for advancement to the headship of the department, and he had served in various important capacities since 1838. Nevertheless, he was a mild man who would be a weak administrator. It is even possible that Panizzi deliberately chose first Jones, then Rye, to fill his former keepership because he knew he could dominate them and so maintain his sway over the department. Ralston was evidently convinced of this, and later, when Rye's term of office was marred by increasing dissatisfaction among the staff, Ralston took a bitter revenge for his rebuff over the keepership.

Richard was still waiting for his expected promotion, and he got it at last in November of 1869, when a member of the zoology department was raised to assistant keeper, leaving vacant his place in the upper section of the senior assistants. Rye and Jones both recommended that Richard be advanced, and the trustees concurred. His increase in salary would be welcome support for a growing family.

William Rossetti's two-volume edition of Shelley's poetical works was published in January of 1870, and Lady Shelley immediately took offense. She wrote in some heat to Richard on 28 January asking him to "run down"[11] to Boscombe to help Sir Percy decide what to do about it, contemplating a letter to the editor, yet not wanting to get involved in a lengthy public dispute. Richard did not go to Boscombe until the end of April, but by then the reviews of Rossetti's work were out and were by no means favorable. Ollier, in the *Daily News*, was the kindest to him, but some reviewers accused him of over-editing, while others regretted his disparagement of Harriet Shelley in the memoir of the poet. Thus Rossetti, as editor and author, was damned for major flaws in both roles.

Now began to blossom one of Richard's dearest friendships, that with Mathilde Blind, a German writer of poetry and prose who was about Narney's age. She had come to London with her mother and her step-father, Karl Blind, in 1853, after he had been exiled from Germany, France, and Belgium for his revolutionary activities. He was making a living in England by writing, and his home was open to all political refugees. Among those who frequented it were Mazzini, Garibaldi, Karl Marx, A. A. Ledru-Rollin, and Louis Blanc. Mathilde thus grew up in an atmosphere of fervent dedication to individual freedom, and though she was sent to school, she learned more from wide reading in European literature. Her appearance was striking: luxuriant, shining dark hair framed classic features, with "glorious eyes that were so eloquent of speech."[12] Her actual speech was marred by a harsh southern German accent, but she "shone principally in conversation, her brilliant things were sparks struck out from the collision of mind with mind,"[13] altogether "a person of extreme beauty and fire."[14]

Richard probably met her in the home of the Ford Madox Browns, with whom she was especially friendly, in 1866, when she was dressed in mourning for her brother Ferdinand, who had tried to assassinate Count Bismarck, the Prussian leader, on 7 May—he had been immediately imprisoned, and had committed suicide in his cell on the following day. Richard wrote that, in her black costume, Mathilde had made an "impression of combined beauty, dignity, and sorrow [that would] never be effaced from his recollection."[15] When he learned that she admired Shelley's works, their friendship was bound to grow. She had been writing poetry since 1859 and had had a book of poems published in 1867 under a pseudonym. Now she was thinking of doing a small edition of Shelley's poems, with a memoir, for the German publisher Tauchnitz's series of English poets.

On 9 January 1870 she delivered a lecture on Shelley which brought her before the public and gained her the sponsorship of John Chapman, editor of the *Westminster Review*. The lecture was also published as a pamphlet, and Richard sent a copy to Lady Shelley, who was very favorably impressed. She thought "Miss Blind's outline of Shelley's life, which covers I think only half a page, a much more truthful one, and describes what Shelley really was a thousand times better than Rossetti's Memoir."[16] Richard quoted this sentence in a letter to Mathilde, adding:

> You see she is not pleased with the said memoir; but pray don't mention this, I should be distressed if it got round to Rossetti's ears and occasioned him any

additional vexation. There is a review in today's *Athenaeum* which will try his equanimity quite enough. It is hard to devote a year to earnest, self-denying labour according to the best of one's light, and meet in return with indifference or abuse. But his is not the first vine which has, to a certain extent, brought forth wild grapes.[17]

Rossetti's *Shelley* was reviewed in the *Athenaeum* for 29 January by Robert Buchanan, a conservative poet and novelist who bore a grudge against the Rossettis. The *Times*, however, had also been critical of Rossetti's work, in its issue for 21 January.

Chapman offered to publish a review of the book by Mathilde, and Richard helped her with it—a little too much, it seems, for she wrote to him on 25 January, "It is really too kind of you to have taken all this trouble to draw up a syllabus of a review for me. I assure you I was quite delighted with it. It will certainly be a great help to me although of course I must think the subject out for myself." In her review Mathilde noted that Rossetti had been able to use original materials found by Richard since the publication of *Relics of Shelley* in 1862. "We must here express how deeply we are indebted to Mr. Garnett and to the liberality of Shelley's representatives, in now being able to offer the results of a more minute examination made since the publication of [Rossetti's] edition."[18] Rossetti seems to have taken no offense at Richard's thus enabling Mathilde to make corrections to his text as published, which had previously been approved by Richard. However, Mathilde joined all other reviewers in regretting Rossetti's tampering with Shelley's grammar and spelling, inadequate as these sometimes were, although she praised his "spirit of affectionate enthusiasm." She commented favorably on the *Shelley Memorials* and harshly on Peacock's reminiscences: a "cold and uninviting work" that showed Peacock's "entire incapacity to understand" Shelley.[19] She then added a new note by praising Shelley for expressing "in a shape of the loftiest loveliness, the most momentous of all our modern ideas—that of the emancipation of women from . . . subjection to men."[20]

It was evident that Richard and Lady Shelley had a disciple who would aid in projecting the proper estimate of Percy Bysshe Shelley. Mathilde proceeded to work on Rossetti's edition of the poems, with Richard's help, while both of them retained Rossetti's good will, so that when a second edition of his work was published by Moxon in 1878, it was more carefully edited and, by general consent, greatly improved.

Richard and Mathilde found that they had much in common besides admiration for Shelley: chiefly their own poetry and philosophy of life, and an interest in the great German poets. They corresponded regularly, Mathilde came to the Museum to chat with Richard, and he called on her at her parents' home. On 21 February 1870 Richard began a letter with "My dear Mathilde (if I may call you so)," instead of "Dear Miss Blind." On 24 February he told her that he was pleased when she assented to his dropping the "Miss," for he said he had wanted to do so "long ago, but there is nothing I so much abhor as the mere semblance of taking a liberty." In the letter of 21 February Richard wrote that Narney "was exceedingly ill last night, but is quiet this morning—worn out, in fact, with pain. The pain is now subdued, and if we can prevent its recurring she will no doubt recover rapidly." He was always ostensibly optimistic about Narney's health problems, which grew more frequent and acute over the years; but there is no way of knowing what ailments Victorian delicacy covered up in veiled references to sickness.

Richard told Mathilde of the inception of his friendship with Edward Dowden of Trinity College, Dublin, which occurred at this time. Dowden had sent Rossetti a pamphlet of Shelley's as a gift; but Rossetti already had a copy, so he suggested that this one might be passed on to Richard, either for the British Museum or for himself. On 20 February Rossetti advised Richard that "Mr. Dowden now very handsomely presents it to you—saying the pamphlet 'of right belongs to him rather than to me, since he knows more of Shelley than I do, and therefore loves him better.' "[21] Richard was deeply touched, but felt that he could not accept so great a gift, and asked to be allowed to return it after showing it to Mathilde and making a copy. Dowden, however, insisted that he keep it.[22]

In March Richard sent Mathilde a copy of *Io in Egypt*, which she praised warmly, comparing some of its lines to some of Keats's. In April he sent her a copy of a story he had written called "The Firefly," which he thought she might like to translate into German and try to publish in a German periodical. He had another story that he would show her when it was "presentably written out." The first tale was about a firefly who was never contented, and a magician's attempts to satisfy her. Mathilde wanted Richard to change the ending. He replied on 18 April, "I cannot consent to omit the end of the story, it would destroy the moral, so far as the Magician is concerned. I want to show that though he regretted the firefly's discontent and would have done his utmost to remove it, he in his heart loved her the better for it. Very inconsistent, no doubt, but true to nature. If inconsistency is an attribute even of wise Magicians—how much more of us ordinary mortals, who are no conjurers!" Mathilde was noted for chronic discontent, so this is a personal allusion.

The second story was probably "A Page from the Book of Folly," which would be published in *Temple Bar* the next year and is about a foolish lover who imagined that his lady remained true to him when he was far away—perhaps another personal message to Mathilde. Although he was trying in various ways to help her write for publication, he assured her that "my regard for you is not in the least dependent upon your fortunes as an author, neither are my opportunities of enjoying your society to depend upon them." He also mentioned that he was going to spend three or four days with the Shelleys during the last week in April. Apparently he found some treasure during this visit, for Mathilde, on 2 May, was delighted with his "news about your Shelley harvest."

Then Mathilde told him of a projected tête-à-tête with the book illustrator J.T. Nettleship, and Richard said on 30 May he would accompany her if possible, but if he could not, he thought it would be respectable for her to go by herself, as no "ill-conditioned person" would be likely to hear of it. "It is one of the arguments which weighs most with me in favour of another life, that there surely must be some place where one can follow one's innocent inclinations and impulses without the eternal checks and circumspections and vigilance which one finds necessary here." This kind of caution he was to feel even more keenly at the end of his life.

In this letter he reported on a party at the Marstons' which he and Ellen had attended. Among the guests were Dante Rossetti, William Morris, the Madox Browns and their daughter, Lucy (who was to marry William Rossetti in 1874), and Dr. Hueffer[23]* (who was to marry Catherine Brown in 1872). "The party might have been made for you," he told Mathilde, "and I regretted infinitely that you could not be there. Morris was very lively, and talked much to Ellen. Rossetti was mute as long as I stayed, but I understood that he waxed eloquent after the departure of the womankind (his taste is widely different from mine) and remained with Morris and two or three men till 3:30. Ellen and I returned at the comparatively Philistine hour of one."

On 19 July Richard wrote to Mathilde from Clitheroe, where he was paying his first visit since his honeymoon in 1863. He was on his way to Wales, but was so warmly received in so many Garnett homes that he was staying an extra day in Lancashire. "It is pleasant to come back after seven years' absence to a place where some of the happiest days of your youth were passed, and to find oneself in the midst of attached friends and relatives, most of whom one has not seen for nearly as long. By reason of the brevity of human life this is not a pleasure one can enjoy very frequently, so I am trying to make the most of it." He proceeded southward to dine with his ailing Uncle Jeremiah, now living at Sale, Cheshire, south of Manchester. It was their last meeting, for Jeremiah died on 27 September.

William John had returned from Egypt in May, recovering from a severe illness, and had consulted a doctor in London. He then drifted about the North of England trying to find gainful employment, but without success. He had speculated in cotton futures while in Mansoura and had ended with a debt of £6000; yet his ventures in 1870 and 1871 only increased his obligations. He was finally rescued by Robert Tennant, who had married Jeremiah's second daughter, Harriette. Tennant came of the landed gentry, had inherited a fortune, and had made another in railways and mines.[24]* He and Harriette and their eleven children lived in a large house near Leeds, called Scarcroft Hall. Robert also had two lodges in Scotland where he took shooting and fishing holidays, and at one of which he once entertained the Prince of Wales for a week. The other lodge, Rose Hall, in Sutherland, had come to him from Jeremiah as part of Harriette's marriage portion. The Tennants not only paid off a large part of William John's debt, but hired him to tutor their fifth and sixth sons, Frederick, eight, and Gilbert, seven. This was a face-saving way of giving William John a home, and from then until 1880 he was with the Tennants most of the time, becoming particularly friendly with the third son, Cecil, and enlivening the household with his natural jollity. The arrangement was a great relief to Richard, yet he was not entirely free from the burden of William John's fate, for the times were bad, with recession striking all classes, and it was impossible for William John to make a good enough income to retire his indebtedness.

Chapter 9

Much Ado about Shelley, 1871–1874

At the beginning of 1871 Narney went to stay with the Patmores at Heron's Ghyll, where she could relax in a happy atmosphere, a congenial environment in which to recuperate from the stress of her social responsibilities and her young family. Richard had been invited to accompany her, but he was not able to leave his duties at the British Museum. Instead, he wrote to ask her when she planned to return, and evidenced some impatience at her absence. However, he had not lacked for amusement, having attended the marriage of young friends. "It was quite a literary wedding. Mr. Poole gave away the bride, young Browning was groomsman, Miss Thackeray one of the bridesmaids, [and] the Hawthornes were present."[1]* Richard and Narney had also been invited to the Blinds' on 31 January in honor of the German poet Ferdinand Freiligrath and his wife, who were going the social round in London. Richard, having translated some of Freiligrath's poems, was delighted to meet him, and Mathilde became a close friend of his daughter Käthe.

In July Mathilde, who had now left her family to live alone, went with the Madox Browns to Lynmouth, Devon, where Shelley and Harriet had stayed for several months. She wrote to Richard from there on 22 July that she had "discovered an old woman who lived with Mrs. Hooper at the time Shelley lodged with her in 1812." Mathilde had spent a morning with the woman, a Mrs. Blackmore, listening to her reminiscences, and learned that she possessed a bill of Shelley's for £30, and a letter from him enclosing £20 and promising the rest; but Mrs. Blackmore said that £5 of it had never been paid (Shelley was notoriously negligent about his debts), and Mathilde suggested that "we lovers of Shelley" pay the amount with £1 interest. Dr. Hueffer offered a single pound and Mathilde another. She was sure Richard would want to help with the remainder.

At the same time that Mathilde was writing to him, Richard was composing a letter to her from his holiday quarters at Littlehampton, Sussex:

64

I have been dreaming about you half the night, and accept the vision as an intimation from the happy Gods that it is time I wrote to you. Indeed, I have been of the same opinion for the last two or three days, but you know that the distractions of a seaside place are not favourable to correspondence. Now don't go and get up a plea on that ground for not writing to me. I trust that you have no distractions, but have taken up some branch of poetry, or philosophy or criticism respecting which you will be only too glad to expatiate to a willing listener. Our communications have latterly been rather too much of a business character for my benefit. I shall always rejoice that I have been permitted to interest myself in your affairs, still I greatly miss the happy days when I used to go up to your little room and talk literature and all translunary matters. I best know how much I have lost by their cessation, and live in hopes of their return—meanwhile if you have any ideas, let me have the benefit of them. I have none. . . . Before concluding . . . I must inform you that my dreams culminated in the discovery of a most useful commodity entitled "Intermediate Morality," by virtue of which we were all to become less stiff than we are while continuing equally respectable. Unfortunately I have entirely forgotten what it was, so the human race must go on stumbling in darkness for the present.[2*]

Obviously Mathilde's friendship meant a great deal to Richard and he regretted the social conventions that made awkward such an intellectual relationship as theirs. He always enjoyed exchanging thoughts and beliefs with a sympathetic feminine mind, and his association with Mathilde was unusually rewarding to him.

The news about Shelley's unpaid account was intriguing, and Richard promised to help discharge the debt, though he had no money to spare at his vacation place, and he gently scolded Mathilde for being too generous with her limited funds. He thought the bill, with the autograph letter, would be worth three or four pounds on the market, and perhaps even more if Mrs. Blackmore would write "paid" on the bottom of the bill, with the date, making it uniquely valuable. He also remarked, on 25 July, "There is another person at Lynmouth in whom I am deeply interested, besides Shelley, and I could have wished that she would have given me some particulars about herself."

Narney was awaiting the birth of her fourth child, Olivia Rayne Garnett, to be called Olive, who was born on 21 August. The other children had remained in Littlehampton, presumably with Chapple, and Richard returned for them at the end of the month. On the 31st Mathilde sent good wishes for Narney and the baby, along with the news that she had contracted with Tauchnitz for the one-volume edition of Shelley's poems, and had asked £35 for it. Then she added, somewhat imperiously, "When are you coming back to town? I should like to have Hogg's life of Shelley, Shelley Memorials, and Trelawny's book, and anything else you may have in that way. . . . I wonder whether you could let me have two more numbers of the Illustrated News and also an Academy . . . . " Richard replied on the same day that he would supply the books and periodicals as soon as he reached London, on the fourth or fifth of September.

The year 1872 began with another Shelleyan flurry when a book was published by the radical "catchpenny" press of John Camden Hotten, who was known for printing sensational writings. It was *The Poetical Works of Percy Bysshe Shelley, now first given from the author's original editions, with some hitherto unrelated pieces: First Series, "Queen Mab" and the early poems, with a memoir by Leigh Hunt.* The words "First Series," promising further publications of the same sort from the same source, were particularly disturbing to Sir Percy and Lady Shelley, as they had not given their authorization for the present edition. The editor was Richard Herne Shepherd, who had published a series of "booksellers' editions" of classics, and also some juvenilia by noted poets, without getting the permission of their representatives. The name of Leigh Hunt, however, as Shelley's good friend, gave the book a certain cachet. Mathilde Blind wrote an anonymous letter to the *Athenaeum* saying that there was nothing new in "Mr. Hotten's Shelley."[3] Hotten immediately replied that the book contained the Stockdale letters verbatim, Richard's account of them in *Macmillan's* in 1860 ("Shelley in Pall Mall") having been "most inaccurate, and therefore of but trifling literary value."[4] Hotten said that he had undertaken his "pocket edition" to answer the criticism, in the *Athenaeum* itself, of Rossetti's over-correcting of the texts of Shelley's poems, by printing them as they were originally published.

Mathilde, this time over her own name, and Richard then replied to Hotten; their letters were printed in the following issue. Richard said:

> As the letters [from Shelley to Stockdale] were originally published by me, permit me to remark that with the exception of one or two such trivial variations as the substitution of "must" for *will*, Mr. Shepherd's text is identically the same as mine. He perhaps meant to imply that, while accurately transcribing Shelley's language, I did not set him the example of copying Stockdale's rubbish also. Such is the fact; the explanation is that in writing for *Macmillan's Magazine* I considered myself to be addressing a refined and respectable body of readers.[5]*

The last sentence explains Richard's censorious attitude toward scholarship all too clearly. In his father's generation it would not have been considered amiss, but things had changed by 1870.

Lady Shelley now invited Richard and Narney to Boscombe. She noted that "on the 4th of March we expect a little visit from Mr. Paul, a clergyman of very enlarged mind & I think it might be interesting for you to meet him."[6] This was Charles Kegan Paul, who was soon to leave the church to devote himself to literature, and eventually to publishing. The meeting was arranged and Lady Shelley asked Richard to bring her, from her London house, Godwin's manuscript entitled "Genius of Christianity Unveiled," which Paul wanted to edit for publication.

Meanwhile Rossetti had had a series of conferences with Edward Trelawny, who was in correspondence with Mary Shelley's step-mother's daughter,

"Claire" Clairmont, in Italy. Claire had lived with Mary and Shelley from the time of their elopement, but she had been on rather bad terms with Mary, which meant that she was *persona non grata* to Sir Percy and Lady Shelley. It was thought that she had gone mad, but actually she merely lived a reclusive life with a niece. Rossetti called on her while in Italy in 1873. For now, he was reading Claire's letters at Trelawny's and was making a summary of the insights he had gleaned from them. He gave this to Mathilde to read, then told Richard about it.

Richard, far from being glad for the new information Rossetti was uncovering, became apprehensive that something unpleasant might be revealed. He asked to see the summary, and, almost predictably, found statements that were as objectionable to him as he knew they would be to the Shelleys. Understanding that Trelawny intended to publish "further Shelley Memoranda supplied by himself and Miss Clairmont, at his own expense, if needful,"[7] Richard prepared a refutation of what he expected Claire to say in the form of two letters to a newspaper. He sent copies of them to Sir Percy and Lady Shelley, apologizing for having quoted without permission passages from letters of Percy Bysshe and Mary Shelley. He had done so, he said, because he "considered that these slanders could not be effectually disposed of otherwise," and added, "I will hurry my own work, and try to answer these calumnies by anticipation."[8] There is no clue as to what his "own work" on Shelley might have been; but he told Mathilde on 28 February that he had prepared his reply in advance to Trelawny "entirely upon my own responsibility, that I might have an answer to those who should accuse me of being merely prompted by the family." He sent her a copy of his "memorandum," saying she could "show it to Swinburne [a good friend of hers], or anybody you think entitled to see it by regard for Shelley; but you must not let it go out of your hands, or allow anybody to copy any part of it [as] I have not Sir Percy's permission to circulate passages from his parents' letters. . . ."

Lady Shelley replied the same day that she had been "buried in papers," trying to find evidence to use in combating whatever Claire might bring up, yet she and Sir Percy were grateful for Richard's concern and wanted him and Narney to come a day early [i.e., 3 March] to talk things over. "What should we have ever done without you!—Your wonderful memory strikes me with awe & astonishment—You always seem to be able to put your finger on the right place at once to knock the attempted slander on the head."[9] Sir Percy, writing the next day, added his "gratitude for the energy and skill with which you have battled that mad creature Miss Clairmont. It was a perverse chance for her that it ever came to your knowledge that this new libel on the dead was in embryo."[10]*

Richard and Narney paid their visit to Boscombe on the appointed date, but Kegan Paul was not able to join them. In the end it was as well, for Richard made a discovery: Mary Shelley's copy of a diary kept by the friend of

Shelley's last days, Edward Ellerker Williams. The diary had been in Williams's pocket when he was drowned with Shelley in the Gulf of Spezia in 1822. Richard copied some of the entries and sent them to Rossetti. Thirty years later the original diary was presented to the British Museum by Williams's grandson, and Richard, who had arranged the donation, also edited the manuscript for publication.

While at Boscombe, Richard was given a poetic assignment. Sir Percy and Lady Shelley had arranged with the occupants of Field Place to have a small memorial plaque placed in the birth room of Percy Bysshe Shelley, and they asked Richard to compose a fitting inscription. He produced the following lines:

> Shrine of the dawning speech and thought
> Of Shelley, sacred be
> To all who bow where Time has brought
> Gifts to Eternity.

The Shelleys were pleased with the lines and had them cut in brass and placed in the room about a year later.

Another person who had known Percy Bysshe Shelley now became known to Sir Percy—a Miss Elizabeth Rumble of Plymouth. She had been a member of the household of a friend of William Godwin's, Mrs. Maria Gisborne, whom Shelley and Mary had visited during their years in Italy. Sir Percy wrote to ask Miss Rumble if she had any papers relating to Shelley and Mary that he might see. She replied, on 24 March 1872, that she had some, but that she was too ill to make a list of them to send. Early in April Richard offered to go to Plymouth and estimate the value of the lady's possessions, and Sir Percy accepted the offer, considering Richard better able to judge in such a situation. "You must have no reluctance," he wrote, "in viewing the financial part of this business with my eyes."[11] Neither Sir Percy nor Richard was a spendthrift. Furthermore, it was Richard who wanted to make use of whatever might be found. He went to Plymouth on 1 May and bought a pound's worth of papers for the Shelleys and five pounds' worth for himself; but the astute old lady placed a price on the bulk of her mementoes that neither man was prepared to pay. Nor would she allow Sir Percy to pick and choose among them, as he would have liked to do.

Five years later Richard was to spend another two days with Miss Rumble, but by then Lady Shelley had offended her by something said in a letter, and at all events, there was no hope of any accommodation between them, because Miss Rumble disliked Mary Shelley. Further, she had said of Percy Bysshe Shelley that he "might be clever as a Poet but as a man he was certainly mad,"[12] a statement sure to anger Richard as well as the Shelleys. At last she decided to put the papers up for auction, and the sale took place at Puttick and Simpson's on 28 May 1878. Sir Percy could then buy as much as he wished, and it turned out that he wished for very little. His agent told Richard that at the Rumble sale he was authorized to bid what he considered a fair price for a manuscript dealing with Shelley and Mary, and he got it for £58, only to discover that Sir Percy was unwilling to pay more than £20 for it.[13]

Richard's most significant accomplishment in 1872 could be said to be the composition and publication of the third of his short stories that were later included in the selection of his tales entitled *The Twilight of the Gods:* "Ananda the Miracle Worker," which appeared in *Fraser's Magazine* for August. It was translated into French and published in the *Revue Britannique* in November, and has been reprinted, in its English version, thirteen times to 1960, making it one of his most popular works. It is a tale of religion, set in India, and describes the career of an apostle who tried in vain to obey his master's injunction against performing miracles. For example, he found a boy lying "in a fit" on the ground, with a group of "Brahmins" trying to exorcise the causative demon. Ananda decided to rescue the lad from the dire exorcism procedures and, at the same time, to acquire merit for himself.

> Yielding to this temptation, he strode forward, chased away the Brahmins with an air of authority, and, uplifting his countenance to heaven, recited the appellations of seven devils. No effect ensuing, he repeated seven more, and so continued until, the fit having passed off in the course of nature, the patient's paroxysms ceased, he opened his eyes, and Ananda restored him to his relatives. But the people cried loudly, "A miracle! A miracle!" . . .

Ananda was thereafter expected to perform miracles, and he soon learned that the way to make converts to his creed was "by perseverance in the path of deceit and disobedience." He managed to escape various torments, from impalement to boiling caldron, by clever ruses devised by an incarnation of his holy master, who appeared at the crucial moments. At last, in punishment for his spiritual pride, Ananda had a dream vision of demons awaiting his entrance to Hell, and, frightened into contrition, he realized that his only achievement as a disciple had been his failure to perform an actual miracle.

In January 1873 Kegan Paul's edition of Godwin's *Essays Never Before Published* came out, and Richard reviewed it for the *Examiner*, signing himself "G." He asked Mathilde on 17 February not to "mention it as mine at present, except to other contributors to the Examiner [she being one of them]. I shall be very willing to write further if they will let me." Only two more reviews by "G" were published in that journal, however, both of them in 1875. Godwin's theology was awkward to discuss, for he had begun as a dissenting minister, then had left the church and become an avowed atheist in 1782; but Sir Percy told Richard that "both my wife and self are very much obliged to you for the kind way in which you have managed to treat a difficult subject—so difficult that I do not wonder that after all you were not entirely satisfied with your work."[14] Sir Percy had gone over Paul's manuscript and had excised a few things, but he and Lady Shelley and Richard all thought the editing well done.

Something impelled Lady Shelley at this time to ask Richard for a list of all the Shelley documents he had, "for if any thing happened to me, Percy would be at a loss to know what had become of them without some memo to refer to."[15] It was May before Richard was able to comply with this request, and he excused himself by referring to his many occupations:

> I am almost afraid I should not even now have mustered up spirit to write, but for two things which I have to tell you. There is to be a new edition of the *Encyclopaedia Britannica,* and, having been a contributor to the last, I have obtained an introduction to the editor of the present in the hope of being enabled, among other things, to revise the article [on] Shelley, and to add others on Mrs. Shelley, Godwin, and Mary Wollstonecraft. It is an admirable opportunity for saying what one wishes, and I trust the negociation may prove successful.[16]

It did not, for the article on Shelley was instead given to William Rossetti, and although Richard contributed twenty-five articles to the ninth *Britannica,* none of those he mentioned was among them.

The second bit of news Richard had for Lady Shelley was that he had been "promised a sight" of some correspondence of Shelley that had been lent to "a friend of mine." This was Rossetti, who had discovered the letters in 1869 in the possession of a gentleman in Brighton, and who was now seeking to include them in an edition of Shelley's letters and other prose writings, to make a kind of autobiography. He was, of course, calling on Richard's knowledge, memory, and influence to aid his project. The two continued to differ, however, over Richard's desire to censor things unflattering to Shelley or Mary. In the end, the book remained unpublished, but a few copies were printed in 1879 under the title *Cor Cordium,* the words inscribed on Shelley's tomb, and it was dedicated to Richard.

There is a gap in the correspondence between Richard and Rossetti from 1873 until 1877, partly occasioned by Rossetti's trip to Italy, partly by his subsequent marriage to Lucy Madox Brown. There was a concomitant hiatus in Rossetti's work on Shelley.

Early in 1874 Richard was contemplating an essay on Mary Shelley's writings, and Lady Shelley hoped he would finish it, because "you are the only one possessing true knowledge of her who is capable of taking in the beautiful tenderness, sympathy, & unselfishness of the character, combined with so much intellectual superiority—In short I believe that your hands alone are pure enough to touch her."[17]

In May Narney was ill again, quite seriously, to judge by a letter Mathilde wrote on the eleventh: "I am indeed grieved to hear that Mrs. Garnett is not better yet. I long to call and inquire but know not whether ringing the bell . . . might not be disturbing to her." Narney was well enough in August to go with the family to Broadstairs, on the eastern tip of Kent, but she remained there for a while after Richard returned on the thirty-first to London to work on his *Encyclopaedia Britannica* articles.

Then, on 2 October, an alarming event shook the neighborhood of St. Edmund's Terrace. The Regent's Canal passed close to the north edge of the park, and just before five o'clock in the morning there was a terrific explosion, when a barge, loaded with five tons of gunpowder, blew up under the north gate bridge, destroying the bridge and the porter's lodge, and killing three bargemen. Considerable damage was sustained by houses in the area: "beds rocked to and fro, doors and shutters were burst open, plaster fell from ceilings, furniture was [moved around],"[18] and glass was shattered. All the windows in the Garnett house were broken, except those in Narney's room. At the zoo much glass was broken, and some birds escaped, though the wild animals and reptiles fortunately remained contained. To add to the pandemonium, there was a "howling wind"[19] and a gas main on the bridge was ruptured, feeding a huge blaze started by the barrels of petroleum that had been on board the barge. The cargo had also consisted of sugar, coffee, and nuts, which rained down on the roofs nearby. Eight-year-old Robert was so frightened that he was put into his mother's bed, and Richard retired to his dressing room, probably to dress and go out to survey the damage. Neighbors called a meeting to consult with each other and try to mitigate the distress of the victims of the blast, while strangers came to gawk at the destruction. Richard returned from the Museum that evening at seven with a bundle of newspapers, and the children were allowed to "come down to dessert"[20] so their father could read the various accounts of the explosion to them.

Richard had offered to help Sir Percy Shelley with an edition of Percy Bysshe Shelley's poetical works, and Lady Shelley was most anxious for him to do so. "I am longing very much for a new edition of the Poems (Shelley's) with a memoir written by you—I feel that you are the only person I should ever like to do it—& I should like to see it done during my lifetime—I know that you would be true & just—giving no fulsome praise & yet appreciating both the man & his writings as no one else can do—first because you understand him &—2nd because you have more knowledge of actual facts than anyone."[21] Yet Richard continued to postpone producing the work he had seemed destined for in 1859.

Chapter 10

Portrait Interlude

On the eve of Richard's fortieth birthday it will be useful to try to paint a verbal picture of him. Well over six feet tall, long-legged and slim, his "build [was] of the loose-jointed Abraham Lincoln order"[1] to an American acquaintance. He gradually began to stoop, as an accommodation to the bent-headed nature of his work and also to the smaller stature of nearly everyone with whom he associated. His square head and blunt features were similar to those of his Lancashire relatives—his uncle Thomas and his cousins William and James Garnett—[2] and were pleasant, yet distinctive and strong. Robertson Nicoll said of him: "He had a ruddy, weather-beaten countenance, and his personal appearance has been well described by the German adjective *rüstig*."[3] Arthur Symons spoke of his "genial, rugged face."[4] His wide-apart gray eyes were not as yet distorted by the round spectacles that marred his later photographs, for he was short-sighted and could read easily without them. Those eyes were generally remembered as kindly, but they were capable of eloquence of a different sort. Nicoll said he had "never heard of his having an enemy," but "this was not because he was blind. Few men had such eyes." Then Nicoll told of a dinner party feting the success of a young author, who proceeded to make a fool of himself, and Nicoll saw Richard's eyes "fixed on him with a cynical, mocking expression. In a moment he dropped his eyes and returned to his roast beef. We drove back together that evening, but Dr. Garnett, though he did not conceal his amusement, had no harsh word to say."[5] It was in his stories that Richard allowed himself the luxury of chastising the fools he met in his daily life, under the guise of a wise man describing faraway places and times.

We have no smiling photographs of him, but his smile was appealing and was commonly remarked upon. Ford Madox Ford recalled that Richard's replies to questions were "uttered with the head a little on one side, with a slightly oblique glance, and the unfailing smile, that seemed to be aroused by some perpetual inward joke no one ever fathomed."[6] Another acquaintance remarked on the "quick, shuffling walk, the abstracted look, the charming and surprising smile,"[7] while his colleague Sidney Colvin, keeper of prints and drawings, called him "the most genially quaint of erudite men, the most helpful, the most smiling and queerly attractive to look at in spite of his stained teeth and bristling russet stubble of a beard."[8] He had grown his short beard and a moustache in the 1860s, possibly to add maturity to his youthful face, but he soon abandoned the moustache, and he failed to keep the beard in trim, so that it was referred to as "untidy" or even "straggling." Despite his height, broad shoulders, and generally robust physique, it was remarked that "he had wonderful hands . . . like the well-kept hands of a woman. They were long and slim and elegant, with tapering fingers; they seemed made to hold nothing heavier than a book."[9] Ford Madox Ford commented on his "odd, caressing gestures of the hand."[10]

Richard was by nature indifferent about clothes. "In London he would wear a black open frock-coat with silk revers, and a broad flat silk cravat. Yet he was by no means a well-dressed man, for he would sometimes wear an old coat with a torn lining, and when he went out he would absent-mindedly brush the nap of his top-hat the wrong way."[11] A story is told "of the maid . . . holding out every morning, in fear and trembling, Dr. Garnett's new hat, and of Dr. Garnett, every morning, taking his old hat and duly and solemnly walking to the Museum with the ancient and battered topper on his head."[12] The hat was obligatory within the precincts of the Museum, except in the Reading Room and the offices.

Richard's voice was thin and high-pitched and did not carry well, but he spoke slowly, and people recognized that what he had to say was pertinent, pithy, and interesting, so they made an effort to listen to him. He was said to have "really talked like a book. His sentences flowed on, unhesitatingly, in lengthy periods, all the commas and semi-colons almost visible to the eye. There was no emphasis, but an unflagging sense of measure, as if he saw the end of what he was going to say before he began it, and had it all arranged and in order" in his mind.[13]

At the same time, "he was one of the most living of men: the warmth and geniality of his disposition was as much a feature of his character as the acuteness of his intellect and the originality of his thought; his conversation was animated and vivid, his laughter infectious; he was always the brightest and most cheerful of companions."[14] He loved to tell anecdotes, and he enlivened his discourse with poetical allusions and quotations in various languages, "though a sturdy British tongue that never could acquire a tincture of a foreign accent forbade him speaking idioms familiar to him as his own."[15] Edmund Gosse recalled: "He would discourse with propriety of the sonnets of Shakespeare, and then, with no alteration in his voice, of those of some Portuguese of the sixteenth century, or some Pole of the nineteenth. He was among the earliest of those who admired Walt Whitman with moderation, Baudelaire with discretion, Heine with enthusiasm."[16] These examples of his literary taste show his interest in all types of writing, tempered by his inability to respond wholeheartedly to the newer voices of his time.

His manner in dealing with the public developed, according to one good friend, from "shy and nervous"[17] to ingratiating but firm, for he was very sure of what he knew. A junior colleague said:

> Gentle, easy of approach, and entirely unassuming as he was, it may be doubted whether any man ever ventured to take a liberty with him; and for myself, to the end of his days, I paid him the unpleasant compliment of stammering more consistently when talking with him than with any other person in the world with whom I was on the same terms. But however long the query took to explain it was always heard with the same benign smile from the spectacled eyes, and when the end came there was usually some modest disclaimer and then a stream of suggestions, not always precisely to the point, but almost always opening up new vistas and pointing out connections I had never suspected.[18]

Another acquaintance also remembered that Richard could be both amiable and frightening: "As with many who have read much he was rather sententious, but his gathered wisdom was pointed by a quiet and gentle wit, and illumined by a pervasive humour. That he might explode never crossed my mind. But at a meeting when a member let out a maladroit word or two he made us all jump by thundering out the word 'Bosh!' A badger had been unearthed and one unfortunate surely craved a cellar to hide in."[19]

His literary judgments were firm and almost unshakable, and he did not hesitate to speak, or write, his mind, so long as he felt he was being fair. To those who were obviously far beneath him in intellect and energy, however, he was always kind—"every one had the same courteous consideration: if there was extra courtesy shown, it was shown to the forlorn-looking: to those not blessed with this world's goods, or this world's success; and in Dr. Garnett's presence no one was allowed to show even the suggestion of a slight to the sorriest conditioned specimens of reading humanity."[20] Nicoll verified this:

> One day I happened to be with him in his own room at the Museum. A poor lady came in with a pitiful and embarrassing story. It was almost impossible not to avoid a smile at the way in which she told it. Dr. Garnett listened with the utmost courtesy, promised to do what he could, and showed her out. Ninety-nine men out of a hundred would at least have exchanged a friendly smile over the interview. Dr. Garnett carefully looked elsewhere, and turned the conversation on to something else. She was a woman and she was destitute—it was enough. . . . It was said of him very truly that there were many whose very subsistence often depended on his kindness. . . . He would rewrite a piece of doggerel; he would touch-up and correct a poor essay, and send it with a letter of recommendation to an editor. Above all, he was ceaselessly endeavouring to get work for the unemployed. His editorial friends were sometimes embarrassed by his persistence. Dr. Garnett thought that everybody was good for something, and credited every one with the same kind intentions as his own. The time and labour he must have spent merely in writing letters, on behalf of those who had no claim upon him but their need are beyond calculation.[21]

His marvelous memory made Richard a valuable ally in any literary endeavor that required research. He deprecated the over-accentuation of this talent, but still he prided himself on being able to recite the names of all the winners of the Derby from 1850 to 1860, as well as the names and dates of the seventeenth-century popes. George Fortescue said that "Dr. Garnett once assured me that he never consciously learnt any passage of prose or verse by rote, but his memory was at once so retentive and so discriminating that any fact, or name, or theory which drew his attention remained stored away in his brain ready for accurate reproduction at the right moment."[22]

Many are the stories of Richard's remarkable ability to find the answer to a query, or a solution to a problem, posed by a reader at the Museum. Arthur Symons wrote:

> His memory was abnormal, incredible. I believe he had read everything, and he seemed to have forgotten nothing. I remember once, when I was talking with him in his room at the Museum, speaking to him about some allusion which had puzzled me in *The Tempest*. He got up and said, "If you will come with me I think I can show you a passage which will throw some light upon it." He led me through many corridors and galleries, and finally stopped in front of a shelf, said, "I think the book is here, on the right hand," took it out, opened it, and showed me the passage. It was an obscure book of travels which he had glanced through many years before, and which contained probably no other passage worth remembering.[23]

In the procedure of placing, Richard had to actually place the books on the shelves, and thus he knew in general where each volume rested. It might be added that his strong memory at times deceived him when he relied on it for his editorial work instead of checking sources, as one not so blessed would do, for it occasionally proved not completely accurate.

At home, Richard was a typical Victorian paterfamilias. The Garnetts lived well, but he frowned on frivolity or extravagance, and he kept Narney on short reins financially. Her pet name for him was "Old Bear." He was indulgent toward his children and enjoyed their company, but he was not as devoted about their education as his father had been with his and William John's. He usually had personal letters to write or literary work to do in the evenings, and he was so fond of parties that he "never refused an invitation if he could help it, and everywhere he was welcome."[24] Therefore May, now eleven, Robert, nine, Edward, seven, and Olive, four, would see him mostly at mealtimes. The table talk was said to have been good, as Richard kept it lively without monopolizing it. "He did not parade learning, and he was never a bore."[25]

There was always a cat in the house and Richard treated it with the same respect he afforded to humans. It was told in the family that if his cat was sitting in his chair when he came down to breakfast, he would take another chair rather than disturb it; and on one occasion he gave a memorably "gentle rebuke to Majestic, his favourite cat, when she was found on the dining-room table, attacking the sirloin when we assembled for lunch. He did not show annoyance or surprise, nor did he remove her forcibly, but after remarking gently: 'Manners, Majestic, manners!' he cut off a bit of outside into which she had bitten and helped her first, depositing her and her helping upon the floor beside his chair before he began carving for his guests and family."[26] Richard's pronunciation of the word "pussy," which he used not only to refer to cats, but as a pet name for Narney, struck many of his acquaintances as unique: he is said to have pronounced the first syllable to rhyme with "bus."[27]

Narney surrounded her family and friends with love. Her daily teas and weekly at-homes were famous, and people who knew the appointed times were free to drop in, usually staying as late as possible because the hospitality and the company were so good. Richard was expected to be present at these parties, which began at four, when his Museum duties had ended, and he found it a convenient way to entertain interesting persons he had encountered or to keep in touch with friends. Narney also attended church and took the children, although Richard seldom accompanied them. She maintained an active intellectual and cultural life by going to concerts, plays, lectures, and political meetings, in addition to sharing Richard's social engagements. She had tried to read the German authors that he liked so well, but her own predilection was for the French language, and she relished the English novels that Richard brought her from Mudie's.

Her moments for relaxation, nevertheless, were few in these early years of marriage, and she was often a victim of "nerves." Her favorite remedy, and that prescribed by her doctor, at times when she was "all unstrung," was to go to visit friends away from London—most often the Patmores, now at Hastings, or the Nobles, near Market Harborough in Leicestershire. In London Narney had a special friend in Christina Rossetti, with whom she conducted a lively correspondence. When Christina was ill, Narney would call on her, bringing the older children. Until 1867 the Rossettis had lived just across Regent's Park from the Garnetts, and even after they moved to Euston Square they were within walking distance. The women's friendship was such that, upon Christina's death in 1894, her brother William saw that Narney received several of her possessions as tokens of her esteem. Richard, on the other hand, found Christina's later religious poetry "morbid" and drew away from her.

Narney tried to contain her emotions, as befitted a good Victorian middle-class matron; but she had a keen sense of humor and an unpretentious attitude that made her very popular. She was said to have carried her parcels home from shopping "in a net bag, a practice otherwise unheard of in her social sphere."[28] This casualness complemented Richard's refusal to partake of any ostentation or to recognize any superiority other than a moral or intellectual one, outside of the obligatory deference to rank. Narney, however, had a sharper tongue than Richard, and there were occasional domestic crises with cooks and maids who lacked proper diligence or competence. She must have relied on her mother to help in retaining control over a household of ten or eleven persons. She could also depend on Chapple to keep the children in order.

David Garnett recalled from his boyhood that "the chief figures were my grandfather, my grandmother, and Chapple. Somehow, though their characters were very different, they were complementary, and the atmosphere of the house was extraordinarily harmonious."[29] Edward James Singleton, when not on military duty, would come to Sunday luncheon, and David was much impressed with his erect bearing and sartorial correctness, as well as by "the gold half-sovereign he pressed into my paw at our first interview."[30] When William John wanted to extend David an equivalent favor, he borrowed the coin from Richard in David's presence,[31] a brash revelation of indigence that David never forgot.

A gift of Edward Singleton to Richard figured in a story that exemplifies Richard's characteristics of prudence and bravery. In the late 1860s bands of "garrotters" infested the streets of London at night, catching their victims around the throat with a piece of rope and stealing their valuables. On one occasion Richard went across Regent's Park to Westland Marston's for a poetry reading by Swinburne. The November night was foggy, and although St. Edmund's Terrace usually stood above the worst fog, the rest of the park was particularly obscure. Richard took along the "stupendous hickory walking-stick"[32] that Edward had given him in 1866. As he made his way back at a late hour, a big man loomed out of the mist and accosted him. Richard promptly struck him with the stick; the man fell; Richard hastened home. The next day a neighbor lady came to tea at the Garnetts' and remarked to Narney that the previous night her husband had been attacked by a garrotter in the park and cudgeled on the shoulder. Narney deduced, to her silent amusement, that Richard must have been the villain in this case.[33]

When not carrying a cane, Richard always had his umbrella with him; and in later years he regularly rose at five in the morning to walk to Covent Garden Market to buy fresh produce for the family table. Once, "when he was in his sixties, he was assailed by three young ruffians in Endell Street and wielded [his umbrella] so vigorously that he put them to flight."[34] His physical strength and his ability to conquer fear served him well all his life; and although courage is not among the attributes most often commended in him, that is because only his family knew of its extent.

In addition to physical courage, Richard had the courage of his convictions, and despite his ostensible modesty, he had a keen sense of his own worth. He knew that his service to the British Museum had been of great value, and he was determined that it should be appropriately rewarded. He had not thus far made a real mark in the world, for his advancement at the Museum had been slow; but he was now, at the end of 1874, about to start moving toward the peak of his career.

Chapter 11

Assistant Keeper of Printed Books, 1875–1878

In late February of 1875 a most unpleasant incident occurred at the British Museum, when men with sandwich-boards, reading "The Clique—Gross Mismanagement—Waste of Public Money," paraded in front of the building in Great Russell Street. They were hawking a pamphlet that purported to reveal scandals in the administration of the revered institution. It was especially vicious against Panizzi and Winter Jones, depicting Jones as Panizzi's toady who promoted staff members according to Panizzi's whim, without regard to qualifications or fairness, and it accused Jones of being largely responsible for the deaths of two assistants because he refused to ameliorate their dangerously unhealthy working conditions, despite their pleas for relief. The author of the pamphlet, which was entitled *The Actual Condition of the British Museum: A Literary Expostulation*, was Stefan Poles, a Polish revolutionary who had been imprisoned in France for being connected with the Communards, had escaped to England, and had been issued a reader's ticket for the Museum Reading Room. He had been outraged when the Department of Printed Books acquired a pamphlet containing a poem denouncing him, and he demanded that the assistant who had brought it into the Museum be disciplined. Jones refused to do this, and although he sequestered the pamphlet, Poles was not satisfied and issued his own pamphlet in revenge. In it he boasted that he had received confidential gossip from members of the staff who were anxious that official malfeasance and incapacity be exposed, and he included complaints from other quarters as well. The tone of the whole was intemperate and carping. Its revelations indicated to insiders that the man chiefly responsible for divulging the information and the opinions in the diatribe was the Slavic expert, W. R. S. Ralston.

Ralston, like Richard in 1866 and 1867, had a double grievance against Panizzi and Jones, for after his disappointment in 1869 over the keepership, he had again been denied promotion in July of 1870, when another man of his rank had been elevated to assistant keeper. He must have borne a grudge ever since, and his resentment must have boiled over during conversations with Poles, who was sick and who died not long after the pamphlet appeared. Through Poles, Ralston was able to express his disgust with what he considered the bias and incompetence of the principal librarian and his close associates. His sympathy was with the assistants, many of whom he considered to be ill-treated and underpaid.

Richard was fortunate in being classed by Poles neither among the deprived nor among those who had been unduly favored. He stood, nevertheless, firmly on the side of the administration. Despite the two previous slights on his abilities, he felt that he was likely to rise to keeper of printed books. He had due respect for the authority of his superiors, as well as the power of old Panizzi, and he was aware of the dangers of rebellion. Beyond these practical considerations, he disliked tattling or any unfavorable comment on the British Museum or its officers. He loyally annotated the department's copy of the Poles pamphlet with facts from his own experience and with commentary on its accusations. He marked several passages with the words "A lie!" and where he himself was described as "a man of letters who ought to have been born in the time of Virgil,"[1] he noted in the margin: "A civil way of saying that I ought to be dead now." The riposte was one he could enjoy, and he was probably not displeased to be cast among the great writers of imperial Rome.

Another of the principal targets of the pamphleteer was the keeper, Brenchley Rye, and although he took the barbs aimed at him with good grace, it was undeniable that many of them hit the mark. His sight had been failing for some time, he suffered from rheumatism, and he had been absent from his office periodically. Since he was not available for consultation, the assistants were obliged to muddle through on their own, or simply to leave work undone. He was obviously not capable of the strong control the department needed.

Poles's pamphlet had its intended effect, for the trustees and Parliament took notice, and the result was an investigation of staffing and working conditions at the Museum that occasioned several changes. The Civil Service Inquiry Commission, which had submitted a report on the administration of the government departments at the end of 1874, continued its investigation into individual institutions in April 1875, concentrating at first on the British Museum. Ralston, having eliminated all prospect of further advancement by his disloyalty, and plagued by both mental and physical problems, left the Museum on 10 April. Rye, realizing at last that it was time to retire, arranged to step down on 14 June, when he was succeeded by George Bullen, the assistant keeper in charge of the Reading Room. This left Bullen's very desirable position open, and Richard immediately applied for it. He solicited testimonials from several influential friends, from Rye and Bullen, and even from the ailing Panizzi, who provided a brief but complimentary recommendation.

Rye gave a fulsome tribute to Richard's qualifications:

> About the year 1857, when I was appointed an Assistant Keeper, Mr. Garnett, who had acquired by this time a knowledge of several European languages, was selected from among the staff of Assistants as the fittest person to aid me in the classification and arrangement of the accessions to the library, but as my time became occupied with other duties, Mr. Garnett performed this important work alone and has since continued to do so most satisfactorily. I ought to say that for the efficient discharge of this duty, which involved the accurate classification of perhaps 30,000 or 40,000 books annually, in all languages and on all subjects, there is required a considerable linguistic knowledge, a wide range of general information, as well as an acquaintance with literary history. . . .
>
> From the long apprenticeship which Mr. Garnett has thus served, to a variety of duties in the Library, aided by a great natural ability, I consider that he is peculiarly qualified for the more difficult and responsible work attaching to the position of Assistant Keeper. I may add that I have frequently derived very valuable assistance from him in replying to questions on points of scholarship and literary history which have been officially addressed to me during my Keepership. It may not be superfluous to say that in point of temper, tact, and courtesy, Mr. Garnett possesses qualifications which are very desirable in an officer of a large public establishment.[2]

Bullen, in his letter, pointed out that Richard had been an assistant for twenty-four years, was "fully acquainted with administration, in almost every respect," and also with the literature of both the modern and the ancient world. He, too, had turned to Richard for help with thorny queries, and expressed admiration for the competent manner in which Richard had been able to implement the complex classification scheme of the library. Sir Percy Shelley said simply, "I do not think it possible that [the trustees] could find any one better fitted for the office than yourself. It is difficult, of course, for me to feel quite impartially in the matter." Frederick Farrar, now headmaster of Marlborough College, said that "by a life of continuous industry [Richard had] acquired stores of knowledge and information such as are surpassed by few men of his own age." David Masson thought Richard's writings showed him to be "one of the most cultured and versatile intellects now in London, and having dealings with books," and Thomas Spencer Baynes, editor of the *Encyclopaedia Britannica*, praised Richard's articles for that publication as "remarkable for their range and accuracy of knowledge, the fulness and value of their literary references, as well as for the clear insight and command of the subject they uniformly display."[3] Patmore, Frederick Locker, and Philip Harwood, editor of the *Saturday Review*, also wrote commendations, as did several other acquaintances.

Needless to say, the trustees were not unaware of Richard's qualities, and he received the appointment on 29 July. He had to supply a surety bond of £1000 from himself, and two more for £500 each from others. Sir Percy offered to sign one of the latter, remarking, "I shall be very glad to secure the Museum authorities from any loss which may result from your natural inclination for theft—That is I will of course sign the document in your behalf whenever I receive it."[4] The second bond was provided by Emmeline Horsfall, through her husband, the Reverend John Henry Hudlestone, and both bonds were accepted on 31 July and "placed in the iron chest."[5]

Narney was at the seaside with the children, so Richard telegraphed the good news to her as soon as he heard it, on 21 July. Then he wrote the details in a letter: "The meeting of the Trustees cannot have occupied an hour, as their decision was communicated to us by Mr. Jones shortly after one. My appointment seems to have given universal satisfaction and I have great reason to ponder the wise saying, 'Take heed of thyself when all men speak well of thee' " [HH]. The next day he wrote again, "A thousand thanks for your affectionate letter, which has given me more pleasure than any other circumstance connected with my promotion," and he continued with information about the disposition of his new salary of £450, mentioning "an act abolishing stamps on civil service appointments passed six weeks since, which will save me £20. I intend to insure my life and I fear that what will remain after this will not do much more than pay my share of the enhanced prices of meat and bread, to which we must look forward. Nevertheless, if Mr. Gosset will paper the dining room, I will not object to paper[ing] the study" [HH].

Mathilde Blind had learned of the event from the newspapers just before receiving the news from Richard himself, she said in a letter of 23 July, and "was wondering whether you would leave to go into the reading room, which I fear would be less pleasant than your [illegible] place below. I should also regret the latter on my own account, as I suppose one could never see you any more in that case." Richard's duties were to be assigned by his superiors, but there was little doubt as to what they would be: he was, indeed, to superintend the Reading Room. Although he was still the official placer of new books, he had to turn most of that duty over to someone else. He was required to sit at a desk in the center of the great domed Reading Room, surrounded by the volumes of the manuscript catalogue of printed books (which were ranged in circular shelving), and to answer readers' questions about the catalogue and the bookstock while also overseeing the attendants who fetched the books. Fortescue, who held the post after Richard, has left a description of it:

> No greater change could well be experienced in the life of an official than to be taken suddenly from the peaceful hermitage of the Library [i.e., the non-public portions of the building] and thrust into the ceaseless toil of the Reading Room, the stock-exchange of literature. The duties of the head of this curious room are so varied and contrasted that it has been said, not without truth, that the perfect Superintendent should combine in his own person the qualities which make a gentleman, a scholar, a police-constable, and a boatswain's mate. In the first two of these capacities Dr. Garnett was obviously the right man in the right place, and

however little he resembled the constable or the petty officer, there was much in his manner and bearing which enforced respect in the minds of all who were brought into contact with him, while among his subordinates the wish to deserve his praise was as strongly felt as the desire to escape his censure.

It was, however, in his ability to guide and help readers in selecting books on a thousand different subjects that his reputation as Superintendent rests. His memory was phenomenal, both for its extent and for its accuracy; his judgement of the value of books was practically final, and his knowledge of every variety of subject was as nearly as possible inexhaustible.[6]

For all its disadvantages, then, the center of the Reading Room proved to be the place where Richard's talents could be most fully developed and where he would make the greatest impact on the reading public. It is hard to recapture the effect of his personality and his spoken words, but he became famous for both before he achieved a comparable distinction for his writings. He came to personify the Reading Room for many scholars and to set its tone of courteous and concerned service.

By September of 1875 Richard had begun to enjoy his work with people instead of books, and he told Mathilde on the twenty-fourth, "I am daily making interesting acquaintances in the Reading Room, among others, Mrs. [Annie] Besant [the Theosophist], who is judiciously letting God alone for the present, and venting her oppressiveness on the inquisition." Three weeks later he said that although he was very busy, he could manage to "spare half an hour, except between three and four. After four I am generally quite at liberty, but we close at that hour after the end of the month." The library closed early in winter because no artificial light was allowed so long as the source of light was flammable.

Richard could always find time for conversation about literary subjects, as another writer recalled. "For [his friends] a day's work in the Reading Room meant a lunch and a chat with Dr. Garnett, when he would enter into all the details of his companion's work, and almost always suggest some hitherto untried source of information, himself looking up the book in question in the catalogue, to ensure quick delivery."[7]

Nevertheless, all was not pleasant in the Reading Room. Readers were protesting the waiting time of an hour and a half to receive a book after the request was handed in, and their complaints were mentioned in Parliament. Richard described the state of affairs in a letter to the principal librarian in 1882:

> The delay in bringing books to the Reading Room was the least part of the evil. Work was disorganised all through the Library, for every man was continually being called away from his proper employment, which remained at a standstill until he returned. . . .
>
> In August 1875 I became Superintendent of the Reading Room, and spent a wretched six months, greatly ashamed of the inefficiency of my department, and powerless to remedy it. All I could do was to get books myself for the readers

whose time I knew to be particularly valuable, which contributed nothing to allay the discontent of the general body [of readers].[8]

In fact, as early as October of 1875 he was asked to submit a report to the Treasury on the state of the catalogue of books as it affected readers, and in that report he proposed the solution that was finally to prevail. He said that the manuscript catalogue was becoming too big for the space allotted to it in the Reading Room, with two thousand volumes already in place and a projected thousand to be added in completing it, not counting the catalogues of maps and music. Many volumes were so thick with pasted-in title slips that they would soon have to be broken up and divided into three, which would make nine thousand volumes, "three times as many as the Reading Room could contain, or the public conveniently consult. The only remedy was to put a check upon the growth of the catalogue by printing all new entries for the future, and to mature meanwhile a plan for converting the entire catalogue into a printed one."[9] This brilliant idea lay fallow for four years while the manuscript compilation of the catalogue of printed books continued as usual. This was because Jones and Bullen were determined to honor Panizzi's insistence that the catalogue be completed in manuscript before printing should be considered.

In December 1875 the Garnetts' fifth child, Lucy, was born, so the nursery was once again the center of Narney's attention; but Mrs. Singleton was quite ill, and she passed away in February of 1876. She was interred in Highgate Cemetery at the lowest level of a grave that would eventually receive Richard's body as well. Her benign influence in the household would be missed by all.

In March of 1876 the trustees took up Richard's suggestion that new entries for the catalogue of books be put directly into print. A special committee considered the matter and decided it would be too expensive to change the system. Yet the readers were still complaining about the slowness of procuring books, and one of the trustees told Richard that something must be done about it. In May the hiring of more attendants was authorized; but Richard found the best temporary solution in an idea brought forward by the most diligent and intelligent of the attendants, John Parker Anderson: that the huge stack area be divided into sections, and each attendant be made responsible for fetching books from just one section. This system would enable the men to learn their own parts of the library so well that they could find and deliver books more quickly. On his own initiative Richard directed Anderson to implement the plan, and it worked admirably. Anderson, who was unable to rise in rank because of deficiencies in his education and social status, was made "Clerk of the Reading Room," and took charge of the book procurement regimen. Richard so admired his work that he tried repeatedly to get him a higher salary, without result.

Richard was a member of the organizing committee of the Library Association of the United Kingdom, which consisted of nineteen London librarians and which first met on 9 April 1877 at the instigation of E. W. B. Nicholson, librarian of the London Institution for the Advancement of Science, Literature, and Art. Nicholson had been impressed by the organization of the American Library Association in 1876 and wanted Great Britain to follow suit. He asked Winter Jones to be president of the association and keeper Bullen to serve on the committee, which subsequently planned the first general meeting of librarians, to be held at the London Institution on 2 October. At that meeting, which attracted international attendance, Richard presented a paper, "On the System of Classifying Books on the Shelves Followed at the British Museum."[10]

One topic discussed during the sessions was the proposal to print the Museum catalogue for general distribution. Jones was against the idea, arguing that such a catalogue would be obsolete as soon as it left the press, when the next book would be bought and could not be entered in it. Bullen expressed pride in the quality of the workmanship in the catalogue and declared himself in favor of printing it. However, he meant only that he hoped it would some day be put into print, when it had been completed in manuscript; for a year later he proved to be adamantly opposed to attempting to print before then. Richard, contrary to his previous view, said he thought printing was a larger project than the staff could handle, but he supported the wish for a subject catalogue of the library.

Jones had been negotiating with the balky Treasury for salary increases for the staff, and the task had been so arduous that his health began to fail, so that in December he was forced to ask for a leave of absence. He retreated to the milder climate of Cornwall and left the administration of the Museum in the hands of Charles Thomas Newton, keeper of Greek and Roman Antiquities, who was a favorite of Panizzi and who was mentioned as a possible successor to Jones as principal librarian. Newton had no desire for that position, but he agreed to act for Jones on a temporary basis. He was strongly in favor of change, and was sensitive to the adverse publicity the catalogue was engendering; so when he found himself faced with a Treasury letter asking for suggestions to expedite the compilation of the manuscript catalogue, he turned to the trustees with an array of evidence. One of the items was a letter, now lost, from Richard to Jones, dated 4 February 1875, to which Bullen had appended some notes. Those notes might have had the effect of neutralizing the gist of Richard's remarks, since the two men were opposed on the catalogue question. Richard was again favoring immediate setting of new entries in type whereas Bullen was promoting the publication of a smaller catalogue in which some of the trustees were interested—one listing books printed in the British Isles, or printed abroad in English, up to the year 1640.

In any case, the trustees were not ready to start the process that everyone knew was inevitable: the printing, leading to the publication, of the British Museum catalogue. They requested that the Treasury allow the Department of

Printed Books to hire "civil service writers" to transcribe entries in longhand, on the theory that more hands would produce more entry slips, and thus the catalogue would be finished sooner. In vain could it be pointed out that the writing of catalogue entries was very different from copying letters in an office. The obvious solution was postponed once again in favor of a highly dubious expedient.

At the same time, the trustees ordered that Bullen proceed to prepare the "early English catalogue." This work had been started under Rye as keeper, when copies of the title-slips for English books printed up to 1640 had been kept in a separate file, to be used for a special catalogue. They needed only to be revised and updated for publication. This task was given to one of the assistants, G. W. Eccles, who worked on it for seven years outside Museum hours before it was completed. During all that time keeper Bullen opposed all attempts to print the general catalogue of books, while Richard Garnett suffered from the resulting inconvenience in the use of the elephantine manuscript catalogue in the Reading Room.

On 16 June 1877 Richard Copley Garnett had been born to Narney, but he was not strong and by autumn he had developed tuberculosis. He died on 6 February 1878 and was buried above his grandmother Singleton in Highgate Cemetery. His father had little time to indulge his distress and grief over the loss of his namesake son, for he was now involved in decisions affecting matters of great importance to the British Museum, and he was being asked to speak on Museum policy, which was taken as an example by the librarians of the world.

Furthermore, Trelawny had finally published his second book of reminiscences, *Records of Shelley, Byron, and the Author*, in which he included information secured from Claire Clairmont about the death of Harriet Shelley and added some hostile comments about Mary Shelley, whereas his previous book had been friendly toward her. Richard immediately took action. He wrote an essay, "Shelley's Last Days," and framed it as a review of Trelawny's book, protesting the errors and "calumnies" he detected against Shelley and Mary. He took advantage of an entrée to the *Fortnightly Review* through an acquaintance with its editor, John Morley, to have it published there in June of 1878.

Trelawny was displeased with Richard's article and he wrote to the editor of the *Athenaeum* defending his ambivalent attitude toward Mary Shelley and sarcastically excusing Richard for his gullibility in accepting Lady Shelley's word: "As Mr. Garnett has his brief from a lady, I have no complaint against him. This lady is said to be an adept in the occult sciences, and, by the aid of mesmerism, she professes to have had direct communication with the spirit of the unfortunate poet. If the lady derives her information from supernatural influences, I have nothing to say. I briefly and simply state things as they occurred."[11]

Upon reading this letter, Lady Shelley wrote to Trelawny, scolding him for turning against Mary, and threatening to remove his portrait and the lock of his hair from her sanctum, as unworthy to be there.[12] She sent Richard a copy of her letter, and when Trelawny made no reply, Sir Percy asked Richard whether it should be printed, and if so, whether he would see to its insertion in the *Athenaeum*. Richard preferred not to publish it. Instead, he sent word to Trelawny, through William Rossetti, that he had not meant to be rude in "Shelley's Last Days," but had merely tried to set the record straight. Rossetti reported that Trelawny did not seem upset about the controversy; but Lady Shelley set about compiling quotations from letters in her possession that formed a flattering appraisal of Mary Shelley's character, and at the end of 1878 she asked to confer with Richard about the arrangement of the family papers, as she was not well enough to undertake the task alone, yet wanted to leave them in order for posterity.

During this period Richard had had two more short stories published. One, "The Purple Head," had appeared in *Fraser's Magazine* in August of 1877. It was about the rivalry between kings for the royal purple dye. Two emissaries who were searching for the source of it got into a fight, during which a flagon of dye was smashed on one contestant's head. That ghastly head was subsequently lopped off by a courtier of another greedy king. The plot was based in part on a comment in a life of the Roman Emperor Aurelian about a gift to him of a beautiful purple robe.

The other story, "The Dumb Oracle," came out in the *Dublin University Magazine* for June of 1878. The plot was taken from a medieval myth, but it was re-set in ancient Greece, and in it may be found some of Richard's favorite themes: the hypocrisies of those who claim the power to intercede for others with a deity; the importance to a prospective devotee of exchanging "abject superstition for common sense"; and the role of divine inspiration in great thoughts and great deeds.

John Winter Jones had come back to his desk at the British Museum in April of 1878, but he was still far from well, and he had made up his mind to retire. He advised the trustees of his decision, and by mid-August his successor had been chosen and approved by the Queen. The new principal librarian would inaugurate a period of reform throughout the Museum, but especially in the Department of Printed Books.

Chapter 12

Dr. Richard Garnett, 1879–1884

Edward Augustus Bond was keeper of manuscripts at the British Museum when he was selected by the trustees as the best person to direct the entire institution, and in his department he had made some healthy changes from the traditional reign of Sir Frederic Madden. He had paid particular attention to the catalogues of manuscripts, his best achievement being a subject catalogue. He was concerned with efficiency and was unafraid of new ideas. He knew the Department of Printed Books and its problems well and was prepared to find remedies for its shortcomings. He and Richard would make an effective team in modernizing the library.

Bond's first project was an attempt to light the Reading Room by electricity: he had a firm of French engineers experimenting with their system during February of 1879, but it was not successful. Next, a German firm with offices in London tried its carbon-arc lamps, and these worked better. By October the boilers were installed and lights could be used in the early evening dark, to the gratification of readers who wanted to stay after four o'clock. Richard reported the good news to American librarians in their *Library Journal* for December, and he must have done so with satisfaction, because he was always eager to utilize scientific and mechanical aids to librarianship. The increased availability of the Reading Room pleased him, even though it meant staffing the room an extra three hours in winter.

His main concern, however, was the catalogue, and he knew that Bond favored putting it entirely into print and intended to work toward that end. The two men were of one mind on the subject and were only waiting for an opportunity to present itself. This came on 8 April 1879, when Panizzi, who had been lingering in a coma for some time, passed away. Richard had admired and respected the old man, and he wrote a generous obituary for the *Athenaeum*. Then he turned his talents to a public presentation of the problem of the catalogue. It was published in the *New Quarterly Magazine*, which had just been bought by Kegan Paul, and it expressed Richard's opinions in an eloquent and convincing manner. It should be said that his arguments for printing the catalogue were not entirely original with him, for suggestions similar to his had been proposed during Panizzi's heyday, notably by John Payne Collier in 1849 before the Royal Commission on the British Museum. However, they had lain dormant until Richard put them into definitive form. He proposed, as he had done before, that entries for new books should be set in type directly and the resulting accessions lists offered for sale to other libraries. At the same time, he suggested, especially lengthy and important sections of the catalogue, such as *Bible*, *Homer*, and *Shakespeare*, should be printed and sold as bibliographies. He was sure that librarians in smaller institutions would be eager to purchase such aids to book selection, and that this would defray part of the cost of printing them.

His best argument for the scheme was that it would save money—the Treasury's primary object—by avoiding double payment for the same work, since resorting to print to save space was inevitable and the longer it was postponed, the more cataloguing would have to be done and paid for twice. The entries for new books could be printed for the Museum and the public at the same time, and they would amount to substantial publications—the new acquisitions were "pouring in at the rate of 40,000 per annum," and by the time the catalogue was completed in manuscript they would amount to "3,000,000 to 4,000,000 titles, occupying from 150 to 200 volumes folio," and would cost £100,000, which might better be spent on printing alone. He then explained why the volumes were so bulky:

> Partly from necessity, partly from oversights, the Museum catalogue is most extravagant in the matter of space. To preserve the alphabetical order of the entries, the titles are necessarily movable, pasted, therefore, on each side of the catalogue leaf, thus trebling the thickness of the latter. It is equally indispensable that wide spaces should be left between the entries when a volume is first laid down, and that when these become insufficient from the number of additions, as is continually happening, the overcharged volume should be divided into three or four. . . . It can only be regretted that part of the available space of every slip is lost in transcription; that scarcely a single transcriber appears to have studied the art of packing; and that the catalogue is overrun with practically duplicate entries of slightly differing editions, transcribed at full length while they might have been expressed in a single line. From all these causes the Museum catalogue is rapidly becoming unmanageable.[1]

Indicating that no other solution than print would ease this situation, he insisted that his object was not to provide a reference work for other libraries—not to *publish* the catalogue, for he knew the trustees and the Treasury would be uninterested in such a goal—but to relieve the crowding in the Reading Room of the British Museum by printing the new entries for the working catalogue only. "Space," he declared, "is the librarian's capital enemy, and the more cruel as it turns his own weapons against himself. The more ample the catalogue, the more liberal the expenditure, the more comprehensive the classification, the greater, sooner or later, are the difficulties from lack of space." Waiting to complete the revision of the catalogue in manuscript, however, meant doubling the expense of each entry. "After paying, let us say, threepence a slip to do its work, the nation [would have] to pay fourpence a slip more to undo it."[2] It was time, he said, to decide on one procedure or the other—not both.

These comments were effective; so was the forceful personality of Edward Bond, who, in May, formally proposed the printing of monthly sheets of "accession titles" to the trustees. He was asked to prepare a detailed plan, and he worked one out with Richard, beginning by determining how many libraries might be interested in subscribing to the printed lists. A sufficient number of favorable responses were received so that, in October of 1879, Bond was allowed to ask the Treasury for a special grant for printing, to be offset partially by the sale of these lists and partially by dismissing the extra civil service copyists, whose efforts seemed to have retarded, rather than speeded, the transcription. In November the Treasury approved the grant. Thus was won the first round in the struggle to get the catalogue into print.

The library world was excited by this development in what was widely considered the leading institution of its kind, and Richard soon became the spokesman for his department. He was recognized as the ablest expositor of the library's inner workings, its problems, and the thinking of its staff on librarianship in general. He was called on increasingly by journals, newspapers, and learned societies for statements and explanations about policies of the British Museum library, about developments in library science, and about the future of libraries, all of which he was pleased to discuss in his clear and elegant style. He delivered addresses to meetings, and most of them were published in library journals afterward. He also contributed articles to the Library Association's monthly, *The Library*, and sat on the association's committees. In fact, he was as generous with his time and energy on behalf of his fellow librarians as he was to his fellow literati and to the patrons of his library.

On the Shelley front, the important news was that Claire Clairmont had died in Italy on 19 March 1879. It was Richard who advised Sir Percy and Lady Shelley of the notice in the *Athenaeum* of 29 March. Harry Buxton Forman, who was compiling an edition of Shelley's prose, and whom Richard had been helping to find materials in the British Museum, also had seen the notice, and he lost no time in sending an envoy to Florence to treat for Claire's papers with her niece and executrix, Paola Clairmont. He had a rival in an American Shelley admirer, Edward Augustus Silsbee, who had been staying in Claire's pension in Florence and trying to persuade her to let him have the papers; but he had only promissory notes to offer whereas Forman offered cash. Therefore Forman got the bulk of the papers and Silsbee had to be content with two copybooks in which Shelley and Mary had made fair copies of finished poems, and one letter of Shelley's to Claire. For these he claimed to have made an insincere proposal of marriage to Paola. Henry James built his story "The Aspern Papers" (1888) around this situation. Silsbee eventually donated his three Shelley items to Harvard College, and one of the copybooks was edited for publication by Professor Woodberry.

Lady Shelley had not given up hope that Richard would produce the definitive work on Percy Bysshe Shelley. She wrote on 19 November 1879, "I wish . . . that you were the Editor of a new and perfect edition of his works—I hope that this may be before I die, which I do not intend to do yet awhile."[3] She and Sir Percy had sublet Boscombe Manor and moved to Shelley House in London for the winter. That gave Richard an opportunity to visit them more often and "converse instead of writing," for writing had become difficult for her. She continued to sort and put in order the family papers, but she had a stiff and sore neck that made the task painful.

Lady Shelley has seldom been given credit for her work on the mass of material Mary Shelley left her, partly because she is supposed to have destroyed some of it and partly because of her fierce partisanship in regard to the content of the letters; yet the arranging was well begun by her. In January of 1880 she asked Richard to return a boxful of papers, and on 2 February Sir Percy reiterated his wife's request that Richard give them his advice on the project. They had received Richard's latest book, *Poems Selected from Percy Bysshe Shelley*, which had been published by Kegan Paul in January. It was said, by Richard in the introduction, to be "practically a reissue of . . . Moxon's edition of Shelley's Minor Poems," and was beautifully printed by the Chiswick Press with color and gold. The Shelleys were "delighted" with the introduction and the dedication to Lady Shelley; but they regretted the inclusion of "Lines Written in the Bay of Lerici," considering it "hardly worth immortalizing—and the proof of their being genuine is not very clear."[4] On this subject the Shelleys seem to have been alone in their reservations, for the verses have been accepted into the canon. Perhaps the missing lines, restored in 1961 by G. M. Matthews,[5] would have convinced Sir Percy of the authenticity of the poem.

By early 1880 Buxton Forman had received the bulk of Claire Clairmont's papers, and he made good use of the material, which consisted of more than two hundred letters, in future publications, eventually selling the originals to buyers in England and America. Richard read the proofs of Forman's four volumes of Shelley's prose which were published later in the year by Reeves and Turner. For this work Forman had had to get Richard's consent, as well as that of the Shelleys, to include several essays; as Lady Shelley said to Richard, "we prefer that you should have the first handling of all papers in our possession, if you wish."[6] The body of this letter was written by Lady Shelley's niece, Florence, who was now Mrs. Leopold Scarlett. She was also helping to copy letters from the Percy Bysshe Shelley papers for her ailing aunt.

In the March 1880 issue of the *[Dublin] University Magazine* there had appeared an astrological article by Richard entitled "The Soul and the Stars," which he signed with his anagram "A. G. Trent," and which attracted attention at home and abroad. He also began editing a selection of Shelley's letters, "designed to include nothing but what is really choice and exquisite,"[7] and to be accessible to students as part of Kegan Paul's Parchment Series. It was published in 1882 as *Select Letters of Percy Bysshe Shelley*.

On 21 February 1881 Arthur Garnett was born to Narney. He became a beautiful child, with blond curls, and he remained handsome as an adult; but he had a severe speech defect which limited his possibilities in life. His was a most endearing personality, marked by good humor and wit, and he was a favorite wherever he went. His upbringing and his need for occupation in his majority caused Richard some concern, but on the whole he was a joyous addition to the family.

At the British Museum the new regime was keeping up a fast pace of change, and Richard was deeply involved. From the beginning of 1880, the printing of the entries for the catalogue of books had been carried on, and although Richard was the most eloquent advocate of the procedure, he had not been given charge of it, as he had a right to expect. Nevertheless, he was helping with it so much that by the end of the year he had almost entirely taken over the supervision of the work. At the beginning of 1881, there began the printing of whole volumes of the manuscript catalogue which were too thick and needed to be divided, and Richard, who had conceived of this as the second stage toward the printing of the entire catalogue, was the overseer, or final reviser, who passed on the printed form of the entries. This is now considered the beginning of his editorship of the catalogue, but at the time it looked to him simply like an extension of the essential work of the department in which he was engaged.

He must have felt unappreciated, for principal librarian Bond, though glad to make use of Richard's literary ability and his intelligent approach to library problems, was slow to show him the favor of control over the catalogue project. Therefore, when the librarian of the Bodleian Library at Oxford died on 8 July 1881, Richard decided to apply for the position. He knew that the university was not likely to choose a self-educated man for the post, but he seized the opportunity to make his superiors aware of his ambition to advance professionally. He received several glowing testimonials from distinguished men, but he was not chosen for the Bodleian. The new librarian there was to be E. W. B. Nicholson, an Oxonian and a much younger man. Richard sent him felicitations, and Nicholson replied:

> Of all the letters of congratulation which I have received, none has touched me so much as yours. I shall never forget having received such a letter from one who was not merely a fellow candidate with me, but who in many respects had claims undoubtedly superior to my own. . . . I feel that you have lost nothing in the *long*

run. There are few people, and I am not one of them, who doubt that some day you will be the head of the library which is beyond rivalry in size and importance even from the Bodleian.[8]

Richard was getting close to that position, as he wrote to Mathilde Blind in October of 1881: "I have been acting for the last three weeks as Keeper of the Printed Books in the absence of the senior officers, and have been so overwhelmed with correspondence that I have not known where to turn." Then, on 11 February 1882, he told her that he was "not going to Oxford. The pros and cons were so evenly balanced that I feel little disappointment if any." Edmund Gosse thought that Oxford had erred in not choosing Richard, but admitted that their failure "is delightful for your London friends. A Reading Room without you would be a maze without a plan."[9]

To ease the tension of his occupations Richard had taken time to write another story, "The Elixir of Life," about a sage who had concocted such a liquid and put it into a phial identical with six others containing lethal poisons. He then invited seven young scholars to choose and drink one of the samples on the chance of getting eternal life. The youths were reluctant to risk death, but one bravely tried to oblige the sage, who had to rescue them all by sending them away. He knew, with the wisdom of his years, that the elixir would be a "fatal boon," and he gave it to a monkey, "where alone it would be innoxious," and himself quaffed one of the poisons. The story was published in *Our Times* for July 1881, the third and last number of the magazine, which, as Richard said, "blasted the elixir's character by expiring immediately afterwards."[10]

In March 1882 Robert Singleton Garnett turned sixteen. He was now ready to leave the City of London School and, like his father at the same age, enter the world of wage earners. He became a clerk in a law office in Gray's Inn, and each morning he and Richard would walk across Regent's Park to the Broadwalk, along it to the Marylebone Road and the Euston Road, thence toward Gray's Inn Road, "and passing the house of Charles Dickens in Doughty Street . . . went through its gate—which, guarded by a jealous functionary in a watch-box, then extended across the grass-grown paved roadway—into John Street."[11] From there Robert crossed into Gray's Inn and Richard went back westward to the British Museum. Although Richard had walked all over London alone at sixteen, he now went out of his way to shepherd his son to work, doubtless relishing every moment of their companionship.

William John had got himself involved in another precarious venture, this time under the auspices of Robert Tennant, who had invested heavily in a company formed to work a silver mine near Lake City, Colorado. At first, William John was hired to be a clerk in the New York office of the associates; then, in March of 1883, he was sent to Colorado to replace the ailing clerk there. He was ecstatic about the fine mountain climate and wrote articles about his environment which he asked Richard to place in periodicals. He also arranged for some verses of Richard's to be published in the *Silver World* of Lake City.

Richard was concerned about May, now nineteen, who had been attending Queen's College and studying German with modest success, and who was attracting young men. One of these was Milnes Patmore, Coventry Patmore's eldest son, a rather wild character, a year older than May, who was destined for a career at sea. Richard did not like him. He was one of the few people who could actually make Richard angry; it is said that the only time Richard was known to slam a door was after an interview with Milnes Patmore. Therefore the whole family was relieved when Guy Hall, a friend of Robert and Edward, became interested in May.

A happy occasion took place in April of 1883, when Richard was awarded the honorary degree of Doctor of Laws by Edinburgh University, where his old friend David Masson was on the faculty. Richard journeyed to Edinburgh for the presentation, and was thenceforth called "Dr. Garnett," somewhat to his embarrassment, for he preferred a less obvious recognition of his accomplishments.

The Shelleys were still in close touch with Richard, for all kinds of people were publishing works on Shelley, and seldom did Sir Percy and Lady Shelley entirely approve of their efforts. However, another of Richard's protégées, Mrs. Julian Marshall, wanted to write a biography of Mary Shelley, and when she told Lady Shelley that she already loved Mary, there was no question of her acceptability.

Then came a small tempest. John Cordy Jeaffreson, who had abandoned writing novels to become a self-described inspector of manuscripts, had discovered some unpublished letters of Lord Byron in the distinguished autograph collection of Alfred Morrison, and he obtained permission from Morrison to publish them in a book called *The Real Lord Byron: New Views of the Poet's Life*, which came out in June of 1883. This was a "realistic biography" that dwelt on the worst aspects of the life of Byron, and it included aspersions on Shelley. The sources Jeaffreson had found were valuable, but his handling of them was sensational in effect, and the book was widely condemned—in the *Quarterly Review* and the *Nineteenth Century*, among other periodicals. The Shelleys were disgusted and Richard disturbed, but not enough to attempt a counterattack.

A more serious blow for the Shelleys was the fire at Kegan Paul's in July, when all the firm's stock was destroyed. The unsold copies of the *Shelley Memorials* perished with the rest. On learning of this, Lady Shelley consulted an old family friend, Sir Henry Taylor, a poet and dramatist who lived in Bournemouth and joined in Sir Percy's theatricals. He recommended that she promote "an authentic memoir" to combat the various "romances" being printed about Percy Bysshe Shelley. She told Richard that Taylor "mentioned Prof. Dowden as having wished to write a life of Shelley—he therefore wrote to him, the result of which has been a visit to us here [at Boscombe]—We like him much, but I have spoken quite openly to him . . . that he must see & converse with you before we could settle about any thing."[12] Dowden, a professor at University College, Dublin, had published biographies of Southey and Browning. He approached biography through psychology: he looked for the dominant characteristics of the subject's mind and temperament, and for manifestations of these in the works. He was particularly attracted by ethical considerations, which would make the study of Shelley difficult for him; but he was eager for the task.

He had been corresponding with Richard since the autumn of 1881, and on 27 July 1883 he wrote to advise him of the Shelleys' proposal and to ask for a meeting in London on 1 August. Richard, in answering, gave his "hearty assent" to Dowden's project and then continued: "[A biography of Shelley] was from an early period my most cherished ambition, but I have long been forced to recognise that the exigencies of my official position, alike by consuming time and preventing concentration of thought, render it almost impossible for me to accomplish such a work so long as I remain connected with the British Museum."[13] Thus Richard relinquished claim to the study he had worked on for so long, and he did so with his customary offer of assistance to his successor. There ensued an exchange of letters between the two, punctuated by Dowden's trips to London to visit the British Museum and to confer with Richard. Their friendship grew apace, so that when the Library Association's annual meeting was held in Dublin in September of 1884, Richard and Narney were guests of the Dowdens.

At that meeting Richard delivered a paper, "Photography in Public Libraries," which contained the prescient suggestion that the British Museum should establish a Department of Photography to make available facsimiles of important and valuable manuscripts and documents—even books—which now could only be seen within the premises. He used the example of Irish materials in the Museum library departments that would be useful to scholars in Ireland if they could be studied there, and he considered the exciting possibilities of an international exchange of documents of various western nations, to be provided through photographic departments in all national libraries. He was also aware of the value of photography as a means of preserving the texts of fragile documents and of insuring against their obliteration by fire or other disaster. All in all, he said, "the conception is so fruitful, its application is so manifold and momentous, that I half recoil, like Fear, afraid of the picture [I] myself have painted."[14] He said he hoped that Edward Bond, having bestowed the twin boons of electricity and printing on the British Museum, would now consider adding photography as a third. Unfortunately, this excellent idea could not be implemented to any large extent until the day of electronic photocopying.

At the beginning of 1884 the catalogue-printing project at the Museum had taken the final step forward: the trustees had agreed to the printing of the entire catalogue, from A to Z, and this meant the fruition of the plan Richard and Bond had sketched out in 1879. The printer, William Clowes & Sons, had become so efficient at the job that it was now cheaper to print the entries than to transcribe them, and with some maneuvering by Bond to secure Bullen's cooperation (for Bullen was still set on completing the catalogue in manuscript first), the Treasury was persuaded to increase the grant for printing.

Richard had edited the printed catalogue entries for some time, in addition to his regular duties, and he felt a good deal of pressure in his daily work. He took proofs of the accessions lists home with him to be corrected at night, and was involved in all the decision-making in regard to the project. He was also being asked more and more to help with the keeper's tasks, because Bullen was deeply involved in overseeing the editing of his catalogue of early English books, the third and last volume of which came from the press in June of 1884. His favoring of this compilation over the general catalogue had caused friction between him and Bond, and Richard had managed to take Bond's side without antagonizing Bullen.

Toward the end of the year, Bond proposed that Richard retire as superintendent of the Reading Room to devote more time to the other work of the department, especially the catalogue, and Richard agreed that the change would benefit the library. It was announced on 8 November, and in the following week's *Athenaeum* there was a letter from the antiquary John Ashton offering to receive contributions for a subscription recognizing Richard's help to users of the Reading Room. Upon reading the letter, Richard wrote to Ashton to say that he could not, under the rules of the Museum, accept any financial reward outside his salary, and that he needed "no outward token" of the kindly feeling behind the proposal, much as he was gratified by it. He had already, he said, received sufficient reward in the friendships he had made among the readers.[15]

There was no proscription, however, on the readers' giving Richard an illuminated address, and this they did in a little ceremony on 2 July 1885. Bond and Bullen attended, and representatives of the readers gave testimony of their appreciation of Richard's services to them. They also praised the improvements he had made in the procuring of books from the stacks, and his addition of a second collection of works of reference to the gallery of the Reading Room. Richard protested that others were responsible for these advantages,[16] but in vain: his friends insisted on giving him the credit.

Despite his disclaimer, Richard was known to have been the moving force behind much of the reform of Reading Room service, and he was far and away the most popular superintendent the room had ever had. Dowden wrote to him on 21 November 1884, "I heard with a pang, yet with pleasure, too, that you are to disappear from the central point of the Universe into some shadowy Altitude, where it may be hard to see your face, when one visits the Valhalla of scholars. I hope it will give you more leisure or what is equivalent to that,—less fatigue. If so, we shall in some way be repaid for your ascension."[17] This hyperbolic phrasing covered a genuine respect, for Richard had, in his nine years at the Reading Room desk, become a legend, known to scholars all over the world as a "walking catalogue" of the library, his mind an encyclopedia of information on an astonishing number of topics. Sir John Ballinger, librarian of the National Library of Wales, recalled "the promptness with which he could draw upon his stores of knowledge" and "the ease with which he moved from one topic to another quite remote," giving as illustration the following incident:

> I was once talking with Dr. Garnett about certain rare Welsh books not in the British Museum, a fact of which he was fully conscious, when we were joined by a distinguished professor of Moral Philosophy, who in the course of conversation referred to some rare books in that subject, which also had been wanting in the Museum Library. Dr. Garnett was able to answer without a moment's hesitation as each book was named. "Yes! we still want that," or, "I am glad to say we have that now, we bought it so and so." Before the conversation ended an eminent mathematician was introduced, to whom Dr. Garnett put the question: "Are there any gaps in the Museum Library in your subject?" A discussion followed on rare books relating to mathematics, and again the answers came prompt: "We have" or "We have not."[18]

The only time Richard failed to answer a question immediately, according to Ballinger, was when Narney asked him if squirrels build nests.

All this mental exercise, however, and all the obliging service to readers, in addition to his diligent work on the printed catalogue, which "he drove through the press with unremitting energy,"[19] had taxed his strong constitution. These combined tasks had "occupied him from 10 A M till past midnight, and probably only his naturally robust health, temperate habits, and a daily four mile walk prevented him from breaking down altogether."[20] He must have felt relief at being able to retire from the imperative demands of the Reading Room, yet he told William John on 11 December 1884 that since he had left it, "I seem busier than ever and have to return to it almost every day to write letters after four by the electric light" [HRHRC]. He was catching up on a backlog of work—dealers' catalogues to scan and other such duties, as well as correspondence. At this time, too, he relinquished the leadership of the Museum's corps of military volunteers, pledged to protect the nation's treasures in case of trouble, either from abroad or at home.

He had moved his workplace to an office off the King's Library, admission to which was gained through a door that was painted to resemble the shelves of books on either side of it. The room was soon cluttered with books and papers, the desk piled high, the mantelpiece topped with his tall hat on more literary debris, the walls hung with portraits of Panizzi and some of his favorite authors. Many men and women of letters visited him there and were given his complete attention, as formerly in the Reading Room. Richard was, in fact, dispersing energy in acts of kindness that a more self-centered man would have used to further his own interests. He had not published a book of his own since his *Idylls and Epigrams* of 1869, having been too much occupied, outside of official hours, with Shelley and his short pieces for the *Encyclopaedia Britannica*, although he found release in writing short stories. He had offered to join the writers who were compiling the *Dictionary of National Biography*, recently started under the editorship of Leslie Stephen, and his first articles were submitted in 1885. Among them were biographies of Percy Bysshe Shelley, Mary Wollstonecraft Shelley, Claire Clairmont, Edward Trelawny (who had died in 1881), and five Garnetts. Not only did he write almost every biography he was asked to write, but he suggested those he felt best qualified to do, and provided lists of persons who might be assigned to other subjects. Richard himself contributed 117 articles to the dictionary.

During 1884 William John's fate again took a turn for the worse. The mining venture in Colorado failed utterly and William John, to Richard's dismay, sued for his unpaid wages. Then he cast about for somewhere else to go. He wanted to move westward rather than return to England, and first thought of helping drive cattle up from Mexico via Arizona, then of mining in Nevada—frontier areas of doubtful safety, in Richard's eyes. At last he got to Tacoma, in Washington Territory, but he found no work there. Richard then undertook to write to a family connection in Melbourne, Australia, David Syme,[21] to ask if there might be something for William John to do on the newspaper of which Syme was the proprietor, *The Age*. By great good fortune, Syme was willing to employ William John as music critic; and so began another chapter in the peripatetic life of Richard's rootless brother, who was forty-eight years old and still far from settled in home or occupation.

Chapter 13

More Shelley, 1885–1887

Richard was now ready to begin a new career of prose writing on literary topics. For Kegan Paul's Parchment Series he edited Thomas De Quincey's *Confessions of an English Opium Eater*, reprinted from the first edition (1821) with an introduction and a postscript, "De Quincey and Musset," about a little-known French translation of the work by Alfred de Musset. The latter included, verbatim, an episode which de Musset had interpolated into his version. The volume came out in April of 1885, and Richard saw to it that Dowden and the Shelleys received copies. Sir Percy, in acknowledging the gift, called it a "beautiful little book"—and added the information that Florence Scarlett had given birth to her fifth son at Boscombe Manor "at 2:30 a.m. on Friday the 10th of April—I note these particulars in case of astrological requirements."[1] Richard cast horoscopes for all the Scarlett children.

Then, in May, there was a storm on the Percy Bysshe Shelley front. Cordy Jeaffreson took his revenge for the criticism of his *Real Byron* by publishing *The Real Shelley: New Views of the Poet's Life*, in which he made up in invective for what he lacked in original sources. He blamed the hostile reception of his former work on Lady Shelley, referring to her influence as "Field Place," the home of Sir Timothy Shelley, where she and Sir Percy had begun their married life. Jeaffreson stated what was generally known about the poet and his two wives as bluntly as possible, and interjected his opinion of Shelley by such phrases as "the chicken-heart and milksop" and "the inordinately blasphemous young rascal."[2] He was obviously outraged by Shelley's defiance, in word and deed, of the hallowed institutions of monogamy, the law, and the church. He was equally contemptuous of Shelley's defenders in the current era. He dismissed Kegan Paul, Buxton Forman, and Richard Garnett as unreliable witnesses, and approved only of Hogg, Peacock, and Rossetti. On Richard he wrote, "I would not be wanting in courtesy to Mr. Garnett of the British Museum, of whom I would say nothing worse than that he is wildly and inexplicably inaccurate."[3]

The reviewers again gave Jeaffreson a drubbing. Rossetti, in the *Athenaeum*, said there was no point in "tarring and feathering" Shelley for his way of life, since he was "one of the greatest poets," but admitted that he was also "one of the most passionate, if also perilous speculative and moral insurgents of this century, or, indeed, of any time."[4] Dowden reviewed the book at length in the *Academy* for 6 June, pointing out thirty "comparatively minor errors" as a test of its validity. Swinburne composed a poem, "Caliban on Ariel" (Ariel being Shelley's epithet), that was published in the *Academy* for 4 July, comparing Jeaffreson to the monstrous slave of *The Tempest*. Richard vented his disgust in a long poem he called "Vampyre or Ghoul? Real Jeaffreson,"[5] giving the surname four syllables to fit the meter of the verse, and circulated copies among his friends. A drawing of Shelley's severed head on a stone, with an owl perched atop, looking menacingly down at the poet, was placed in Narney's album, and similar drawings, apparently by May Garnett, adorned the copies sent to Dowden and the Shelleys.

Lady Shelley decided to avoid the book. She learned from Dowden that it was "odious" and told Richard, "I shall trust that you & he will expose any misstatements & I will not look at it—as I should only be made ill & miserable which would do no good to any one."[6] Sir Percy was so impressed with Dowden's review of *The Real Shelley* that he considered printing it as a pamphlet to send "to all notable & literary people in this country and America."[7] Both Dowden and Richard advised against this, considering it better to make no public response to Jeaffreson.

Dowden was progressing with his biography of Shelley, and in June he sent Sir Percy his ninth chapter, dealing with the separation of Shelley and Harriet. As expected, there were objections and specific recommendations, and Dowden asked Richard to intervene to effect a compromise. Sir Percy sent the chapter to Richard, who read it and wrote out a memorandum of commentary. He supported Dowden in his determination to maintain a disinterested approach to the subject, and was able to mediate an amicable accommodation of the differences. "In estimating Professor Dowden's work," he told Sir Percy, "we must always remember that he is not writing as an advocate, as I did in the Relics, but as an historian: and that it is a great gain to have the favorable verdict of a competent and impartial judge: even if it does not go quite so far as one could wish."[8]

At this time Richard was revising his attitude toward Peacock. While continuing to deplore Peacock's writings on Shelley, he now claimed to have "a very kindly feeling towards his memory, and [I] am at present trying to get some of his posthumous papers published. I have secured insertion for one in the 'National Review,' and hope to publish some more."[9]* He had borrowed these papers from Peacock's granddaughter, Mrs. Edith Nicolls Clarke, but the rest of them never got into print under Richard's name.

Meanwhile he was composing a "Note on the Printing of the British Museum Catalogue," to be read for him at the annual conference of the American

Library Association in September and to be published in *Library Journal* for September–October 1885.

At the end of 1885 F. J. Furnivall and some others founded the Shelley Society. Furnivall, whose physician father had delivered one of Mary Shelley's children, had already organized societies for the study and appreciation of Shakespeare, Chaucer, Wycliffe, and Browning, and Richard was apprehensive about the taste with which the latest of these groups would be conducted, Furnivall's chief characteristic being unbridled enthusiasm. Richard advised Sir Percy not to take any committee assignment, even if he wished to join the society. Richard wanted no risk of encounter with Jeaffreson, who, he thought, might become a member, nor to face the necessity of resigning if Jeaffreson should appear at a meeting; so he declined membership. However, his fears were not warranted, for the man who had written so bitterly of Shelley did not choose to associate with Shelley-lovers; and at the second meeting, on 4 April 1886, when William Rossetti had to cancel his assignment to the chair upon the death of his mother, Richard consented to take his place. The speaker was Buxton Forman, on "Queen Mab." In November of that year Mathilde Blind spoke to the society on Shelley's view of nature, contrasted with that of Darwin, and in December Rossetti was the speaker, with Richard again in the chair.

The publication program of the Shelley Society was being handled by a young man who was to make a large impact on the literary world, at first brilliant, then disgraceful: Thomas James Wise. With only a moderate income, Wise had been able to acquire early editions and personal papers of important English writers, and he amassed a superb collection called the Ashley Library, which was sold to the British Museum after his death. Richard was helping him to find books and papers of the Romantic poets, and in the spring of 1886 Wise brought out a private edition of Shelley's "Prologue to *Hellas*" with Richard's introductory note from *Relics of Shelley*, where the verses had first been published. Only twenty copies were printed and Richard got at least two, for he gave one away in May. It was one of several works by Shelley that were published in 1886 under the aegis of the Shelley Society and the ambitious Wise, who was also secretary of the organization.

This pamphlet was genuine, but Wise was already embarking on a program of producing and offering for sale small printings of works of popular authors, advertising them as first, private, or otherwise rare editions. Nearly fifty years later these were proved to be forgeries, and Buxton Forman was implicated in the massive fraud.[10] In the 1880s, however, Wise was known as a book lover with an ingratiating personality and a reputation for generosity toward other scholars who wanted to consult his library. He also compiled excellent bibliographies of individual poets, based on his holdings. His prominent position in London's book world gave him both protection from suspicion and advantage as a purveyor of rarities which he claimed to have discovered.

Richard was taken in by Wise, as were all his contemporaries, yet he did not purchase one of the forged pamphlets sent him by Forman in 1896: he had the foresight to inquire about it from its purported publisher, Bell and Daldy, the firm that had issued his *Io in Egypt* and *Poems from the German* in 1859 and 1862, respectively. Now called George Bell & Sons, the publishers disowned the pamphlet, which was William Morris's *Sir Galahad*, part of his *Defence of Guinevere*, with a date of 1858. Richard did not purchase it. Yet either he or Bullen must have allowed Wise special privileges in the British Museum library, for it was discovered after Wise's death that he had abstracted hundreds of leaves from volumes belonging to the Museum to perfect his own copies or copies he had sold. Wise was generous in donating his publications to the library, which has now, in all, twenty-seven of the forgeries, eighteen of which came as gifts from Wise, and eight of these during Richard's keepership, while Richard authorized the purchase of seven more.[11]* On 9 November 1898 Wise wrote to Richard about a faked reprint of a work by Shelley that he claimed to have exposed,[12] a clever cover-up of his own devious practice.

In November 1886 Dowden's *Life of Percy Bysshe Shelley* was published by Kegan Paul, Trench & Company. Richard quickly congratulated the author on "the skill with which you have handled such copious materials, and the self-restraint you have exhibited in dealing with them."[13] Eleven days later he had finished reading the two volumes and was "thoroughly satisfied."[14] The reaction of the Shelleys is not directly known, but they remained on friendly terms with Dowden and approved of his issuing a shortened version of his work in 1888.[15] It remained the standard life of Shelley for over fifty years.

Critical comment on the book was not entirely favorable. The harshest reviewer was Matthew Arnold, who said he regretted its publication, and took the occasion to express his adverse impressions of Shelley and his poetry. Although admitting Shelley's personal attractiveness and good will, he contended that "the Shelley of actual life is a vision of beauty and radiance, indeed, but availing nothing, effecting nothing. And in poetry no less than in life, he is 'a beautiful and *ineffectual* angel, beating in the void his luminous wings in vain.' "[16]* This quotation has become firmly attached to Shelley, more because of its pictorial quality than because of its aptness. Dowden and another Shelleyan, Stopford Brooke, protested Arnold's estimate of the poet, and Richard, in his entry for Arnold in the *Dictionary of National Biography*, while praising Arnold's brilliance as a critic, added: "He inherited his father's ethical cast of mind; conduct interests him more than genius."

Arnold was not alone, however, in criticizing Shelley's writings, for two of Richard's best friends were doing the same thing in November of 1886. Edmund Gosse, a former colleague in the Department of Printed Books, now Clark lecturer on English literature at Cambridge University, gave a series of lectures about Shelley between 30 October and 15 November, and the one on 8 November was entitled "Poems Written at Pisa." In it he condemned

"Epipsychidion" as an expression of calf-love and self-pity, of "effeminate and selfish sensuality," and Shelley's influence as tending to undermine the social law and order. Coventry Patmore discussed this lecture for the *St. James's Gazette* of 13 November in an article called "The Morality of Epipsychidion," supporting Gosse's view that some of Shelley's poems were insidiously immoral: this particular poem, written to a young woman in a convent, was considered a continuation of Shelley's unorthodox amorousness. Patmore also wrote two articles on Shelley that were published in his *Principle in Art, Religio Poetae, and Other Essays* in 1889. The title of one of them, "Bad Morality Is Bad Art," was a sentence he had used in his review of Gosse's lecture, and was the antithesis of Richard's credo. The second article appeared in the *St. James's Gazette* for 2 December 1886, and it reviewed Dowden's biography of Shelley in a negative way. Richard's feelings must have been hurt by these pronouncements by men he liked and admired; but he would have to make the best of many more severe criticisms of Shelley before his days were done.

He had continued his affiliation with Edinburgh University, and had attended the tercentenary celebration in April of 1884. Now, in 1886, the students gathered literary contributions for a volume to be published and sold for the benefit of the Student Union, to help them acquire a house to meet in. They called the book *The New Amphion*, after Amphion of the Greek legend, who raised the walls of Thebes by the music of his lyre. Some distinguished writers, such as Robert Louis Stevenson and Robert Browning, donated special works. Richard sent a short story called "The Philosopher and the Butterflies" that depicts the attitudes held about the origins of their respective species by a butterfly and a caterpillar, and constitutes a brief lesson in the interpretation of Darwinism.

For nearly two years Richard had been engaged in writing a biography, not of Shelley, but of Thomas Carlyle, another of his favorite authors. He had told Mathilde Blind on 16 February 1886, "I am absorbed in Carlyle and grudge every moment that I cannot give him." Indeed, he became too engrossed in his subject and wrote much more than was desired by the publisher, Walter Scott, so that the text had to be "drastically reduced" before it was printed in 1887. It was not meant to be a full-scale biography, but was intended for those readers whose time and needs did not require complete detail. It was part of the Great Writers Series edited by Eric S. Robertson and Frank T. Marzials, brother of Richard's colleague at the Museum, Théophile Marzials. Richard was to write two more biographies for this series—the *Life of Ralph Waldo Emerson*, published in 1888, and the *Life of John Milton*, 1890. Each book had a bibliography of the author's works compiled by J. P. Anderson, the Museum attendant whose career Richard promoted.

These three monographs were very favorably received by critics and have been standard sources in libraries ever since their appearance. Cosmo Monkhouse, poet and art critic, called the Carlyle biography "a masterpiece of lucid narrative and well-balanced judgement, guided by a sensitive taste and penetrated by that keen but good-natured irony, which is one of [Richard's] finest endowments."[17] Richard was confident that this work was good, but was less sure about the other two. The reviews of the Emerson were pleasing, however, and William Rossetti said of it, "I think it extremely good; & in point of writing one of your best compounds of solid sense with a bright & indeed brilliant touch—a combination in wh[ich] few of our contemporaries can rival you now."[18] The Milton was written partly to counteract the effect of another book on the poet, and it quoted extensively from previous biographies, especially David Masson's six-volume classic life. *The Nation* called Richard's work "the best starting-point for a study of Milton,"[19] which is what Richard had aimed to produce. A large part of his literary fame stemmed from these three books.

At the British Museum the printed catalogue had been proceeding apace, and in order to release some of his time for other pursuits, Richard had acquired a skilled helper with the editing. This was the assistant Arthur William Kaye Miller, who had been put on the catalogue as reviser in 1882 and who had proved so competent as to become an unacknowledged assistant editor. Miller was more particular about the details of the entries than Richard was, Richard's compelling motivation being speed—to get the catalogue into print before the enabling funds could be withdrawn. There was a scare in 1886 when the Conservatives formed a government and immediately began to retrench on finances, cutting the Museum's budget for the following year by £10,000, £4000 of that to come from Printed Books. Yet Richard had won a point at the initiation of the printing program that was to save it from the budgetary axe and that he explained to his fellow librarians succinctly: "By making the printing a portion of the daily life of the institution, a piece of administrative routine like cataloguing or binding, we escape alike ambitious professions and ambitious failures."[20] Richard had devised a schedule for preparing the entries, delivering them to the press, and having them processed and returned that assured a swift and steady accomplishment of each phase. The accessions sheets had sold moderately well, but the main source of income was the Treasury, and despite the backsliding in 1886, Richard thought that, on the whole, the Museum had been generously treated.

On 5 June 1886 the trustees had received another catalogue, the *Subject Index of the Modern Works Added to the British Museum Library in the Years 1880–1885*, which had been compiled in spare time by George Fortescue, Richard's successor as superintendent of the Reading Room. This was a much-desired publication, one that Richard had been especially eager to have. What was really needed was a subject reference key to the entire library, but such an enormous work was out of the question, so everyone was thankful to have at least a partial means of access by subject. It had been made possible by using the printed accessions lists to arrange entries according to the classification scheme used for shelving the books.

One of Richard's proudest achievements was the installation of movable bookcases in the stacks of the British Museum library. This took place between July and November of 1887, but the preparations had begun in November of 1886, when Richard had visited a small library that had just been renovated, at Bethnal Green in the East End of London. He was much impressed with a space-saving device the librarian had installed to hold patents—a wheel on the bottom of a bookcase that allowed it to be kept flat against another case and easily moved out on the wheel when access to the books behind it was desired. Richard immediately began to investigate ways the idea might be adapted to the Museum's stack area. He approached Henry Jenner, the placer, whom he knew to be anxious to increase the storage capacity of the building, and Jenner was more than receptive: he visited the Bethnal Green library and then sketched out a version of the device for the Department of Printed Books, to be hung from above, rather than wheeled on the floor, for the floors consisted of iron grillwork to supply light. Bullen approved of asking the trustees for working models and, with Bond's support, got their consent. Bullen had to take money from other parts of his budget to finance the sample cases, but they worked so well that everyone was pleased. The only rub, to Richard's mind, was that Jenner got all the credit, and a bonus of £100, whereas Richard had made the suggestion and therefore felt he deserved recognition for it.[21]*

An amusing sequel to this episode was recorded by a man who was a student in the Library Association's summer school in the early 1890s, when Richard was still smarting from the acclaim received by Jenner. Pointing out that at the sessions of the schools he had attended, he had found Richard the "star performer," who had "stirred" his audience and was "memorable on Literature," while his two lectures on Victorian prose and poetry "were among the best I have heard," the author continued: "At an earlier School Garnett, usually genial, loomed like a tempest, tried to fold his angry face into his beard, as he listened to Henry Jenner garrulously mixing a discourse on the B. M. classification and hanging bookcases with flouts and jeers at authority in the Museum: a cunning, and, to us [students], deliciously funny revelation of institutional domesticity."[22]

Richard delivered an address on the hanging, or sliding, presses at the annual meeting of the Library Association in September of 1891,[23] after many more of them had been installed throughout the library and two different types constructed. They proved, however, to have a serious drawback, for careless handling of the enormously heavy cases caused damage to the books they held, as well as to those in the cases against which they were fitted (or slammed, as was all too often the practice). Nevertheless, they remained in use into the 1930s and were the ancestors of today's compact shelving.

In October of 1887 Richard read to the Shelley Society a paper on "Shelley and Lord Beaconsfield," which was printed in their *Papers*, Part 1, 1888, and as a separate under the general title of Centenary Studies by Richard Clay &

Sons, printers to the society. Richard later included it in his collection *Essays of an Ex-Librarian* (1901). It was a nice example of literary detection, tracing the influence of Shelley's writings on Disraeli's *Revolutionary Epick* (1834) and *Venetia* (1837).

Chapter 14

The Twilight of the Gods, 1888–1889

In the Garnett household things were both good and bad in 1888. On the darker side was a "tedious indisposition" that kept Narney "confined to her room."[1] When Dowden arranged to visit London in June to speak to the Goethe Society (of which Richard was also a member), Narney and Richard would have liked to return the Dowdens' Dublin hospitality, but although Richard made a tentative offer of a room, Dowden declined to impose under such circumstances. At the end of October Narney was still suffering from this illness, which was "gradually wearing itself out, but the process is slow, and she will be an invalid for an indefinite time yet."[2]

On the brighter side, Edward, now twenty, had fallen in love with a young woman who was to bring much pleasure to the family, and also to add distinction to the name of Garnett. This was Constance Black, who had been one of the first students at Newnham College, Cambridge, when it was opened for women, and had left it with honors in 1883. After this she had tutored for a while, and then had taken a position as librarian in the People's Palace, a recreational and educational institution for working men and women in the East End of London.

Constance had first come to tea at St. Edmund's Terrace in 1886 with her sister Clementina, whom Richard had been helping with research at the British Museum. Constance's friendship with the young Garnetts ripened quickly, and when she and Edward became committed to each other, Edward set about finding a source of income. He had been idling around home after finishing school, and was most interested in literature, but had given no serious thought to a career. Richard was at first too much occupied with his own cares to do more than suggest that Edward learn shorthand in order to get a job reporting for the *Manchester Guardian*; but Edward did not relish the prospect of newspaper work, so Richard spoke to the publisher, T. Fisher Unwin, and Edward took a place in the shipping department of that firm. It was not long before he had shown his exceptional talent for literary criticism, and he became a reader of manuscripts for publishing houses, his very successful lifetime occupation.

Constance had introduced Edward to the vivid atmosphere of the industrial East End, where she lived as well as worked, and to the Fabian Society and other socialist groups. One result of this new environment for Edward was a novel, *The Paradox Club*, which Unwin published in June of 1888. Richard proudly sent a copy to Dowden, who praised its "delicate craftsmanship."[3] Richard replied:

> The book is certainly a most remarkable one for so young a writer: the chief drawback to it, indeed, to my mind, is that it has so few of the errors of youth. When I think what nonsense I should have perpetrated at Edward's age I don't know whether more to envy him or to pity him![4]

The book had serious social themes, but these were much more Constance's preoccupation than Edward's, and he published only one more novel, *Light and Shadow*, in the following year. This work has been described as "a barren wilderness of despair where Hardyesque pessimism, without the Hardy genius, imbues the doom-laden life of Maurice Driscoll, the central character."[5] Richard said of it to Rossetti, "I am very much of your mind about Edward's book. I take it, however, that this unwholesome pessimism is but another aspect of the general tendency of youthful genius towards the cadaverous, which produced 'Zastrozzi' [a Gothic horror story by Percy Bysshe Shelley as a youth] and the like in their day. The present phase of the disorder is worse for life but better for literature: for Zastrozzi and such like performances have no truth and no merit, while Edward's analysis of Driscoll's feelings, granted the situation, is wonderfully true to nature."[6]

The month of June 1888 brought another change to the British Museum, when Edward Bond retired as principal librarian. Several people outside the Museum thought that Richard should be Bond's successor, but instead the position was given to Edward Maunde Thompson, who had followed Bond as keeper of manuscripts. Thompson was an equally dynamic man, but with a quite different personality. Richard was able to establish a good relationship with him immediately. At this time, too, the grants for the Museum began to be raised by the Treasury, so that much of the recent financial pressure was eased.

To Richard, however, the most important event of the year was the publication, by Unwin in October, of a collection of his stories under the title of the first of them, *The Twilight of the Gods*. Four of the stories had appeared in magazines; all had been written as recreation during his scarce free time and were the products of his imagination at its most sportive. The book constitutes his *chef d'oeuvre* in the minds of many of his admirers, for it is not only different from anything else he wrote, but it is unique in English literature. It is an expression of the essence of Richard Garnett, and it betrays an aspect of his character that was hidden from most of the people with whom he came into contact. This was his wry attitude toward the petty faults of men, his disdain for the violence which often results from selfishness, and his amusement at the prevalence of tawdry sentiments and irrational behavior in everyday life. An impish wit hides in casual phrases, delighting the reader who fathoms the author's meaning, although that is often unexpected and may require interpretation.

A common theme of these tales is the overcoming of noble impulses and recognized ethics by such human failings as greed, jealousy, and pomposity, where lip-service is paid to what is known to be right while wrong is being done. The settings are always remote in time and place, but the analysis of psychology and motivation is applicable to any era and any locale. Richard was chiefly concerned with religion and philosophy, taking a detached attitude and making his points calmly but trenchantly. His *bêtes noires* were priests, rulers of all kinds, magicians, and any others pretending to special knowledge or unusual powers. He consistently made such characters look ridiculous; yet his manner was so controlled that it is hard to take offense at his revelations of their humbug.

The title story in *The Twilight of the Gods* is about Prometheus, the demi-god who created Man, at Zeus's command, and then gave him divine fire (inspiration), which made Zeus jealous. Richard's Prometheus has just been released from a lengthy punishment meted out by Zeus, and is discovered by a lovely maiden, a priestess of Apollo who has been driven from her temple by a Christian mob. Prometheus reveals his identity to her, though he is now a man ("I am rewarded for my love of man by becoming myself human") and tells her that man is the "preserver or . . . destroyer" of the gods. "He looks up to them, and they are; he out-grows them, and they are not." The world is now Christian, and Prometheus and his lady find it expedient to pretend to be of that faith, since there is no longer room for their own religion.

The second story is "The Potion of Lao-tsze." It begins:

> In the days of the Tang dynasty China was long happy under the sceptre of a good Emperor, named Sin-Woo. He had overcome the enemies of the land, confirmed the friendship of its allies, augmented the wealth of the rich, and mitigated the wretchedness of the poor. But most especially was he admired and beloved for his persecution of the impious sect of Lao-tsze, which he had well-nigh exterminated.

Sin-Woo wanted to live forever, since he was so good, and when he learned that the secret of the Elixir of Immortality was known only to the few surviving followers of Lao-tsze, he ordered his minions to find it for him, on pain of death for failure. One of them discovered that a woman who knew the secret was, with her mother, in a cave guarded by a tiger (tigers did not eat Lao-tszeans) and he took a party there. When he entered the cavern he saw a withered old woman, whom he promptly slew, and a lovely young one, whom he carried off to Sin-Woo. She was in a trance induced by the potion, and everyone waited years for her to awake, only to find, when she did, that it was the older woman who had known the recipe. The young lady became empress and tolerated the followers of Lao-tsze. "Since, however, they have ceased to be persecuted by man, it is observed that wild beasts have lost their ancient respect for them, and devour them with no less appetite than the members of other sects and denominations."

"Abdallah the Adite" is set in Arabia, where the hermit Sergius practiced religion and alchemy. The prophet Abdallah had been his pupil and had been sent out into the world as a proselyte for his holy teachings. The first time Abdallah returned, he was "covered with weals and scars, and his bones protruded through his skin," from having been beaten and starved in a dungeon. The hermit was delighted with such signs of devotion in his disciple. After another expedition Abdallah returned "covered as before with wounds and bruises, but comely and somewhat fat": he had promised a Caliph's wives that for feeding him secretly "each of them in the world to come would have seven husbands."

"How knewest thou this, my son?" . . .

"In truth, father . . . I did not know it; but I thought it probable."

"O my son! my son! . . . thou art on a dangerous road. To win over weak and ignorant people by promises of what they shall receive in a future life, whereof thou knowest no more than they do! Knowest thou not that the inestimable blessings of religion are of an inward and spiritual nature? Did I ever promise any disciple any recompense for his enlightenment and good deeds, save flogging, starvation, and burning?"

"Never, father . . . and therefore thou hast had no follower of thy law save one, and he hath broken it."

After a third term of preaching to the ignorant, Abdallah persuaded Sergius to teach him how to breathe fire and walk "over nine hot ploughshares," so as to impress people. This earned him the title of prophet and won him disciples.

On his next visit to the hermit he brought a blanket full of bones, proclaiming them "the bones of the camel of the prophet Ad, upon which his revelation was engraved by him." The message, however, had been obliterated by time, and Abdallah wanted Sergius to "write it over again," which he reluctantly did. He was careful to forbid polygamy, yet Abdallah dictated a gloss on the Book of Ad that allowed nine wives—but not ten. Then he had become enamored of a young lady for whom he would have to repudiate one of his present wives. Unfortunately, the wives knew that "the revelation of the blessed Ad is not written upon the bones of a camel at all, but of a cow," and since Ad was not known to have ridden on a cow, they would have to be placated. Sergius achieved this at the price of marrying the cast-off wife, an old and ugly one.

Abdallah then became very powerful and slaughtered unbelievers in great numbers, as he proudly showed Sergius. One of them blasphemed by saying that the Book of Ad was written on the bones of a cow, and he was about to be burned at the stake when Sergius protested that he had told the truth. Abdallah agreed, but claimed this was an unforgivable sin, whereupon Sergius retreated to his hermitage in despair at the ways of the world.

No summary can convey the real flavor of these stories, whose charm derives from the style and from the continual drollery of which Richard was a master. Of the remaining stories in *The Twilight of the Gods*, the one called "The Poison Maid," about a beauty whose magician father had fed her from infancy on various poisons, thus rendering her immune to them (her name was, understandably, Mithridata), was made into an opera, "The Poisoned Kiss, or, the Empress and the Necromancer," by Ralph Vaughan Williams, with a libretto by Evelyn Sharp. Several others have been anthologized, "Ananda the Miracle-Worker," "The Dumb Oracle," and "The Elixir of Life" being the favorites.

The major critical journals responded quickly to *The Twilight of the Gods*, giving it first-page attention. The *Academy* praised it: "Mr. Garnett proves himself to be an artist in literary satire. He has exceeding culture, a wide range of sympathy, the rare faculty of serene irony, and a style at once delicate and vigorous, concise, and yet vividly illustrative." The *British Weekly* said that "this volume takes rank, for imagination and delicate humour, above most of the literary work of recent years. Every tale is crackling with wit, and if imagination and style compose the true elixir of literary life, *The Twilight of the Gods* should live." The *Scottish Leader* said, "The literary workmanship is characteristically graceful and finished." The contrary *Athenaeum*, however, had grave reservations about the book, protesting that it was "flippant" about "departed gods and goddesses."[7]

Friends and colleagues were enthusiastic. Richard sent Dowden a copy, remarking diffidently, "I hope you may find some entertainment in my stories: they are, I think, LITERATURE; more I must not say."[8] Dowden was too busy correcting examination papers to read the "Götterdämmerung," as he called it, upon receipt, but when he did, he enjoyed it immensely. He later remarked, "You are a very complex person and without these tales a good deal of the Garnettism of Richard Garnett would not have gained a permanent form. The irony is intellectual and wise, and . . . one seems to know human nature better after having read your Tales, and not to care less for it, but to accept it—far from sentimentally—with its infirmities. . . . I wish I had found as happy a medium for things in me that have never got into print, and never will."[9] Edmund Gosse recalled in 1903, "I was one of its very warm admirers when it first appeared in 1888, and I have often expressed the wish that it could be more widely known. It is a book of uncommon beauty, full of the delicate irony which is so rare in England, and so persistently discouraged by the vulgar. I hope that [it will have] the career as a little classic which it richly deserves."[10]

That career started very gradually. In early 1889 Richard wrote to William John in Australia to say that he should have received his copy, and added, "The sale is very slow, but notices are constantly cropping up in unexpected places, showing that it has made its way where it was never thought that it would go" [fragment, HRHRC]. He should not have expected a large sale of a book that evinced such disdain for popular institutions and beliefs; but its special audience has always cherished *The Twilight of the Gods*. Lord Lytton, who was then British ambassador to France, wrote an unsolicited letter of praise for the book that gave Richard great satisfaction.[11]* The stories, both individually and as a whole, were eventually translated into French, German, Italian, Portuguese, and (in 1967) Russian. Richard arranged for translators and helped to find publishers for the translations. On 19 April 1897 he wrote to his daughter Olive, "If I rightly understand my Portuguese translator, the complete version of the Twilight of the Gods is ready for publication, but has not yet found a publisher. She had wished to print it in the Azores, which would have made me an African author!" [HH]. He also tried to arrange for a Chicago edition in 1896, but the book was not published in the United States until 1924.

A touching sequel to Richard's report of the lack of sale of the stories was told by Alfred Pollard of the British Museum. In 1891 the publisher, Unwin, delivered the unsold copies to a remainder house to be marked down. "When the remainder-man's catalogue was received in the Printed Book Department, it was promptly taken the round of the different rooms, and the resultant order for twenty-five copies so surprised the vendor that he refused to execute it except at the very advance of price it was partly intended to bring about."[12] As a consequence of this loyal and warm-hearted gesture, Unwin retrieved the copies and had some bound with a new set of advertisements.

However, it was only a temporary solution. In the *Academy* for 4 September 1897, E. V. Lucas reviewed *The Twilight of the Gods* as the second of "Three Neglected Books," when he discovered that it was available as a remainder, "new at a shop in Holborn at a fraction of its original price; yet there must be in London alone many persons eagerly on the watch for a book containing such excellent fun . . . both fun and mischief—illustrious alliance. [Garnett's] great joy has been to get philosophers and prelates into tight places." Noting that Richard's other work was all "in the direction of erudition," Lucas continued:

> But somewhere he cherishes a fund of sardonic humour, and this humour runs through and underlies the stories in *The Twilight of the Gods*. The book is the fruit of wide and varied reading and a keen sense of irony. . . . And the result is a kind of saturnine fairy-tale, or mordant "morality." The moral, however, seldom lies near the surface: Dr. Garnett knows so much that one must tread delicately in following him. A learned man of ironical bent is a dangerous companion when his tongue is in his cheek.[13]

Although Richard's stories have often been compared to those of other writers, it is pointless to do so, for they are clearly in a class by themselves. They are his special contribution to English literature, and are the most characteristic product of his subtle and penetrating mind. He was in a fever of creative composition during these years, his mental energy released by the easing of pressure at the Museum, and his cogitations about human nature stimulated by his work in the Reading Room.

On 30 April 1888 Richard had written to Dowden: "Do you know a magazine for damsels, called 'Atalanta'? They publish there a series of papers on the chief English writers, adapted to the capacities of their readers. I have already written one of Coleridge, and am to write another on Hawthorne. They have asked me to recommend some one to write on Matthew Arnold, as a poet, I take for granted, and I have named you. I hope you may find it possible to undertake this little work."[14]* Not only had Richard contributed biographical sketches of these authors, he had published one of his tales, "The Rewards of Industry," in *Atalanta* for August 1888. This story, quite sophisticated for girl readers, concerns the worldly rewards to inventors of games, such as chess, compared to the hostility with which some more powerful inventions, such as printing, have often been received in the past: "For the world is a big child, and chooses amusement before instruction." The last sentence of the story, however, indicates Richard's respect for the mental effort, above mere amusement, involved in the game of chess.

In the issue of *Atalanta* for September 1890 was Richard's story, "The Talismans," about a daydream of "a magnificent palace, guarded by goblins, imps, lions, serpents, and monsters whose uncouthness forbids description," wherein Time guarded the worn-out ancient talismans. It describes the effects on society of the suspension of Time and Mutability. A series of four very short stories, entitled "New Readings in Biography," was Richard's contribution to the *Scots Observer* in 1889.[15]* They were witty "revisions" to the standard histories of noted people.

These six stories joined the others for a second edition of *The Twilight of the Gods*, which was brought out by John Lane in May of 1903. It contained, in addition to the original sixteen tales, twelve more, most of them written in the interim. Press notices were again very complimentary. The *Times Literary Supplement* for 5 June 1903 said: "The book bubbles with laughter: it is one of the few books that make the reader envious of the writer; for, delicious as the reading is, the conception must surely have provided a more exquisite joy.... [Garnett's] sense of humour has a wide range ... being precise, suave, and logical in the most ridiculous situations." Arthur Symons considered Richard's book much more serious in its potential, saying, "It is a text-book of intellectual anarchy; it is loaded with symbols of revolution; but the air of our century is proof against it, it will never go off with the least damage to our idols."[16]

The second edition enjoyed better sales, and three more impressions of it, as well as several other editions, followed.[17]* The finest of the latter was an elegant one illustrated by Henry Keen and introduced by T. E. Lawrence, who paid tribute to Richard's professional expertise in the library, and then to his creative imagination:

> Courteously and unerringly Dr. Garnett would advise [a reader] upon bee-keeping or bimetallism, while inwardly his mind was picturing Caucasus or Pandemonium and little themes of Albert of Aix or Hesychius were running through his head. Never did he abdicate from his chair of scholarship. In this book are his *obiter scripta*, reactions of his spirit against drudgery, and what a bouquet and flavour they have![18]

This edition reappeared in John Lane's Week-End Library series in 1927. C. A. Watts & Company's Thinker's Library series published one of the tales in 1940, with a foreword by David Garnett. There was also a Penguin Book of 1947 which comprised the sixteen stories of the first edition. An American library reprint house, Darby Books, brought out a facsimile of the 1903 edition in 1975, the only edition now in print. The stories are small masterpieces that should not be allowed to fall into obscurity.

In addition to all these creative works, Richard was writing on the British Museum catalogue[19] and on other subjects for the *Universal Review*, which had begun publication in 1888. To this magazine he contributed four articles, a story, and a note, between October 1888 and the end of 1890. His January 1887 address to the New Shakespeare Society was printed in 1889 and was called "The Date and Occasion of 'The Tempest.' " In it he gave evidence to support a theory that the play had been written and performed in celebration of the wedding of the eldest daughter of King James I in 1613.[20] Unfortunately, there was too much evidence that the play dates from 1611 for Richard to convince his audience otherwise. The next article was "On Translating Homer,"[21] in which he gave as examples his own translations of five scenes from the *Iliad*. His third contribution was the story called "The Wisdom of the Indians,"[22] which suggested, under the guise of the adventures of two young men, that the knowledge of the world contained in Buddhist scriptures came from Greek philosophy.

Richard's translations from the *Iliad* were also included in his *Iphigenia in Delphi: A Dramatic Poem, with Homer's 'Shield of Achilles' and other Translations from the Greek*, published by Fisher Unwin in his Cameo series in 1890. The book was divided into three sections: dramatic, epic, and idyllic. The drama had been written in 1861, though probably not in final form, and had been published in the *University Magazine* in 1879. The epic was the Homer, and the idyllic, eight idylls from the *Idylls and Epigrams* of 1869 (the epigrams would be reprinted in the Cameo series in 1892). In the meantime, seventy-two such translations by him were incorporated into an attractive little book called

Selections from the Greek Anthology, edited by "Graham R. Tomson." This was the pen name of Mrs. Arthur Tomson, a beautiful young woman who was a clever rhymester and an ornament of literary teas. There is no doubt that Richard took an important part in the compilation and publication of this work, probably suggesting some of the other contributors from his wide acquaintance.

Edward was now progressing in his work at Unwin's. He and Constance had been married in August of 1889, and May and Guy Hall had become engaged. William John, however, had been very ill since February of that year, and by August he was despondent about his health and his future. In contrast, Richard was on the verge of the best years of his life.

Chapter 15

Keeper of Printed Books, 1890–1892

Two deaths saddened the turn of the year and the decade for Richard. Sir Percy Shelley died on 5 December 1889 and Westland Marston died on 5 January 1890. Marston had been in dire financial straits after his last play had failed in 1895, and his friend Henry Irving had given a benefit performance of Byron's *Werner* for him. All Marston's family had pre-deceased him, so that Narney now had only her brother Edward left of all her kin in London.

Early in January William Rossetti informed Richard that he was working on an annotated edition of Shelley's "Adonais." Richard responded in his generous fashion that he was "very glad to hear of your undertaking," and added, "I have sometimes thought of editing Shelley myself, with a more elaborate and illustrative commentary than he has received hitherto. Someone will have to do this some day, and meanwhile your work will be a welcome instalment."[1]

In June a long-anticipated event occurred at the British Museum when George Bullen retired as keeper of printed books. Richard, having known of his intention the previous August, was ready to apply for the position. He could claim extensive experience in all the affairs of the department, for as early as February of 1888 he had had "everything to do"[2] in Bullen's place for two weeks, while Bullen was ill. From that time on, Bullen had left more and more of the administration in Richard's hands. There was no serious contender for the keepership, and Richard was given the position on 8 March. He turned over the chief responsibility for editing the printed catalogue to A. W. K. Miller and named Alfred Pollard to help him, although Richard himself "continued to supervise it closely."[3] The printing was supported by a grant of £3000, and Richard hoped that it could be completed by the end of the century, as, indeed, it was. However, no extra staff had been provided, and the work was becoming a severe drain on departmental resources.

One concomitant of the keepership of printed books was a dwelling within the Museum building, so that the keeper, in rotation with the other keepers, could be responsible for the safety of the collections after closing hours. The Garnetts' home was to be one of the two middle apartments in the east wing, its door facing Montague Street. In April, while its rooms were being prepared for new occupancy, Richard was "entirely overwhelmed with official business," the "principal achievement" of his first two months in office being "the acquisition of [a] unique Caxton,"[4] along with several other valuable purchases, in which he took great pride.

The family moved to the Museum early in June. It was somewhat difficult for Narney to adjust to having her household part of a large institution. The house had four bedrooms and five attic rooms, but with five children, all but one of them grown, to accommodate, along with a cook, two maids, and Chapple, it was quite full. Its drawing room soon began to receive guests for tea every day and for the usual open house on Thursdays. "Our ground floor is really almost as public a place as the grass plot [in the forecourt]," Olive commented.[5] The younger Garnetts made themselves notorious for unorthodox behavior: they not only played without hats on the grass, but Olive and Lucy climbed out through an attic window onto the roof with a parasol to seek relief from a hot summer day indoors. This shocked the caretaker who spied them. He reported the incident to the principal librarian, who warned Richard to see that it did not happen again.

In his official capacity, Richard had within a few months to deal with an awkward situation in regard to the Private Case. This was the large collection of erotica that was kept in the Arch Room in locked cases, its use restricted to readers who could prove a legitimate purpose. Even the catalogue of its contents was secluded from the general public. A former assistant in the Department of Printed Books, Wilfrid J. Wilberforce, sent a letter to the archbishop of Canterbury, a principal trustee, protesting the expenditure of public funds for such works and the maintaining of them in the library. The archbishop forwarded the letter to Principal Librarian Thompson, who presented it at a meeting of the standing committee of the trustees on 8 November. Richard had to report on department policy on the acquisition of erotica, and he said that it had been the custom to purchase only works that were important as literature or were illustrative of manners, not simply because they were pornographic. He promised to be very careful in supervising the accession of this kind of publication, which he said a national library was bound to have. The trustees were satisfied with his assurance and made no attempt to satisfy Wilberforce's demand for the elimination of the Private Case collection.

Richard missed his daily walks across the park, but his duties were so heavy that he had scarcely any more time at home than before the move to the Museum building. He continued to write in the evenings, and Narney began to include Olive, now nineteen, in her attendance at meetings, concerts, and plays. Olive was pleased when Mrs. William Rossetti bought from Richard the leasehold to No. 3, as it was now numbered, St. Edmund's Terrace,[6*] and when the family moved there in the fall, Olive was free to visit her old home, for which she always retained a sentimental attachment. This circumstance also aided the development of the friendship between Olive and Ford Hueffer, age seventeen, the son of Francis Hueffer, who had died in January of 1889. Ford, his brother Oliver, and his sister Juliet went to live with their grandfather, Ford Madox Brown, at No. 1, St. Edmund's Terrace, and Juliet later joined the household of her aunt and uncle at No. 3. Ford, at loose ends without his father, was a constant caller at the Garnetts' British Museum home. He was "In and out every day and all day long. Their hospitality was as endless as it was beneficent."[7] He played chess with Richard and became like a brother to Olive.

Ford gave Richard credit for starting him on a career of novel-writing when, at a tea party, Richard provided a clue to a good subject (the trial of a pirate) and directions where to find information on it in the British Museum library. Reluctant at first, Ford eventually took the advice and succeeded. The resulting book was published in 1903 as *Romance*, on which Joseph Conrad collaborated. Richard seemed very old-fashioned and rather stuffy to Ford, but the younger man always regarded the older with "gratitude and affection."[8]

There had been no let-up in Richard's literary production during the great change in his home life. He was preparing an edition of Mary Shelley's stories, the first collection of these to be published, which came out at the end of 1891.[9*] From 1891 through 1893 he contributed fifteen memoirs of poets to Alfred Miles's *Poets and Poetry of the Nineteenth Century*, a twelve-volume compilation published from 1891 to 1897. Richard's entries included those for Carlyle, Patmore, Peacock, and Mathilde Blind, to whom he wrote on 7 May 1891 that the volume covering Peacock was out and he was "not dissatisfied with the figure I make in it." As a poet, he himself was represented in the sixth volume by seventeen selections.

At this time Richard took an opportunity to make amends to the memory of Peacock by producing a ten-volume edition of his novels for J. M. Dent. Dent's son Hugh, who succeeded his father as head of the firm, wrote of the inception of this project:

> In the early part of 1891 my father's old friend, Mr. F. H. Evans [a bookseller] ... suggested that it was time for a new edition of Peacock's works. Further, if my father would take up the suggestion he would get him the ideal editor. The Chief having agreed to do so, Mr. Evans waited until Mr. Edward Garnett's next visit to his bookshop, and over a cup of tea requested him to tell his father that he had a job for him. On being told of the new project Dr. Garnett said it was the very thing he would like best to do. I believe that Dr. Garnett greatly enjoyed the work and I know that my father gained much pleasure from the friendship he made with his editor of Thomas Love Peacock.[10]

In the introduction to *Headlong Hall*, the first novel of the set, Richard made an apology to Peacock, saying he regretted his "unjust and uncharitable" words about him in *Relics of Shelley*, although he could not feel them "to have been inexcusable." Richard's grandson, David Garnett, said that the text of the novels in this edition "proves, on examination, to be corrupt and unreliable,"[11] but he conceded that his grandfather had done well to collect the best of the fragments and essays by Peacock. Richard, never known as a meticulous editor, had derived his text from a previous edition, without taking care to make it definitive; yet his introduction and notes were good enough to be reprinted by David in his own edition of the Peacock novels. Another recent scholar, Carl Van Doren, said that Richard is "one of the men who have done most to keep Peacock from neglect,"[12] by means of his long article about him in the *Encyclopaedia Britannica*.

On Saturday evening, 30 January 1892, Samuel Butler, author of the utopian novel *Erewhon* (1872), gave a lecture at the Working Men's College on "The Humour of Homer," and Richard, at Butler's invitation, attended. Butler was an iconoclast who delighted in teasing conventional Richard, though he liked him and appreciated Richard's help at the British Museum—he had dedicated his *Unconscious Memory* (1880) to Richard "in grateful acknowledgement" of that help. In the lecture he took a homey, human view of the *Iliad*, stripping the chief characters of their heroic aura, making the gods seem to be ordinary men and the goddesses termagants. Then he claimed that the *Odyssey*, being a gentler story, less flattering to men, and displaying a suspicious ignorance of such masculine pursuits as agriculture and seamanship, must have been written by a woman. His delivery was light-hearted and the audience of working men and women was highly amused, although Butler was quite serious about his theory and later expanded it into a book.

Those among his listeners who were learned, however, were taken aback by the performance. Richard could not be expected to accept such an interpretation of the great classics of Greek literature. When Butler called on him at the Museum next day, Richard was unusually taciturn, and could only admit that it was just possible that Mrs. Homer was the model for the wily and heartless goddesses her husband depicted. Butler thought Richard's reaction would be typical of that of the dons at Oxford and Cambridge, "cautious and academic," and Fortescue confirmed to him that "Garnett hates anything downright and outspoken."[13] Butler added that Richard was "one of the most brilliantly humourous and in all respects fascinating writers of the time, if not the very best we have, for I know not who can be placed above him." This remark referred to *The Twilight of the Gods*, rather than to Richard's other writings. In that work, of course, Richard had been disrespectful of some of the Greek pantheon and had been rebuked for it by the *Athenaeum*. But he had not made fun of Homer. When Butler's lecture was printed as a pamphlet, he sent a copy to Richard, who thanked him for it with the wry comment, "I shall read [it] with no less pleasure than I heard it." Butler put a note on the letter: "I. e. 'which I hate as much as when I heard the lecture delivered.' "[14]

Richard wrote a review of the book version of Butler's theories, *The Authoress of the Odyssey* (1897), for the *Athenaeum*, dismissing the arguments for a woman author with his own less exalted opinion of the capabilities and characteristics of women, but praising the work as "ingenious and entertaining . . . . Indeed, the book is full of clever things."[15]

Spring in 1892 was inaugurated by the birth of a son, David, to Edward and Constance, on 9 March, at her parents' home in Brighton. Constance wrote to Olive that he was "long and fat and resembles Arthur" [ALM], which indicates that he was a pretty baby, and he soon became the pet of the family. But Constance was very weak after the birth and was ailing for a long time. It was the end of her child-bearing.

Lady Shelley wished to raise a monument on Percy Bysshe Shelley's grave in Rome, and she had asked Richard to serve as a trustee to carry out the work if she should die before it was completed. However, the cemetery plot had been purchased by Trelawny, and his daughter opposed the plan; so the monument was instead offered to Oxford. Richard had obtained a contract for it from the sculptor Onslow Ford, and on 23 March 1892 Lady Shelley invited him to view the finished piece in Ford's studio. On 10 April she invited him to Boscombe to meet with representatives from Oxford, and on this occasion she arranged to donate a large number of Shelley's papers to the Bodleian. Among these were several notebooks with jottings and fragments from which *Relics of Shelley* had been compiled, and Lady Shelley gave three of them to Richard in token of his long service to the family. Two of the three had been crudely bound in vellum, the other was a plain blank book, and all were kept in green morocco cases. They became the most treasured part of Richard's personal library.

In March of 1892 the trustees of the British Museum created a separate Department of Oriental Books and Manuscripts, relieving Richard of "many thousand responsibilities."[16] Such relief would be especially welcome because he was being asked to assume new duties by various groups, one of them the Liberal Association, which was meeting in Paris that year and wanted Richard to be its president. He declined, for he had a more important reason for going to Paris from the ninth through the eleventh of May: the second sale of the Heredia library, where he was to make purchases of Spanish books for the British Museum. There were four sales of this large Spanish collection of Ricardo Heredia, comte de Benahavis. At the first, in May of 1891, the Museum had bought one rare book and a number of extremely rare pieces of music. At the second sale, Richard and assistant R. E. Graves purchased seventy-five books, "the majority," said Richard, "of the greatest rarity, including the two oldest Spanish cancioneros. A great step has been taken towards rendering the Museum library the finest Spanish library out of Spain."[17] This ambition echoed that of Panizzi, expressed in 1848, to make the library the best in the literature of all countries outside their boundaries.

For the conference of the Library Association in Paris in September, Richard composed an address to be read for him. He chose to present a new version of the idea of a universal catalogue of literature which had been discussed during the seventies. His title was "The British Museum Catalogue as the Basis of a Universal Catalogue," and he proposed that the printed catalogue of the British Museum's books be used as the beginning of one, even though he recognized the problem that would be involved in such an ambitious undertaking:

> It could no doubt be performed by a sufficiently numerous body of competent persons, working under efficient control, guided by fixed rules, and influenced by such consideration in the shape of salary and pension as to induce them to devote their lives to it. There is not, however, the least probability of the endowment of such a college of cataloguers. If the Universal Catalogue is ever to be attained, we must submit to proceed by gradual approaches, and to be content with something very far short of perfection in the execution of the work. We must take the printed catalogue of that library which most nearly approaches universality as a basis, and we must appeal to the administrators of other libraries to supplement its deficiencies; without insisting upon too rigid a uniformity of method, which could not be enforced.[18]

Richard knew at the time he wrote that the British Museum catalogue of printed books was the largest one available, expected to have at its completion about a million entries. "If its contents do not comprise a majority of the books existing in the world, they undoubtedly comprise a very great majority of the books which it is really important to catalogue." Therefore he hoped to stimulate public pressure to have the catalogue reprinted as soon as possible, so as to have the accessions made since its inception incorporated for use by a universal cataloguing committee. The establishment of a center for this work would amount to a "universal literary registry," such as the standard book numbering system has become for current publications in the late twentieth century. More elaborate schemes for implementing Richard's dream, notably the Institut International de Bibliographie established in Brussels in the 1930s, foundered from their own weight and from the interminability of the commitment of both energy and finance necessarily involved. We can only marvel, nevertheless, at the vision of an ideal, combined with the practical sense to tell how it could be realized, that Richard Garnett displayed in his exposition of this possible use for the printed catalogue of the British Museum's books.

During the year one of Richard's "literary ladies," as Olive called them—feminine friends from his Reading Room days—had begun to come to the Garnett house for lunch or dinner: Beatrice Harraden, whose novel *Ships That Pass in the Night* would soon make her famous. She, with Arabella Buckley and her sister Elsie, Agnes Clerke and her sister Ellen,[19*] and several others, were welcomed to Narney's hospitable table. Arabella Buckley used to walk from the Museum to her bus stop with Richard when he lived on Regent's

Park. She told Olive one time that when the Museum was about to close in the afternoons, "I put my bonnet on and stood at his elbow till he came. He was always buttonholed by someone," so at last she said to him, "You *must* introduce me to your wife and get her to ask me to dinner,"[20] which he did. Miss Buckley became a favored guest—Olive liked her better than the others. So, it seems, did Richard, for he and she carried on a regular correspondence when she was out of town. Other people were aware of their walk to the bus stop: Samuel Butler recorded that his own lady friend, Elizabeth Mary Ann Savage, had seen Richard and Miss Buckley "flirting down Berners Street (quite innocently, but good square flirting)." Butler thought Arabella a "silly tattling log-rolling mischief-making woman and I dislike her very much."[21] But as he and Richard differed on nearly everything, their tastes in women would hardly have been similar. They behaved, in fact, as friendly enemies; and whereas Butler had only Miss Savage, Richard had a whole coterie of female intellectuals whose company he could enjoy at work or at home.

Nevertheless, Richard was an old-fashioned man in his attitude toward women in general. Olive recorded in her diary his comment on woman suffrage: "My father says that it will give power to the classes who have power enough already, priests and doctors"; and it was a magnanimous gesture for him to offer Olive, when she turned twenty-one, "an allowance of £20 a year paid quarterly as long as he could afford it."[22] She never married, and she lived in her parents' home until her father's death, so she had her basic needs supplied; but to have a little spending money must have been very pleasant for her. May, on the other hand, was married to Guy Hall in August of 1893 and went to live in Rio de Janeiro, where Guy was employed by a British coal company.

Chapter 16

Poems and Problems, 1893–1894

Richard was president of the Library Association of the United Kingdom in 1893, and when he addressed the annual conference in Aberdeen, Scotland, in September, he reviewed the developments of the sixteen years of the association's history. He gave credit to the American librarians who had joined in the inaugural British meeting in 1877 for bringing with them the infectious "esprit de corps" that is characteristic of the members of an organized profession who are "recognised and honoured as such." He then took up the topics that had been discussed at the first meeting and gave his opinions on their progress—chiefly cataloguing and binding, but also the use of photography in libraries, which had been first suggested by Henry Stevens of Vermont. Richard noted the establishment of a photographic department at the Bodleian Library and hoped for one at the British Museum. He ended with praise for the spread of free public libraries, of the study of bibliography, and for the high quality of the students in the association's library school, each of them a future "minister of culture."[1] He was chairman of the education committee for several years.

Henry R. Tedder, librarian of the Athenaeum Club and the moving spirit of the association, recorded that Richard, after his "admirable" address,

> frequently joined in the discussions, speaking with great rapidity in a somewhat low tone, and as he had a habit of bending his head, at times he was scarcely audible. Another quaint but not unpleasing peculiarity was a kind of rhythmic rise and fall of tone, and an occasional reminiscence of his native midland tongue. He delivered his remarks in well-balanced sentences, of precise literary form, without a break, and apparently without preparation. Words, phrases, or facts never failed him. He was always informing and interesting, full of knowledge, good sense and good feeling, never dry, technical, or pedantic. He rarely spoke without a well-told anecdote, or neat quotation, and his most informal speeches were brightened with many a ray of wit, and warmed with a vein of sly humour peculiar to himself. Indeed he was equally apt with speech or pen, and the exercise of both faculties appeared to give him real pleasure.[2]

After the Aberdeen meeting the delegates were invited to a nearby estate for socializing, and two of the company remembered with special praise Richard's little speech of thanks to their host. One man called this "the occasion on which I thought him at his brightest and happiest," adding: "No one who was present can forget the grace, the gaiety, the felicity, the absolute rightness with which Dr. Garnett conveyed to [the host] the warm and grateful appreciation [of] the Association.... The speech formed a worthy crown for an unforgettable day."[3] Another said, "If a record of that speech is available it ought to be printed as an illustration of the apt and graceful way in which Dr. Garnett could use his wide reading for the adornment of life."[4]

On 30 November 1893 a selection of Richard's best poems was published by the arts-and-crafts-oriented firm of Elkin Mathews and John Lane at the sign of the Bodley Head. In April 1894 it was issued by a similar firm in Boston, Copeland and Day, which had just been inaugurated.[5]* A well-designed book, it had a title page embellished with a floral wood-block print by J. Illingworth Kay. Included in the text were the poems from *Io in Egypt* and sixty-three others. Several of the new poems were about the sea, several about fairies, and several about the tropics, which Richard had never seen. One was about Nausicaa, Samuel Butler's alleged authoress of the *Odyssey*, whom Richard portrayed, to Butler's pleasure, as asking to be taught to sail a boat so that she might follow Ulysses and live near him.

Richard sent a copy of the book to Mathilde Blind, who was packing to go to Egypt for her health, and who promised to read the poem "Io in Egypt" again on the spot. She was to spend the winter at Aswan, and on 23 January 1894 she wrote to Richard from there to ask that he send her two books. She also mentioned that in Cairo, at Shepheard's Hotel, she had met William John. It seems that he had written an article for the *Age* in Melbourne that was so biting as to cause a threat of a suit for libel, and this was not his first such offense. Therefore David Syme had decided it would be wise to dispense with his services. William John had stopped in Cairo on his way back to England and was looking for work. He was unsuccessful, for in July he was living in London, apparently with the Garnetts at the British Museum. Olive wrote in her diary that they were all ready to go to Charmouth for vacation when William John secured a position as sub-editor of the *Egyptian Gazette* in Alexandria, and was to get "£250 a year and 25 per cent of the profits!!! We are all dancing with joy."[6] Olive added that William John had said good-bye only to her, "evidently disgusted with everyone else." This indicates that there had been a breach between the brothers over William John's disgrace in Australia. Richard's filial devotion certainly lessened at this time. Furthermore, William John's health, which had been poor in Melbourne, deteriorated in Egypt, and it would not be long before he was unable to work at all.

Richard himself had been in the throes of a harrowing libel suit in the early part of 1894. It was the third and most serious of eleven cases involving censorship that marked the nineties at the British Museum.[7]* The first had occurred early in 1892, when Hypatia Bradlaugh Bonner had asked that a scurrilous biography of her father, Charles Bradlaugh, be removed from the shelves and the catalogue of the library. Richard, with the trustees' permission, had acceded to her request. The second case, in 1893, was settled easily when libellous statements about an Irish member of Parliament were deleted from a new edition of the book in question, which could then be shelved in place of the original. Richard had asked for guidance from the trustees, but had received none. Therefore he was doubly distressed when a legal action was brought against the British Museum and its officers by Victoria Woodhull Martin, an American feminist and free-love advocate, who had led an adventurous life in the public eye, promoting her unorthodox ideas in lecture halls and capping her career by running for President of the United States four times. Her activities in New York had been so notorious that many publications denounced or ridiculed her.

The Department of Printed Books had acquired six pieces that unfavorably mentioned this prominent lady, who by now had married a respectable Englishman named Martin, and the Martins asked that the offensive items—four pamphlets, a magazine, and a book—be withdrawn from the library as libelous to her. Their argument was that the library was "publishing a libel" when it allowed these works to be circulated to readers.

Richard opposed censorship in principle, but practiced it when he felt his own standard of values was violated. He acceded to the Martins' request to the extent of sequestering two pamphlets that he judged obscene. These were put either in the keeper's office, in a locked case, or in the Arch Room with the erotica. More important, Richard had the entries for the pamphlets removed from the Reading Room catalogue. Still, Mrs. Martin was not satisfied and threatened to bring suit. Richard advised Maunde Thompson that it would be unwise to set a precedent by suppressing what he considered "valuable" works—those whose contents were worth having in the library, even though a brief passage or two might be considered libellous by someone mentioned unflatteringly in them. Individual issues of periodicals, he said, could not reasonably be removed from circulation, but passages in them might be deleted. He suggested that if expurgated editions of any of the protested works were published, the library should acquire these and dispose of the original editions. His opinions appealed to the trustees, who ordered that a mollifying letter be sent to the Martins in the hope that it would end the matter.

Instead, the Martins insisted on having a public apology from the trustees and, when none was forthcoming, initiated a suit. It was heard at Queen's Bench No. 2 on 23 February 1894 before Sir Charles Edward Pollock.[8]* The Museum was represented by the Treasury solicitor, whose defense was that the offending materials had been legitimately acquired and that libraries could not reasonably be prevented by outsiders from allowing such works to be read. George Bullen had been keeper of printed books when the items under litigation had been purchased, so he was called to testify, as were Thompson, as head of the institution, and Fortescue, as superintendent of the Reading Room, where the items were given out to readers. Last of all, Richard had to testify about the pieces he had suppressed. Olive, who went to court to hear the proceedings, wrote in her diary: "Mr. Thompson, Mr. Taylor [private secretary to the principal librarian], the Treasury solicitor, Mr. Fortescue, Mr. Bullen and Papa sat in a row together" and "Papa, as a man of letters and student, [was] withdrawn from consideration [of] petty details of scandal etc; concerned for the honour of the great library; a little nervous, very conscientious, a picture of integrity."[9]

The jury was swayed by the immense personal appeal of the attractive Mrs. Martin and by the unchivalrous behavior toward her of the defense attorney, and they awarded her damages of one pound. The judge, however, found for the Museum on 5 March, occasioning, Olive said, "great jubilation" there. Then Richard had to advise the trustees on the disposition of the items Mrs. Martin had objected to. He advocated eliminating permanently the three obscene pamphlets from the shelves and the catalogues, but retaining the others.

It was obvious from this experience, however, that the officers of the Museum needed firm guidance in deciding whether or not a work was libellous, and he asked the trustees to establish a policy in regard to the matter. They were unable to do so, but Richard continued to plead for some legal aid for librarians faced with problems of censorship. He privately consulted Sir Frederick Pollock[10]* about a parliamentary act that might cover this kind of contingency, but was discouraged in any hope of help from that source. Then he went to the Library Association meeting in Belfast, in September, and presented his view that libraries needed protection under the law from contentious persons dissatisfied with characterizations of themselves in print. No relief came during his tenure in office, but in 1900 a revision of the Public Libraries Act, brought before Parliament, contained a clause of exactly the sort he advocated; and although the clause was eliminated before passage of the act, it seems to have inhibited any further actions against libraries for libel.

During this time Richard had been beset by another anxiety: Constance had left on New Year's Day 1894 for Russia, to stay in St. Petersburg with a woman she had met in London and to get acquainted with some of the Russian literati, chief of whom was Count Tolstoy. She had been translating from the Russian for some time and was interested in increasing her contacts in the country. A nursemaid had been found for baby David, and Edward had resigned himself to loneliness. Richard had bought Constance a fur-lined coat to wear, and wrote frequent letters to her while she was away. There was unrest in the Russian capital, making him apprehensive for her safety. He gently chided her for leaving Edward, in a sonnet which he submitted to a new periodical, *The Yellow*

Book. This avant-garde magazine, whose proprietors bowed to conventional taste to the extent of soliciting poems from established writers such as Richard, quickly became the subject of gossip; yet during the next two years Richard contributed to it twenty-seven poems and a story.

Constance returned at the beginning of March, and Richard rejoiced. He noted, at the end of a letter to William Rossetti on the fifth, that "the Russian police laid its paw upon her, but took it off again."[11] She had been delayed at the frontier and so arrived a little later than expected. On the twenty-fifth she and Edward dined with Richard and Narney, and Olive wrote in her diary that Constance looked very well, despite her strenuous trip. Edward had actually suffered more and was forced to take leave from his work for two months to calm his nerves.

Another romantic episode involved the Garnetts in Ford Hueffer's marriage to a seventeen-year-old former schoolmate, Elsie Martindale, whose parents objected to the match. In despair of obtaining their consent, Elsie ran away from home by eluding her sister in a railway station and taking a train to Bath. When Ford learned of it he consulted Robert Garnett as a legal adviser, and Robert arranged for Elsie to go to some Garnett cousins in Bristol. On Easter weekend he went to Bristol and took her to stay with Chapple's family in Gloucestershire. He managed to hold Elsie's father at bay until late May, but then Mr. Martindale started proceedings to make Elsie a ward of the court, and Ford hastened to her and took her to a registry office, where, by lying about their ages (Ford was only twenty), they succeeded in getting married. They had a short honeymoon, then came back to London and moved in with the Garnetts at the British Museum.

Richard and Narney were obviously sympathetic, but they probably did not feel that they were living in a novel, as Olive did. There was a private trial in June, and Ford and Elsie were forced to separate: Ford left to stay with his mother, but Elsie remained with the Garnetts. The case was soon decided, for there was no recourse from the fact of the marriage, and the Martindales bowed to fate and let the young couple start their life together. They moved to Mrs. Hueffer's, and the Garnetts were able to settle back into a calmer routine.[12]

Disturbing to Richard was a series of three articles published in mid-year by Mark Twain upon reading Dowden's biography of Shelley, which Twain called "the strangest book that has seen the light since Frankenstein," for its sidestepping of Shelley's guilt in deserting Harriet. He quoted Hogg's book and Shelley's poems to make his point that Shelley's behavior would be, in other men, called "a grave crime," and that there was no evidence of Harriet's responsibility for it. He pretended to be shocked that America's young women were being given Lady Shelley's version of Harriet's story in the book when it was used as a college text.[13] About this new anti-Shelley blast, Richard restrained himself to expressing his reaction "pretty freely" to his friend Professor George Woodberry of Harvard on "Mr. Twain's astounding impertinence."[14] It was, of course, Richard who was directly responsible for Dowden's careful handling of the problem of Harriet's tragedy; but he was no longer ready to act the gallant champion of Mary Shelley, nor would his position as keeper of printed books at the British Museum allow such public altercation as he had once indulged in. He did publish an article called "Shelley in Italy" in the *English Illustrated Magazine* for December 1894, the occasion for which was the erection of a monument to Shelley in Viareggia, Italy, between Pisa and Lerici, and in which he discoursed on Shelley's travels in Italy as mentioned in his letters, and the influence of the country on his poetry and that of other English poets.

On 30 October he had arranged for the exchange of a book in the British Museum library for another recently published. His friendship with William Morris may have influenced him, but his conscience would not have let him make a bad bargain for the Museum. Under copyright, the Museum received a plain paper copy of every work published by the Kelmscott Press, but Morris offered a vellum-bound large paper copy of one of three newly printed books if he could have ten leaves from a duplicate incunabulum in the King's Library, apparently in order to copy some woodcuts from them for a future publication. Richard investigated and found that the leaves desired were not among the original donations of the King, but had been purchased separately and were not needed. Therefore, although the procedure was most unusual, he recommended the exchange, and it was made. In fact, he managed to increase the advantage to the Museum by securing two, instead of just one, of the three Kelmscott books.[15]

Chapter 17

Richard Garnett, C.B., LL.D., 1895

When the Queen's New Year's honors list was announced on 29 December 1894, Richard's name was on it for Companion of the Bath. The active force behind the nomination was the Prime Minister, Lord Rosebery, with whom Richard had been friendly for several years, and who sent him a note to advise him of the honor. Their acquaintance, originated by David Masson, had been enriched by a mutual love of poetry and history, liberal politics, and horse racing—Rosebery won the Derby in 1894, 1895, and 1905. He was also the author of several biographies of English statesmen.

    Richard was formally notified of his selection by means of a letter, signed by the Queen, to her "trusty and well-beloved Richard Garnett" [HRHRC], and was later summoned to Windsor Castle to receive the insignia on 25 February 1895. Olive objected that "the levée dress savours of the theatrical and seems unsuited to the dignity of a learned man like Papa and worse still it is quite unsuited to this cold weather."[1] He and the others to be honored had luncheon with the Queen, then were invested in the White Drawing Room. The oval gold medal of the order, with symbols of England, Scotland, and Ireland, hung from a "red ribbon with a gold safety pin and above it a hook, which the Queen hung on a pin fastened in his coat."[2] The occasion provided a rich reward for Richard's long service to the Crown, and he received eighty-six letters and telegrams of congratulation [HRHRC], which added to his pleasure in the honor.

    In January he had joined Leslie Stephen and others in a movement to preserve Thomas Carlyle's house, becoming a member of the council of the trust. He wrote to the editor of the *Nation*, Charles Eliot Norton, a Carlyle scholar with whom he had some contact, a letter soliciting subscriptions from Americans.[3] This was one of several letters Richard sent to Norton that were published in the magazine during the 1890s.

    At the end of January he reported to the principal librarian on the successful result of an experiment to test a new device, called the telautograph, a "printing telegraph" or teletype that could be adapted to send, instantaneously, the titles of books desired by readers in the Reading Room to the stacks. Since time was the crucial factor in the procurement of books for readers, Richard was anxious to find a means of speeding the process, and having done what he could with the human factor (Anderson's sectioning of the stacks), he was ready to try a mechanical one. He urged Thompson to bring the matter before the trustees,[4] but there was no result. He was many years ahead of his superiors in his concept of efficient library service.

Now occurred what one writer has called "one of the saddest events in all Victorian literary history,"[5] a persistent story involving Richard with attempts by the first Mrs. Thomas Hardy to suppress the publication of her husband's *Jude the Obscure*, which she considered scandalous. The exact time of the alleged meeting between Mrs. Hardy and Richard is vague in all sources reporting it, the original version having been written down by Ford Madox (Hueffer) Ford years later. Ford's reputation for embellishing facts with his literary flair has made the story suspect; yet there must be a grain of truth in it.

We have no record of an acquaintance between Richard and Narney and the Hardys until 1901, when the two couples belonged to a literary group called the Whitefriars Club; but Hardy had studied at the British Museum for some of his writings, and he and Mrs. Hardy, although they lived in Dorset most of the year, spent a good deal of time in London, so they could well have encountered the Garnetts before then.

The publishing history of *Jude the Obscure* complicates the interpretation of the incident because the novel first appeared serially between December 1894 and November 1895 in *Harper's New Monthly Magazine*, entitled first "The Simpletons," then "Hearts Insurgent." As with his earlier novel, *Tess of the d'Urbervilles* (1891), Hardy had to expurgate some of the most daring passages to get the story into print at all. Then, on 1 November 1895, the complete *Jude the Obscure* was published in London in hard covers by Osgood, McIlvaine & Company, and the reviewing press burst into invective. Such phrases as "Jude the Obscene," "Degenerate Hardy," and "a titanically bad book"[6] issued from both sides of the Atlantic, and even Hardy's friend Edmund Gosse was revolted by the grim story. At least one reviewer, however, saw more in it: the *Illustrated London News* said that "the reader closes this book with a feeling that a huge pall has blotted out all the light of humanity," yet: "In one way, that sensation is a tribute to Mr. Hardy's mastery of his art . . . [the book] is manifestly a work of genius."[7]

Emma Hardy had been excluded from helping her husband with *Jude*, although she had followed the development of the other novels, and her fury when she read it revealed Hardy's wisdom in keeping it from her. It is said that she "threw the pages away from her in disgust"[8] and threatened to burn them, if necessary, to keep them out of print. If she was not allowed to see the actual manuscript, the word "pages" may refer to the issues of *Harper's*, where she most likely would have read the story for the first time. Her object then was to try to prevent its being published in England, and to this end, the story goes, she wrote to Richard Garnett, asking him to try to dissuade Hardy from his intention to do so. When her letter elicited no satisfactory response, she made a "special trip"[9] to London to consult Richard. What ensued was recorded thus by Ford:

> Then a storm burst on the British Museum. The young Garnetts went about with appalled, amused, incredulous or delighted expressions, according as the particular young Garnett was a practising Anglican, an Agnostic or a Nihilist ... It began to be whispered by them that Mrs. Hardy, a Dean's daughter, ... had been calling on Dr. Garnett as the Dean of Letters of the British Isles and Museum to beg, implore, command, threaten, anathematize her husband until he should be persuaded or coerced into burning the manuscript of his new novel—which was *Jude*. She had written letters; she had called. She had wept; like Niobe she had let down her blonde hair ... The Agnostic and Nihilist young Garnetts rejoiced, the Anglicans were distraught. Doctor Garnett had obdurately refused.[10]*

This highly colored story sounds too fanciful for authenticity, yet Emma had reason to feel desperate. As recently as 1889 the publisher Henry Vizetelly had been imprisoned for issuing the works of the naturalistic French novelist Emile Zola. He was charged with "bestial obscenity" and "obscene libel," terms Emma thought applicable to *Jude the Obscure*.[11] She therefore feared that her husband might be answerable to the law if the book were published in London.

However, Ford must have embroidered the facts of the Garnetts' involvement in the matter. If there had been weeping in the parlor of the Garnett house, the young people could have overheard it, but Edward now had his own home, Robert was at his office in the daytime, and May, the strictest Anglican in the family, was not in England; so it would have been Arthur, fourteen, Lucy, twenty, or, most likely, Olive, now twenty-four and Ford's friend and confidante, who told him whatever he had learned of it. If the incident had taken place in the keeper's office, it is unlikely to have been overheard by anyone, although if it had been, it would quickly enough have "got around in the Museum."[12]* On the other hand, Ford's opening sentence may have caused his readers to deduce that the whole institution was aware of Mrs. Hardy's visit, rather than just the Garnett household there. Richard was too chivalrous to have publicized a lady's distress, except possibly to have mentioned it to Narney and Olive in private. Olive made no mention of the affair in her diary, and there is nothing in the existing correspondence of the Hardys or the Garnetts to corroborate Ford's account.

The date of the event is equally hazy, but the most likely time seems to be the spring of 1895, by which time the arrangements for publishing *Jude* must have been underway. Osgood & McIlvaine were bringing out a collected edition of Hardy's novels, and he went to London alone, early in April, to consult with them and to look for a house he and Emma could occupy for the summer; but Emma's visit to the city must have occurred before that if she hoped to forestall publication of the book.

As for her reason for approaching Richard Garnett, we can only guess that his position in the literary world, so pithily put by Ford, was the chief factor in her selection of him to take her side, for there is not the slightest evidence that Richard might have had any influence over Hardy. He might have been asked to speak to the publisher, and he might have done so, but that would have been distasteful to him, and surely ineffective. The most he could do was to reassure Emma as to the improbability of an action against the book under the obscenity statutes, and if he had read the chapters in *Harper's*, as he is likely to have done, he could have spoken on that score. (He is not likely, however, to have admired *Jude the Obscure*, for he was as conventional a Victorian as Gosse.) If the interview described by Ford did take place, Richard, with his gallant attitude toward women, must have been able to calm and reassure the lady, as publication of the book proceeded without incident, and the only punishment meted out to Hardy came from the critics. However, early in 1896, when the playwright Alfred Sutro visited the Hardys at their country home, "Max Gate," he made the mistake of praising *Jude* over luncheon, and Emma stiffened. She told him she would never have allowed the book to be published if she had had any say about it, and that it "had made a difference to them... in the County."[13] Emma came from a social class above Hardy's and had greater concern for the good opinion of her peers.

In the midst of all his duties and responsibilities, Richard took time to locate a book describing various obelisks that Mathilde Blind might view on her next sojourn in Egypt. She sent Robert a copy of her *Birds of Passage*, just published, and he told her she should also send one to William John to review in the *Egyptian Gazette*, since it contained several poems about Egypt. This opportunity for publicity had to be forgone, for on 27 May 1895 Richard wrote to Mathilde, "We are at present in a state of expectation on account of my brother, who is suddenly returning from Egypt, I am sorry to say in bad health." William John remained in England from then on, very feeble at first, and only slowly regaining strength over several years. Richard had to support him, with the help of the Tennant cousins, who had offered to pay his fare home and were kind and attentive to him during his illness.

In the spring of 1895 the brilliant career of Oscar Wilde came to an abrupt end. The Marquis of Queensberry had accused Wilde of ruining the marquis' son, and Wilde sued him for libel. As a result of the trial, Wilde was indicted for sodomy and condemned to two years in prison. The sentence was pronounced on 25 May, and when it appeared in the papers, Ford Hueffer rushed to the British Museum to discuss it with the Garnetts. He recalled, many years later, that as he went up the steps of the main building, on them I met Dr. Garnett . . . a queer, very tall, lean, untidily bearded Yorkshire figure in its official frock-coat and high hat. I gave him the news. He looked for a moment away over the great yard of the Museum, with its pigeons and lamps and little lions on the railings. Then he said:

"Then that means the death of English poetry for fifty years."

I can still hear the high tones of my incredulous laughter. At the moment he seemed to me an old obstinate crank, though I knew well how immense was his North Country common sense. . . . On this occasion he held his top-hatted head obstinately and deftly on one side and repeated, with half-closed eyes:

"That means the death-blow to English poetry. It will not be resuscitated for fifty years."[14*]

Ford may have laughed at the time, but he came to concede that Richard was right, for the "electric" literary atmosphere of 1890s London, which Ford so enjoyed, soon quieted and, to his mind, never quite recovered the excitement of those days when Wilde reigned over a coterie of English and French wits.

The recently launched *Yellow Book* also suffered from Wilde's conviction. Although Wilde had had nothing to do with the magazine, his taste was evident in its pages, and it was thought of as part of his aesthetic movement. Mathilde's friend Arthur Symons was about to start a rival publication, the *Savoy*, and had asked Mathilde for a contribution. Richard warned her to "watch the course" of the magazine "very narrowly," but he thought that "under the circumstances you do right to let Symonds [sic] have your poems: even if there is a scandal you will hardly be made responsible."[15*] The *Savoy* was intended to promote the work of the French and English decadents, and was a project of Leonard Smithers, who was noted for publishing erotica. It lasted for only a few issues. Arthur Symons had gone to France and fallen under the spell of the French *décadents*, writing poetry in their vein of "receptiveness to all experience," especially that of the seamy side of city life. His article "The Decadent Movement in Literature," in *Harper's* for November 1893, had been very influential; but, Richard continued to Mathilde, "I detest his last volume [of poems, *London Nights*, just published by Smithers], and all the more because there is real poetical power in it. The erotic poetry of the ancients and the great moderns I can tolerate and even admire, but I cannot stand the nauseous effeminacy of our 'decadents.' "

Symons was an able critic, however, and was about to have the second of his introductions to Shakespeare facsimiles published—a task he had first undertaken at age nineteen under the sponsorship of Richard and Furnivall. He had also edited the Henry Irving Shakespeare, to which Richard had contributed his article on *The Tempest*.

Richard's own brush with the law in 1895 was, fortunately, of a more amusing than serious character. On 4 July he received a summons to appear in county court because a reader named Alexander Chaffers was "claiming damages from: the Prince of Wales [a trustee], Edward Thompson, and Sir

Richard Garnett, for maliciously refusing to renew Plaintiff's ticket of admission to the Reading Room of the British Museum."[16]* Chaffers had been, it seems, "forcibly prevented from entering the Room" because his permit had been revoked; he sued in order "to test the legality of the absolute discretion of the Trustees, and claimed nominal damages for a technical assault."[17]* The Treasury solicitor had to undertake another defense of the policies of the Museum administration, the case dragging through several courts until a parliamentary act against "vexatious" legal action was passed in 1897. Richard was doubtless amused to have his C.B. mistaken for a K.C.B., but relieved not to have to defend himself against the ex-reader, who must have done something reprehensible to have been banned from the Reading Room.

Happier news for the Garnetts in June was Lucy's engagement to William Harrison Cowlishaw, a young architect and a Fabian, whom all the family liked. The laggard Robert had also become engaged, in December of 1894, to Martha Roscoe, a literary-minded descendant of William Roscoe, the Italophile book collector who had befriended the youthful emigré Panizzi in the 1820s. She was the daughter of Richard Roscoe of the legal firm Robert now belonged to. Robert also had a strong literary bent, and not only did he and Martha write independently—he, reviews and essays; she, reviews and novels—but in 1917 they collaborated in editing Richard's correspondence about Shelley. Richard was extremely fond of Martha and gave her some of his most prized books.

Early in October of 1895 Richard's eight-page *William Blake, Painter and Poet* was published by the *Portfolio* in its Monographs on Artistic Subjects series, with many illustrations, some in color. In it Richard praised Blake as a spontaneous poet who had appeared after a long period of artificiality in art, and called him "the morning star which announced the new day of English poetry," although he was less impressed with Blake's painting. The young William Butler Yeats reviewed the book from the point of view of mysticism, in which he was deeply involved, and faulted Richard for having failed to study that subject. Despite Richard's interest in astrology, he distrusted the other occult arts, claiming that, unlike them, astrology was not "hidden," but rather was manifest to reason and experience, the influence of the planets on human affairs being, to his mind, easily demonstrable. Richard's book on Blake, nevertheless, made frequent references to Yeats's edition, with E. J. Ellis, of the literary works of Blake (1893), which interpreted them from the esoteric point of view.

Late in the year, George Bell & Sons issued Richard's *The Age of Dryden* in the series Handbooks of English Literature, with an index by J. P. Anderson. It has been among his most widely used texts.

Also in 1895 Richard had been elected president of the Bibliographical Society for a two-year term, and he took his responsibilities therein very seriously. He felt compelled to decline a third year, but often acted for his successor, the earl of Crawford. Richard always attended meetings when the speaker was from the British Museum, a courtesy to his colleagues that is not typical of institutional officers. Alfred Pollard remarked, "It is no exaggeration to say that his presence by itself sufficed to make a meeting a success, for he chatted delightfully with everyone who went up to him, and could always be relied on for an interesting speech."[18]

Chapter 18

The Old Order Changeth, 1896–1898

The year 1896 brought many important events in Richard's life. Some of them were sad—the loss of two dear friends; some were rewarding—honors and publications; some were happy—Robert and Martha's marriage in June; and some were disturbing—Olive's long visit to Russia and Narney's failing health. In the spring, and possibly also in the fall, Richard called on Lady Shelley, who grew feebler each year.

His first publication that year, translations of 124 sonnets from Dante, Petrarch, and Camoëns, came out in May and was dedicated "To Professor Charles Eliot Norton, the first commentator in English on the Vita Nuova." Norton had published *The 'New Life' of Dante* in 1859 and Dante's *Divine Comedy*, translated into English prose, in 1891–92. Richard's book was printed in the distinguished style of the Bodley Head and Copeland and Day, and had a title page illustrated with Illingworth Kay's portrait medallions of the three poets, which were repeated on the cover in gold. Richard had composed a sonnet to honor each poet as an introduction to each section.

In June the *Portfolio* brought out, as part of the twenty-seventh of its "artistic monographs" (this one consisting of three sections), Richard's *Richmond on the Thames*, a hundred-page essay on the history of the area, covering natural features and the connections of royalty, art, and literature with Richmond. It was illustrated with numerous photographs of works of art in which scenes, buildings, and persons were represented, and it has been one of his most lasting works, remaining in print in Britain longer than any of his others.

Arthur Symons wrote on 18 July to ask Richard for a story for the *Savoy* [HRHRC]. He hoped that there was one like those in *The Twilight of the Gods* lying in Richard's desk, ready for publication; but either there was none, or Richard preferred not to lend his name to a journal of such questionable respectability, for he shortly afterward published two stories elsewhere. One was "A Handful of Dust," a "prose poem" about cremation, printed in the *Pageant*;[1] the other was one of his most popular stories, "Alexander the

Ratcatcher," a fable about the worldly Borgia Pope Alexander VI, which appeared in the *Yellow Book* in January of 1897. It was included in the second edition of *The Twilight of the Gods* and has been several times anthologized.

Olive was determined to travel to Russia, where a friend of Constance's found employment for her as a governess. Richard was unable to understand her interest in that country, though he knew of her close Russian friends in London. He said to Dowden, "It is curious that both she and my daughter in law should have taken up Russia, an uninteresting country to me; but it is right that the new generation should fill up the *lacunae* of the preceding."[2*] Olive left in August and was gone for nine months.

On 28 June 1896 Justin Winsor, the noted historian and librarian of Harvard College, had written to Richard to acknowledge a copy of *Dante, Petrarch, Camoëns: CXXIV Sonnets*, and to say that Richard should bring Narney to the United States and, as he put it, "let Harvard give you a doctorate. If you could only say you would come, I think I could bring about the rest" [HRHRC]. This pleasant prospect could not be realized, but Winsor helped secure Richard's election, on 10 December 1896, as a corresponding member of the Massachusetts Historical Society, presumably for his biography of Emerson.

The honor came at a gloomy time, for Richard had recently lost two of his best friends. Coventry Patmore and Mathilde Blind had died on the same day, 26 November. Richard had published a rather uncomplimentary article on Patmore for the *Bookman* series Living Critics,[3] but he wrote a long and fair obituary for the *Times* and one for the *Saturday Review*.[4] Mathilde had been failing for some months, and had gone to Cambridge earlier in the year in search of an educational institution worthy of receiving a legacy from her. She chose Newnham College, which both Constance and Martha had attended; then she retired to a rest home in London, where she slowly grew weaker. Five days before her death she received friends, probably among them Richard and Robert, who was her legal executor, and Arthur Symons, her literary executor. She was peaceful and resigned at the end. To Richard she left his choice of six reproductions of paintings by Ford Madox Brown, and also her own portrait by Lucy Madox Brown Rossetti.[5*] So it was that as Richard's sixty-first year drew to a close, he saw two cherished chapters of his life ended.

Narney, too, had been unwell again. In January of 1897 she had to go to the country for a month to recover from what the doctors called nervous exhaustion. By the end of February she was enough improved to be able to visit Edward and Constance at their new country house in Kent, "The Cearne," designed by Harry Cowlishaw. On 12 April Lucy and Harry were married and went to live in a farm house not far from "The Cearne." To recover from the wedding, Narney stayed with friends in Somersetshire; but when Richard took her to Southwold in September, she was still "ill and uneasy about herself."[6] The rest and change soothed her symptoms, but, unfortunately, did nothing for their source.

Richard himself had begun to feel his years. During the Southwold vacation he told Olive, "I have not rambled far. The cause is a sore foot now getting better, which has limited my walks very much."[7] This was a severe inhibition for him, and one he was to endure more and more as time went on, until he was obliged to lean on the cane he had been using for more aggressive pursuits, and his step became slow and halting.

July of 1897 had brought extra work but a pleasant distraction in the form of the second international conference of librarians, held in London from the thirteenth through the sixteenth. The attendance was nearly three times that of the first international conference in 1877: fourteen governments and 313 libraries were represented by 641 delegates from all over Europe, the United States, the British colonies, and even Japan. Included in the program of meetings, receptions, dinners, and parties were an exhibit of library appliances and a special performance of *The Merchant of Venice*, with Sir Henry Irving as Shylock and Ellen Terry in her famous role as Portia.

Richard was not only in charge of the committee on papers and discussions, but was on the committee to edit the transactions, and had prepared an exhibition of American books and books relating to America which the delegates could visit during British Museum hours (10 a.m. to 6 p.m.) throughout the conference. He was ready to welcome them himself when he was on duty. Forty-six papers were delivered during the conference, covering nearly all aspects of library science, its history, and its contributions to culture. The Bibliographical Society was a co-sponsor of one session and, as its president, Richard spoke on a bibliographical subject, "The Introduction of European Printing into the East."[8]

At the British Museum George Fortescue had been removed from the superintendency of the Reading Room in order to help Richard with the administration of the Department of Printed Books, "which was already too big a burden for one man, however able."[9] Fortescue was continuing to compile the subject indexes to the catalogue of printed books, and Richard wrote an introduction to the first volume of these to be printed, which covered the accessions from 1890 through 1895 and was published in 1897. Richard also provided prefaces for several other Museum publications during his keepership.

Indeed, his pen was seldom idle. He edited and introduced Robert Browning's poems for George Bell & Sons' Endymion series, and contributed an article on "The Early Italian Book Trade" to *Bibliographica*, as well as one on "The Manufacture of Fine Paper in England in the Eighteenth Century" to the *Library*.[10] Of this last he sent a copy to his cousin Jeremiah of Otley, who was still running the Garnett paper mill. He finished entries for the *Dictionary of National Biography* on Percy Bysshe and Mary Shelley, and undertook to edit a series of books on librarianship for George Allen. Five volumes were published in this Library series, all with introductions by Richard, and the last volume was his own *Essays in Librarianship and Bibliography* (1899). This work contains a broad sample of his professional interests: "Paraguayan and Argentine Bibliography," "On Some Colophons of the Early Printers" (read at the annual meeting of the Library Association in London in October 1889), "Subject-indexes to the Transactions of Learned Societies," "The Telegraph in the Library," "On the Protection of Libraries from Fire," "On the Provision of Additional Space in Libraries" (read at the annual meeting of the Library Association in Belfast, 1894), and biographical sketches of bookmen.

He was also working on a *History of Italian Literature*, which was to be the fourth of a series called Short Histories of the Literatures of the World, edited by Edmund Gosse. Richard had been asked to postpone a projected life of Heine in order to concentrate on this project. Gosse wanted 90,000 words, about 300 pages, and offered £150 for them. In November Gosse was writing editorial advice to Richard and asking him to re-translate a poem that he thought had been badly done by the translator Richard had chosen. Richard agreeably set about making his own English version of the poem, and Gosse accepted it, adding, "You must now write a seductive Preface, an austere Bibliography, and a modest Index. I wish you joy, for these are hateful tasks."[11] The preface, which Gosse emended somewhat, was dated December 1897, and the book appeared, under the imprint of William Heinemann, early in 1898. It was reprinted in America in 1973 and has always been a well-regarded source.

Richard had also been invited to write a biography of Edward Gibbon Wakefield, which was to be subtitled *The Colonization of South Australia and New Zealand*. It was to be published by Fisher Unwin in London and Longmans, Green in New York as Volume 4 of the Builders of Great Britain series, one of Edward Garnett's ideas. Richard found it a challenging assignment, involving much time-consuming correspondence between London and the colonies down-under, and when it came out, in November of 1898, he was pleased to have a descendant of Wakefield's tell him, "You have made the *man* come to life."[12]

In January of 1898 Richard sent to the editor of the *Athenaeum* a variant version of the first stanza of Shelley's "To Constantia, Singing," which had been transmitted to him by Edward Silsbee, now back in the United States. Claire Clairmont is generally considered to have been the subject of the poem, and in one of the copybooks Silsbee had acquired from her estate were several emendations to the verse as previously printed. Silsbee had met Richard through Rossetti while in London in the fall of 1877, and by 1895 he had become well enough acquainted to have attended an at-home on 12 December, as recorded in Olive's diary. The *Athenaeum* published the poem in the issue of 15 January.

The two men combined forces in June of 1898 to arrange for the donation to Oxford of a guitar which had been given by Shelley to Jane Williams in Italy. It had become available upon the death of the daughter of Jane and Thomas

Jefferson Hogg in 1897, and her nephew wanted it to be placed in a public institution, but Silsbee was also anxious to have it. Richard suggested that Silsbee buy it and present it on deposit to the Bodleian, a plan that satisfied both parties. To carry it out, Richard joined the two donors in the trip to Oxford, where E. W. B. Nicholson provided a glass case for the guitar. It was a handsome object, having been made by Bottari of Pisa in 1816, with a front of Swiss pine, a back of mahogany, and a fingerboard of ivory inlaid with flowers.[13]*

Richard was involved in the presentation of another Shelley discovery in 1898—the juvenile verses of Percy Bysshe Shelley and Elizabeth Shelley that had been suppressed by Stockdale in 1810. Those copies of *Victor and Cazire* that had already been distributed, mostly as gifts by Shelley, had vanished without a trace. Now, suddenly, one had come to light, bound with some works of Byron, in the possession of a descendant of the person to whom Shelley had given it. It was brought to John Lane, who decided to publish a facsimile under the editorship of F. B. Money-Coutts, whose grandfather was mentioned in one poem.[14]* But when Money-Coutts learned that Richard had identified the work in 1860 in "Shelley in Pall Mall," he suggested that the edition be turned over to him as a fitting sequel to the earlier article. Richard at first demurred, then allowed himself to be persuaded to write an introduction and notes for the facsimile.

Original Poetry by Victor and Cazire was published by Lane in October. In his introduction, Richard quoted documents and letters to establish the authorship of the young Shelleys, and then apologized for the poor quality of the poems: "Seldom have the beginnings of a great poet been so destitute of merit as [Shelley's] early lyrics." The reason for publishing them again was that they constituted "the final chapter of a romance, and a bibliographical event." There is no doubt that somebody else would have brought them out if Richard and John Lane had not done so, for anything written by Shelley was considered important, and the verses have since been included in the Shelley canon. Yet Lady Shelley was not pleased to see the reprint. She acknowledged the copy Richard sent her with regret that this "boy's first scribble" should be given to the public, despite her opinion that Richard's introduction would be "of value to the world & I rejoice that it was given into your hands."[15] Richard had promised to visit her in the summer of 1898, and at that time he should have told her of the projected publication; but her letter begins, "What a surprize! [*sic*] and how grateful I feel to you for sending it to me yourself and writing your name in it which enhances its value." So the friendship of forty years between Richard and Lady Shelley remained firm, despite disagreements, yet Richard was now acting independently in regard to Shelley.

The original book, from which the facsimile was made, was keenly desired by Richard for the British Museum, and by Buxton Forman for himself, but it went instead to T. J. Wise for £150.[16] Wise later acquired another copy and sold the first one to John Henry Wrenn of Chicago, whom he was helping to build a literary collection. He told Wrenn he had paid £255 for it.[17]*

An Italian scholar now entered the Shelley fold, and Richard seems to have sponsored him. This was Guido Biagi, the librarian of the Biblioteca Mediceo-Laurenziana in Florence. He had been in correspondence with Richard for some time and was interested in Shelley's life in Italy. He had investigated municipal records to try to shed light on the capsizing of the sailboat that caused Shelley's death. There had been a rumor that pirates had attacked the boat, thinking it belonged to Lord Byron and would have valuables aboard, but Biagi and Richard discounted the idea. Biagi found evidence to confirm the cause as a sudden storm, combined with Shelley's recklessness in proceeding under full sail. Biagi produced a book on the subject, *The Last Days of Percy Bysshe Shelley: New Details from Unpublished Documents*, and Fisher Unwin published an English translation of it in 1898. Presumably in recognition of Richard's *History of Italian Literature*, Biagi proposed his name for membership in the Società Bibliografica Italiana, and he was duly elected in October.

Chapter 19

A New Century, 1899–1900

As another London winter began to set in, Richard realized that Narney would never be well in the city and that he must let her have the benefit of pure air and quiet in a rural environment. He therefore informed Maunde Thompson that he wanted to retire as soon as possible, even though the civil service regulations entitled him to another full year in the Museum. His own health was no longer robust, for it had begun to weaken under the steady pressure of his position in the library and literary worlds. He confessed to Dowden, early in 1899, that "my eyes ... have given me some uneasiness of late"[1] and, indeed, he had been to an optician, who had prescribed two pairs of spectacles, one for reading and one for distance [HRHRC]. Obviously, his long and intense labors over print and handwriting had taken their toll, and on the eve of his sixty-fourth birthday he could only look forward to a steady deterioration of his vision.

This prospect would have added to his wish to retire, if any addition had been needed. He therefore "laid his resignation before the Trustees" on 11 February, when, said Olive, "the Prince of Wales, the Speaker [of the House of Commons], the Bishops of London and Winchester, Sir John Lubbock and Mr. John Morley and Mr. Fortnum came."[2]* These gentlemen accepted the resignation with regret, and Thompson was directed to express the trustees' appreciation of, and thanks for, Richard's long and "faithful" service. The event was announced in the press and there was a stir among Richard's friends. Two of his staff, Alfred Pollard and Robert Proctor, planned an exhibit of three hundred notable books acquired by the library during his keepership, along with a printed volume describing them, with a frontispiece portrait etched by William Strang. The project had to be rushed through in ten weeks, and it was remarkably well done under the circumstances.

The portrait closely resembles Richard's photographs, but one person disliked it: J. Y. W. MacAlister, who, as editor of the *Library*, wanted a likeness of Richard for "an appreciation of his life and work" in that journal. He wrote to Narney on 14 September, "I have never seen the Doctor's face except wearing either an amiable smile, or a pleasant, thoughtful expression, and Strang's portrait seems to me to make him as severe and hard as a mediaeval inquisitor" [HRHRC]. To others, the portrait gives an appealing impression of weariness or sadness.

The book contained sixty other illustrations and had, on the red cloth cover, an impression of Richard's monogram in a filigree cartouche drawn by Laurence Housman. It was printed at the Edinburgh University Press and bound in London by Joseph William Zaehnsdorf's fine bindery. The annotated entries were arranged in sections, by country and by century, with a miscellaneous division at the end. One copy was ready for presentation on Richard's last day as keeper, 20 March 1899. Among the 162 subscribers were nine libraries, twenty librarians, six bookmen and collectors, eight publishers, three noblemen, and many other distinguished persons. The editors described it as an "entirely private and unofficial . . . souvenir of Dr. Garnett's Keepership" in which only a few very choice volumes were listed, and pointed out that "a Keeper's purchases are dictated, not only by opportunity and his own tastes, but by what his predecessors and the great benefactors of the Museum have left for him to do. As this list will show, Dr. Garnett has been able to enhance the prestige of the Museum collections even where they were richest, and to bring at least one of the less flourishing sections, that of early Spanish books, to the level of the rest. The Editors can wish no better fortune to the Museum Library than that future Keepers may attain as much success."[3]

This book was a precious gift, for Richard was proud of his acquisitions, not only of early Spanish, but also of early English printing, his purchases of which, he claimed, amounted to more than those of the previous forty years. Among the latter were "five new Caxtons. Five may seem a small number," he told an interviewer, "but I mean five Caxtons which the Museum did not already possess."[4] There were also thirteen Wynkyn de Wordes and eight Pynsons, forty-one sixteenth-century books, twenty-nine from the seventeenth century, and four from the eighteenth. The nineteenth-century books included three Shelley works, one of them donated by Lady Shelley; rare first editions of Carlyle and Emerson; and one of the trial copies of Tennyson's *Idylls of the King* that Richard had seen in sheets at Moxon's in 1857, entitled "Enid and Nimue." This had corrections in the author's hand and was donated by F. T. Palgrave. There were numerous purchases from 1894, indicating a substantial budget in that year, when Lord Rosebery was prime minister. Several works came from the sales of Lord Ashburnham's library in 1898.

The London press took notice of Richard's retirement with tributes for his long years of work for the nation. Typical was the comment in the *Sketch* that "his retirement from a post in the Civil Service which he has rendered exceptionally illustrious is universally regretted."[5] On 14 March Maunde Thompson advised Richard that the trustees had awarded him a pension of £602.15.6, and added, "Long may you live to enjoy it!"[6] On 13 April a dinner was given by his staff at the Freemason's Tavern, where Richard was presented with a gift of Narney's choice—silver spoons and forks.[7] Thompson gave the main address.

An official oil portrait by John Collier was also commissioned by a committee whose secretary-treasurer, A. H. Huth, accepted subscriptions from friends of the subject. Other members of the committee were Lord Acton, Sidney Lee, Leslie Stephen, and the Bishop of London, Mandell Creighton. The portrait was over-subscribed, so forty-seven volumes of reference, chosen by Richard, and specially bound by Zaehnsdorf, were added to the gift, and all were presented on 23 June at an assembly of the subscribers in the rooms of the Society of Arts. Leslie Stephen, in the chair, told Richard the gifts were "an expression of a genuine, a very widespread, and a very strong sense of gratitude and esteem for him, and carried with [them] the most cordial good wishes for his future health and happiness."[8] Sidney Lee also spoke, remarking that Richard could hardly need forty-seven reference books, "as he must already know every thing."[9] The portrait was displayed at the British Museum for two days, then it was turned over to the family.

Richard's friends were quick to suggest literary endeavors to keep him occupied in retirement. Fisher Unwin wanted him to write his reminiscences, but Richard doubted that they "would be of much interest to the public,"[10] and in any case he could not attempt them for some time because he had other commitments. He was already helping with a big Byron project—an edition of Byron's poetry being done by Ernest Hartley Coleridge for John Murray. The first volume had come out in 1898, the last would appear in 1904, becoming the standard edition for a time. Byron's letters and journals were being edited by Rowland Prothero to complete the comprehensive oeuvre, and when the first volume of each had been published in 1898, Richard had reviewed them favorably for the *Bookman*.[11] Prothero wrote a note of thanks, saying, "Praise from you is, I think, the best reward a man can have."[12]

In February 1899 Richard had received an invitation to speak on Shelley at a ceremony dedicating the home of the late Lord Leighton as a museum of art. He replied, "I am a bad lecturer, my voice being weak and my delivery ineffective. If your committee enlist me it must be at their peril."[13] However, he was willing to contribute a talk on Shelley's views on art if he could have enough time to prepare it. He found the time and was ready on 27 April. The lecture was published in the *Anglo-Saxon Review* for September 1900 and also in his *Essays of an Ex-Librarian*.

Early in 1899 Lady Shelley had purchased a number of letters from the Hogg family, a few of them actually from Percy Bysshe Shelley and Mary Shelley to Thomas Jefferson Hogg and Jane Williams Hogg. Others were of Trelawny, Claire Clairmont, and Edward Ellerker Williams. "I wonder if it would be possible," she wrote to Richard, "for you to spare me a day or two before I die, that I might consult you as to what I ought to do about Hoggs letters?—It is eighty years since I was born so that there is but little time."[14] This last proved to be quite true. Richard visited her at Easter, 28 March, and on 7 April she wrote to thank him for a photograph of himself: "I can't think how you have found time just now when you have so much to do with regard to your removal from the Museum—but then, of course, you are a wonderful man."[15]

It was her last letter to him, or, at least, the last one that has been preserved, for she died on 24 June. Richard apparently did not attend the funeral, although he was invited by Shelley Scarlett to stay at Boscombe if he so desired;[16] but he sent his sympathy to Florence Scarlett, who replied on 3 July that she had not had time to write to all Lady Shelley's friends before the news had reached the public, as the final illness had been so short that Florence herself had arrived only after her aunt's death. She added that she was glad she and Richard had both been with Lady Shelley at Easter, "for it drew old links together again in a way I have missed much latterly; & feel that few live now who know so much of the former Shelley life (from papers) as you did, & I may say, I did, who had copied so many.... I am sure your kind offer of help in any arrang[emen]t of papers, will be much appreciated by Shelley, my son, who inherits everything—of course I told him of it at once—.... Robert, who was left the Cottage and everything in it . . . has therefore your latest photograph, with which my Aunt was so very much pleased; & had three."[17]

Richard and Narney had found a house on the edge of the city that seemed ideally situated for them. It was at the back of Parliament Hill, north of Regent's Park, on the edge of Hampstead Heath, and close to the Hampstead Heath railway station. The address was 27 Tanza Road. It was a modest semi-detached house with a small garden at the back and a gate in the high fence that shielded the houses from the heath. They moved into it in April.

On 14 April the centenary of the Garnett mill at Low Moor, Clitheroe, was celebrated, but Richard was unable to travel there for the occasion. He was arranging to sell some of his books because the space he had for them in the new house was smaller than that of the Museum house, and on 10 May Hodgson's disposed of them by auction. Some other volumes and some manuscripts, including letters of Edward Gibbon Wakefield, were donated to the British Museum.

The Library Association, at its meeting in September, presented Richard with a testimonial signed by the members, along with an aneroid barometer and a gold watch engraved with his monogram. The *Library Association Record* reported that the committee for the presentation, chaired by Lord Crawford, had been hardly regular in its constitution, as "the members elected themselves." The subscriptions were "limited in amount" so that all might contribute toward "recognising Dr. Garnett's services to librarianship and bibliography in general, and their own Association in particular." There were 277 signatories, representing all ranks of the association, as well as branches in Canada, the West Indies, Cape Colony, and Rhodesia, and also foreign members from

France, Italy, Norway, and the United States. "All this showed that those who knew and respected Dr. Garnett were to be found at the uttermost parts of the earth, and that his great reputation had penetrated throughout the world of books and libraries. . . . As long as [he] was spared to them, they would feel that they might look to him for advice and encouragement, and he would always live in their memory and the memory of those who would come after them as the model of what a great librarian should be."[18]

In October three concerts were given in which Richard's poem "Where Corals Lie" was featured as one of Edward Elgar's "Sea Pieces." So far as can be determined, no member of the Garnett family attended the concert in London on the seventh, even though they should have been aware of the event, for in July Elgar had written to Richard asking to use the poem in the series of songs he was composing for the popular contralto Clara Butt. The songs were well liked from the first presentation at the Norwich Festival on the fifth, and "Where Corals Lie" soon became the favorite. Later in the month a command performance was given at Balmoral for Queen Victoria. Elgar was just entering the best period of his career, his first works having been performed in 1890, and 1899 being the year of his "Enigma Variations." Three years later, in 1902, he asked to be allowed to set to music one of Richard's translations from the *Greek Anthology,* noting that the success of "Where Corals Lie" had been great and hoping that Richard had heard it sung well with orchestra.[19]* His phrasing indicated that "Sea Pieces" had been performed by others besides Clara Butt in the interim. Still, we have no evidence that any of the Garnetts heard them on any occasion.

Also in October, Richard wrote a report for the *Times* on the approaching end of the printing of the *Catalogue of Printed Books in the British Museum,* the final volume of which came from the press in December. Of it he said: "It is a marvelous work, built up, like the cathedrals of the Middle Ages, by the labours of successive generations. It has no rival in the world, nor can it have, until some library as large as that of the British Museum has been catalogued with equal thoroughness."[20] The catalogue has had only one rival, the Library of Congress *National Union Catalog*, but, with further editing and correcting, Richard's work has survived as a bibliographic tool of unique importance throughout the twentieth century. He took pride in his accomplishment and that of his colleagues and was content to have guided the entire project through the press in the allotted time and so to have produced the first printed catalogue of a national library that approached completeness.

Another extensive compilation of which he was the general editor was a twenty-volume anthology of the world's great writers, from ancient times to the current era—the *International Library of Famous Literature,* containing "over a thousand masterpieces," with essays on the literature of different nations and epochs. His co-editors were Leon Vallée, Alois Brandl, and Donald G. Mitchell.[21]* The set was contracted for by an American syndicate and was first published in 1899 by the *Standard* of London. The work was issued several times, with minor variations, the principal other title for it being *The Universal Anthology*.[22]* Richard contributed an introduction, "The Use and Value of Anthologies"; five of his sonnets; ten of his translations from Camoëns and one from the Italian; two short stories; a selection from *Iphigenia in Delphi*; and eighteen "Gleanings from the Greek Anthology" translated by him. The earliest example of world literature was the "Assyrian Story of the Creation," from a Babylonian clay tablet, while among the nineteenth-century authors represented were Dowden, Farrar, Gosse, Henry James, Andrew Lang, Maurice Maeterlinck, Bret Harte, and Emile Zola, the latter two being resident in London at the time.

Richard got praise for this huge work from scholars and librarians, one of whom thought that a set should be put in the library of every girls' school, for he was sure most educated young women were deficient in literary knowledge. A greater testimonial came much later from D. H. Lawrence, who recalled from his youth the "lasting importance" to him of a household set of the *International Library*, from which he said he had learned more than he had from the schools he had attended. He thought it "brilliantly selected" and a good "basis for a generous liberal education."[23]

In his first year of retirement Richard turned out a number of other publications, of a rather astonishing variety. One that was close to his heart was the memoir of Mathilde Blind, prefixed to Arthur Symons's edition of her poems, which was published by Fisher Unwin in 1900. He joined the Hampstead Historical Society and began to research the famous literary figures of the past who had lived in the area. The *Hampstead Annual* for 1899 had the first of several articles by him, "Notes on Some Poets Connected with Hampstead." He edited the *Complete Works of Charles Dickens*, in thirty volumes, for Chapman & Hall; edited orations of British and American orators, each in two volumes, for Fifth Avenue Press; cooperated in editing *The Library*; and wrote an introduction for a book called *What Makes a Friend?*[24] in which he expressed his belief that friendship was governed by the planets and that compatibility was predestined by the nativities of the individuals involved. He continued his large personal correspondence and wrote to the editor of the *Times* protesting that another letter, published earlier, had given him too much credit for the publication of the *British Museum Catalogue*.[25] He went back to the Museum almost daily for several months, then less often, and finally as the kind of visitor he had spent his life in serving there.

Chapter 20

Journeys and Publications, 1901–1902

Two more books by Richard were published in 1901. The first was *The Queen and Other Poems*, which was brought out by John Lane. The title poem consisted of four sonnets on the death of Queen Victoria in January and there were four more about royalty. Twenty-five new sonnets joined an equal number from *Poems*, and one was a more mature tribute to Shelley than that in *Io in Egypt*. The second book was a collection of prose writings, *Essays of an Ex-Librarian*. It consisted of twelve essays, addresses, and introductions by him to works by others, all in the field of "literary history and criticism, and [all] having preluded their appeal to public interest by interesting the author himself."[1] William Heinemann published the compilation in the autumn.

The most unusual occurrence of the year was the visit Richard and Narney paid to Thomas and Emma Hardy. It came about through a pilgrimage made by the members of the Whitefriars Club, "a convivial society of writers and journalists,"[2] to see Hardy's "Wessex," the area in which he lived and about which he wrote. A hundred people went, not all of them known to the Hardys, who were to receive the group at their home for tea. Hardy wrote to Richard on 23 June, hoping that he and Narney would be of the company, and adding the wishes of Emma in a postscript.[3] This is a clear indication that the two couples were by now on friendly terms, probably as a result of membership in the club. However, the Garnetts were unable to get away at that time, and Richard suggested that they might pay a separate visit later on. On 27 June Hardy returned a gracious welcome "for a night or two,"[4] when, as the only guests, they could have a more leisurely time for conversation. On 16 August Richard and Narney went by train to Dorset to stay at Max Gate for the weekend and then to proceed to the seaside for their normal summer holiday, visiting other friends on the way.

Hardy was not a good host, for he customarily retired after breakfast each day to write in his study upstairs, and he tended to be taciturn under the best of circumstances. It took some ingenuity to draw him out, as Alfred Sutro discovered when he could get a response from the silent Hardy at luncheon only by mentioning an unusual kind of bird he had seen.[5] The Garnetts, on the other hand, were always good company, and Mrs. Hardy was a loquacious hostess who entertained her guests with drives about the countryside. The fact that the Hardys had several cats would have created an immediate bond between the couples, and the men had a number of topics of mutual interest to discuss. One, of course, was literature, especially poetry, for Hardy was working on some verses which he let Richard read. He had sent Richard a copy of his *Wessex Poems* in 1898, and Richard now encouraged him to give the new poems to a publisher. Writing on 8 September to "My dear Garnett," instead of the more formal "Dear Dr. Garnett" of earlier letters, Hardy said that he had occupied himself since the Garnetts' departure in mailing off the manuscript to a firm in London, despite his fear of adverse criticism when it was published. This was to be *Poems of the Past and Present*, which was released by Harper and Brothers at the end of the year.

Another topic of conversation for the men was the variation in English country dialects and colloquial terms, about which they continued to correspond for a while. A third topic was Hardy's garden, and he expressed an interest in acquiring an old sun dial for it, possibly two, an "erect and direct" one and a horizontal one.[6]* Richard, with his usual assiduity, upon his return to London hastened to look up dealers in second-hand dials and send their addresses to Hardy. He also sent Hardy a copy of his own *Idylls and Epigrams* of 1869, which Hardy acknowledged in a letter of 8 September as "a real prize."[7]

The *Magazine of Art* for September 1901 carried Richard's "Portraits of Shelley at the National Portrait Gallery," a discussion of the two paintings said to be of Shelley—one of them, an oil by Amelia Curran, had gone to the gallery on the death of Lady Shelley in 1899; the other, on the death of T. J. Hogg's daughter in 1900—along with a third at the Shakespeare Memorial at Stratford which Richard considered spurious.

During the last half of 1901 Richard was in correspondence with Thomas Greenwood, the publisher and promoter of public libraries, about a projected monument to Edward Edwards, one of the pioneers of the public library movement in Britain and a former assistant in the British Museum library, who had ended his days in loneliness and penury on the Isle of Wight. Greenwood had approached Richard knowing that Edwards's diary and some of his personal papers had been acquired by the Museum at Richard's suggestion. The Library Association had considered a memorial to Edwards, but had done nothing more, and Greenwood wanted Richard to join him in creating one. The letters exchanged by the two men from July to December [HRHRC] show a deep concern for the details of the monument and the inscription to be placed upon it. After much discussion, all was arranged, Greenwood and Garnett bearing most of the expense of the undertaking, and on 7 February 1902, a cold, gray day, the anniversary of Edwards's death, a group assembled in the church yard at Niton, on the Isle of Wight, where the monument was unveiled. Richard addressed them, and his remarks were published in a pamphlet describing the occasion, then later in Greenwood's biography of Edwards.[8]

Richard's literary work failed to diminish. He had agreed to do a project for children—two volumes of *Nelson's Literature Readers*, "selected and annotated by Dr. Garnett, with numerous illustrations"[9*]—and had made the selections during 1901. On 3 February 1902 he was asked to write the introduction and notes for each selection in the first volume. The chief principle he had employed in choosing examples was "freshness" or newness to the average reader. It was the sort of thing he could be counted on to do well and that he enjoyed doing. Another publication of 1902 was "Rome and the Temporal Power," chapter seven in Volume 1 of the *Cambridge Modern History*, a work at first edited by Lord Acton, who had solicited Richard's contribution. In February of 1902, however, Acton turned over the project to a group of editors, one of them Prothero, and they asked Richard to make a few changes in the chapter before finally accepting it.

In April Ernest Hartley Coleridge provided Richard with an introduction to the family now occupying Field Place, Major and Mrs. Travers and their daughter Rosalind.[10*] Richard was quick to take advantage of it because a Shelley heir, descendant of Percy Bysshe Shelley's younger brother, planned to take possession of the house in September, and access would then be more difficult. He also suggested that Dowden make a trip to Field Place before the Traverses left it, but Dowden was unable to do so.

After his usual autumn visit to the seaside, Richard had "a severe cold which for a time," he said, "incapacitated me for any intellectual exertion"[11] and confined him to the house; but as soon as he began to improve he hastened to perform a reference service for two literary friends, Katherine Harris Bradley and her niece Edith Emma Cooper, who wrote poetic dramas under the pseudonym Michael Field. He gave them an annotated list of sources for the Borgias, entirely from memory, apologizing for being unable to resort to the British Museum for a more extensive list. Richard enjoyed the ladies' dramas, which were usually set in remote eras, such as that of imperial Rome or ancient England. He also read proofs of their publications, as he did for many other friends.

At the end of the year Elkin Mathews published *The Journal of Edward Ellerker Williams, Companion of Shelley and Byron in 1821 and 1822*, edited with an introduction by Richard Garnett. Williams's original journal had been discovered and presented to the British Museum by his grandson, John Wheeler Williams, along with a number of letters written to E. E. Williams by T. J. Hogg, which Richard had gone through and separated as "noteworthy" or not. He conceded in the last paragraph of his introduction to the journal that "some few circumstances have been omitted, which appeared altogether too insignificant for publication; and it has been necessary to pass over others—not numerous or apparently of much importance—on account of the illegibility of the MS. from the fading of the ink, caused by its immersion in the wreck of the Don Juan [Shelley's sailboat]."[12] This statement was naturally objected to by the critics, and it further detracted from Richard's reputation as an editor among the younger scholars who were concerned with the availability of complete and exact texts. There was an exchange of letters in the *Athenaeum* for 14 February 1903 in which Richard accepted blame for some omissions; but recent scholars have damned him fiercely for over-editing the journal.[13]* He had gone to considerable trouble to get the work published, three publishers having rejected it before Elkin Mathews agreed to undertake a small edition, and Richard insisted that all the royalties go to Mr. Williams. By July of 1905, 360 copies had been sold.

Edward Dowden had twice tried to get Richard employment for his leisure hours by recommending him for an American-sponsored history of English literature; but Richard could not accept because he had already committed himself to cooperate with Edmund Gosse in writing one for William Heinemann. This work was to become the popular "Garnett and Gosse" illustrated history,[14] a standard source in college courses and libraries for many years. Richard approached it without enthusiasm, for he had been assigned parts of the history that he knew less well than others. He was to write all of Volume 1, "The Beginnings to the Age of Henry VIII," and in Volume 2, chapters one through six, "From the Age of Henry VIII to the Age of Milton," on Elizabethan poetry and prose. Gosse took Volumes 3 and 4, the latter containing Peacock and Shelley. When Volumes 1 and 3 were published, in 1903, Richard told Dowden, "I am painfully aware that my knowledge [especially of Anglo-Saxon writings] is far from up to the mark, and that I am vulnerable on every side to the attacks of experts in special departments."[15] The critics were, indeed, harsh on flaws in the work of both authors and were lukewarm toward the whole. The *Athenaeum*, however, for once made a generous comment: "Dr. Garnett has given such an account of our literature as hardly another man of our times could have written from his personal knowledge."[16] Dowden's only criticism was that the work would be excellent for students, "except for its costly form."[17] It was printed on coated paper with countless illustrations, some in color, and the top edges of the pages were gilt. The books weigh about four pounds each. Yet illustration was the heart of the project and in that it succeeded admirably.

Richard's family had diminished in one way—Chapple, who had retired, but had been staying with the Garnetts, died in April of 1902—but it had increased in others. Two more grandchildren had been born in 1901 and now, early in 1903, May and Guy Hall returned to England from South America, intending to remain, although Guy had no remunerative position to look forward to. They moved in with Richard and Narney, filling the Tanza Road house to the brim. This made life for the rest of the family rather difficult, and the situation was to last for well over a year because the Halls' belongings arrived only in March of 1904, and Guy was a long time finding permanent employment. Olive was particularly discomfited by their presence, as she and May were not very compatible.

Ellen had been to London to see a heart specialist, but she was living alone in a residential hotel in Scarborough. William John was in a nursing home, still weak from his fever, and he was being supported by Richard, Cecil Tennant, and the younger Charles Cumberland. Tennant, now a London banker, took the chief responsibility for the arrangements and visited William John more often than Richard did. It was five years before William John could manage on his own again, and from then on, till his death in 1923, he lived a quiet life, having some connection with the Royal Colonial Institute, for which he had worked abroad.

Chapter 21

An Ending and a Beginning, 1903-1905

In May of 1903 *The Twilight of the Gods and Other Tales* was issued in a "new and augmented edition" by John Lane. A handsome book, it attracted further critical acclaim. The *Speaker* called it one of the most interesting of the new editions: "In these tales, with which many readers are already familiar, Dr. Garnett draws on the vast store of his learning and illuminates what he finds with odd fancies and witty and picturesque ideas. Truly, the recreations of a scholar are seldom so likely as these to become the recreations of a larger public."[1] *The Outlook* said of the author: "Filled with learning culled from all ages, but cheerful as a schoolboy's holiday and whimsical as the 'Bab Ballads,' he has all kinds of fun at his disposal, and all good and all human."[2] However, Richard told Dowden, "I am not likely to find gaiety for any more of these trifles, and am thankful to have been able to bring them together into so pretty a volume."[3]

His premonition that his life was beginning to run down toward its end was accurate, but he seems to have had no such feeling about Narney, or else he dared not admit to worry over her health. She had continued her normal activities with what had become normal indispositions; but she must have repressed a great deal of discomfort. She instituted her traditional at-homes in the new house, always on the last day of the month, unless it were a Sunday; and for one large party on a Monday, Olive named in her diary sixty-eight guests, noting that "about twenty people who were asked were unable to come."[4]

Toward the end of June 1903, Narney had been feeling poorly and had decided to take her usual cure—a trip to the country. On the twenty-first she went to visit Lucy, who was newly pregnant, in her second home in Kent, Four Elms Farm, and had been there only a day when Lucy wrote to Richard that her mother was "in bed with a chill."[5]* The next day Richard had gone into the city and Olive was about to go out, at two o'clock, when a telegram arrived: "Consider Mrs. Garnett's state very grave. Come this evening to Four Elms."

An Ending and a Beginning

Olive packed a bag for Richard, who returned at four and left for the country on the five-fifteen train from Charing Cross. Another telegram reached Tanza Road at 8 p.m. It read: "Operation so far satisfactory." It seems that Lucy's physician had been called and had insisted on operating immediately, there on the kitchen table. The only identification of Narney's ailment that can now be deduced is a strangulated hernia. If this was truly the case and surgery seemed necessary, the operation by a country doctor in a farm kitchen was extremely risky.

Richard telegraphed Olive on the twenty-fourth: "Matter most serious. Come with Edward if you think well." They went, and Arthur too, but they arrived too late, for Narney had passed away at about nine in the morning. Olive went upstairs to see her mother and wrote in her diary afterward, "She looked most lovely, like a queen. I never saw her look so handsome and calm in life." This simple testimony reveals the strain under which Narney, like so many women of her time, had spent her days as a matter of course.

She was buried in Hever church yard, a short distance from Lucy's home. The ancient church stands at the top of a hill amid fair fields, with the gateway to the grounds of Hever Castle on one side and the rectory on the other. The grave yard is not crowded, even today, and a Celtic cross marks Narney's resting place. It is inscribed at the base: "Children and the building of a city continue a man's name, but a flawless wife is counted above them both." Lucy was sure that her mother wished to rest in this peaceful spot and she, with Robert, Edward, and Arthur, made the funeral arrangements. On 27 June, Richard, May, Guy, Olive, Robert (Martha was pregnant and did not attend), Edward Singleton, and Mr. and Mrs. Moir, old friends, went down by the 11:15 train and were met at the station at noon. At Four Elms, along with Lucy and Harry and a nurse, were Edward and Constance and Arthur. They unpacked a load of wreaths and placed them in the hearse for the procession to the cemetery, where they were joined by ten people from London, one of them Charles Cumberland. Ford Hueffer arrived just as the burial was ending. They all drove back to Lucy's and then directly to the station for the London train.

Narney's sudden and unexpected death was a severe blow to the entire family. Lucy carried her daughter, Olivia Margaret, to term, but the child was retarded, presumably because of Lucy's extreme distress at such an early stage of its development. Olive had previously been unwell and was "completely prostrated for some time" after the funeral.[6] Then she gave up her attempts to write stories based on her adventures in Russia and devoted her energies to keeping house for Richard and Arthur. Arthur had been casting about for employment, his chief interest being in horticulture. Richard finally found him a place at Kew Gardens in February of 1904, and Arthur was contented there. He was very popular among his co-workers, being of a sunny disposition and having the Garnett sense of humor. He was also a skillful writer and contributed articles to nature magazines.

Richard took solace in reading and writing. A curious product of this period was his cooperation with G. K. Chesterton, then at the beginning of his career, in a book on Tennyson, published by Hodder and Stoughton. Richard's part in it was an essay, "Tennyson as an Intellectual Force," which was the title given the book when it was re-issued three years later in the series Little Books for Bookmen. Richard and Chesterton were an unlikely duo, and Chesterton's biographers make no mention of their collaboration. Chesterton was probably responsible for the illustrations, and the book bore little relation to his later writings. The previous year Richard had commented to Dowden that in Chesterton's projected book on Browning "we may expect brilliant paradoxes."[7]* Edward had worked with Chesterton for a time at Unwin's, but it is most likely that the Tennyson project was conceived by Robertson Nicoll, editor of the *Bookman* of London and resident of Hampstead, for whom Richard had written articles and for whom Chesterton was reviewer of art books in 1903.

In this time of sorrow it happened that there was a new friend in Richard's life that would help to mitigate his loss. A letter had come to him in April that began a relationship of great importance to his waning years. The letter was from Violet Eveleen Neale,[8]* a young woman who was living with her mother at Ilfracombe on the north coast of Devon. She had borrowed William Rossetti's edition of Shelley's poems from the local lending library and had become so enamored of it that she had copied a hundred foolscap sheets of poems and introductions. She had then found Trelawny's *Last Days of Shelley and Byron* and, next, Richard's edition of Ellerker Williams's journal. After reading these, she wrote to Richard, in care of Elkin Mathews, to ask why he had omitted so many passages from the journal that had been quoted in Trelawny's work.

Richard's reply welcomed a new Shelley admirer and enclosed a snippet of Shelley's handwriting from a manuscript in his possession, while explaining his editing to Violet's satisfaction. The correspondence waxed more and more cordial as more points of mutual interest were revealed. The two exchanged views about the soul and the spirit, and Richard began to explain astrology. Violet was compiling a selection of *Thoughts from Shelley*, which was to be published in Hampstead by Sydney Mayle as a Priory Press Booklet, and Richard was bound to have much to say about such a work. He invited her to visit him at Tanza Road when she came to London, to see the notebooks and other relics of Shelley he had acquired. He also offered to recommend her sister, Ethel Neale, who lived in London, for a reader's ticket to the British Museum Reading Room so that she could do research for Violet.

In June, after a jaunt along the Devon coast, Violet enclosed in a letter to Richard "a sprig of myrtle picked in the garden of Shelley and Harriet's honeymoon cottage at Lynmouth, which bush Shelley planted."[9] This token arrived on the very day of Narney's funeral, and Richard carried it to Hever and placed it on her casket. He then wrote his thanks to Violet and suggested that, if she should happen to go to Lynmouth again, he would like to have another sprig from Shelley's myrtle bush. This was duly procured and sent. In July Violet came to London en route to Canada, to visit relatives, and she arranged a meeting with Richard on the twenty-eighth. She was somewhat startled to find that he looked just like a photograph in a book that had frightened her as a child, although he no longer appeared in any way threatening to her. Richard was equally surprised to discover that Violet had a fresh beauty, with large brown eyes and abundant brown hair. He must have been reminded of Mathilde Blind, whom he had already mentioned to Violet. At this meeting Violet gave him a copy of her Shelley booklet.

Upon her return from North America she settled with her mother in Bournemouth for a while, and there she made a point of visiting the grave of Mary Shelley. She and Richard continued to exchange opinions on life, religion, literature, and art. On the latter topic Richard could find much to say because his favorite painting, Titian's "Sacred and Profane Love," had been the subject of a series of letters to the editor of the *Nation*, begun by an Italian columnist for the magazine who had a new theory about the meaning of the work. Other theories were suggested by readers, and Richard gave his own idea by adding a new title to those already suggested for the picture—"Chastity and Desire."[10] He denied that the subject could have come from the *Argonautica* of Valerius Flaccus, as the Italian and several art experts in England averred. One of the latter was Lionel Cust, director of the National Portrait Gallery and a former colleague of Richard's at the British Museum. He and Richard were friends, and Cust may have been instrumental in Richard's recently having been made a trustee of the gallery in recognition of his lifelong interest in both art and biography.

One more letter in the *Nation* series came from a lady in Concord, Massachusetts, who said that the text used by Titian for his subject was obviously the "Pervigilium Veneris," the ancient love poem found in Catullus and other early writers. The "Vigil of Venus" was an ode to spring, dating from the first century B.C., a passionate celebration of love and renewal at the goddess's festival. Richard objected to this interpretation of the painting on the grounds that Catullus's work was first printed in Paris in 1577, whereas Titian had died in 1576, and that the picture dated from about fifty years earlier. He also noted that the landscape did not suggest springtime.[11]

This exchange served to call Richard's attention to the old poem, which he would soon use as inspiration for a work of his own. The subject of love had been discussed early in his correspondence with Violet Neale, beginning with Shelley's written comments, moving to those of Mathilde Blind, and then to his and Violet's respective opinions about it. Violet felt that she would bring misfortune to anyone with whom she might become intimately connected, thus stimulating all Richard's sympathetic and protective instincts. She was interested in clairvoyance, and though Richard could not believe in it, he was supportive of all her investigations of mysticism. Only two of their letters from 1903 are extant—one of his and one of hers—but the friendship had grown steadily, so that in January of 1904 he began his letters with "My dear Violet."

He was still very busy professionally. Writing to Violet on 28 January 1904, he reported on his trip to Keighley in Yorkshire to speak to the Brontë Society on "The Place of Charlotte Brontë in Nineteenth Century Fiction."[12] In his speech he recalled his Yorkshire ancestors, who had lived just a few miles away, and remembered reading *Jane Eyre* until two o'clock in the morning, after a full day's work, because he could not put it down. He told Violet he had had "a large and appreciative audience for my address, and an agreeable stay with my host at Haworth." He did not say he had visited his cousins in Otley, but he may well have done so.

To a meeting of the Dante Society he discoursed on "The Vicissitudes of Dante's Literary Reputation,"[13] and in April he spoke to the Shakespeare Society on "Plays Partly Written by Shakespeare."[14] The *Times* reported that the latter talk had been greeted by cheers. At the end of April he was elected vice-president of the Royal Society of Literature for 1904–5. His biography of the year was *Coleridge*, in George Bell & Sons' Miniature Series of Great Writers, another of the very creditable minor works that helped to supplement his income. He had also started on a biography of William Johnson Fox, the Universalist preacher of the Reverend Richard's day, whose papers had been willed to Richard by Fox's daughter.

On 31 May he closed a letter to Violet by saying, "I have written three letters today to ask favours for other people—a thing I abhor—and feel quite a relief to be able to write to you." Soon afterward, Violet and her mother moved to London, where they joined her grandmother and an aunt in a house at 89 Fellows Road, Hampstead, not far from Tanza Road. Richard found himself responding to Violet's revelations about herself with increasing emotion. His loneliness without Narney caused a vulnerability to feminine friendship of which Violet, who had always been lonely, could not resist taking advantage. Richard encouraged her to impose on him, and went out of his way to write long letters full of understanding and advice. He also selected books and ran errands for her. Then he cast her horoscope and was astonished to find that it complemented his own, so that they shared some daily auspices. If he needed evidence that fate had sent Violet to him as the solace of his declining years, here it was.

In July they met twice, on the fifteenth and the twenty-second, and discovered that they were in love. There are significant lacunae in the collections of both his and her letters at this time. In August Richard took Olive on a holiday as far as Wales and returned on 9 September. Next day Richard addressed a letter to "My Violet" and she replied to "My own dear Dr. Garnett," the greatest degree of intimacy she allowed herself in writing. They made arrangements to meet on a day when Mars was not afflicting their astrological charts. This was to be one of many meetings, often in a park, sometimes in the "tubular" railway station, sometimes at Madame Tussaud's, and occasionally at the British Museum, beside the Rosetta Stone. At least once they met at Tanza Road, probably when Richard was alone there. His letters to her were posted to arrive early in the morning so that the maid would bring them directly to Violet, and neither her mother nor her grandmother would see them. This circumspection was necessary for Violet to avoid parental interference and possible censure, whereas Richard had no illusion that his children would look kindly on an intimate relationship with a woman just a year older than Lucy, just a year after Narney's death. Besides, he was too proud of his high reputation to jeopardize it with a public romance. Yet he was desperately smitten. He compared Violet to his concept of Goethe's Mignon, and sent her his translation of "Mignon's Song" from *Wilhelm Meister*. They also exchanged photographs and described at length their feelings, their concepts of love (Richard assuming the role of teacher that he enjoyed so much in relation to women), and the expressions of passion in poetry, prose, and art.

By November Richard had accumulated a number of thoughts and epigrams composed in reaction to the strong emotions he was experiencing. He gave them to Violet for herself alone, but she soon persuaded him to share them with the world, although he insisted on anonymity. The two went over them in detail for several months, concerted a selection of the best, arranged them carefully for publication, and Richard got Elkin Mathews to agree to bring them out. The book was to be called *De Flagello Myrteo*, in honor of the sprig of myrtle from Shelley's bush that had brought them together, and the opening quotation was to be from the *Pervigilium Veneris*: "Implicat casas de flagello myrteo."[15*]

During this period Richard had also completed a poetic drama, *William Shakespeare, Pedagogue and Poacher*, which was read on 8 November 1904 at the Victoria Hall and Bijou Theatre. The star of the performance was the distinguished actress Florence Farr Emery. Richard gave her a signed copy of the play, which had been printed by John Lane. The story is an elaboration of the tradition that the bard had often been caught poaching deer on the lands of Sir Thomas Lucy, near Stratford-on-Avon. Richard imagined Shakespeare as well known to the Lucys and Lady Lucy as enamored of her dashing young neighbor, who was bored with teaching a few boys in his Stratford school and longed to go to London to play on the stage. He was also eager to escape his nagging wife Ann. One night he took the schoolboys on a poaching expedition and they were caught and brought before Sir Thomas. Lady Lucy pleaded for him, but he was rescued from a flogging and imprisonment by a courtier sent by Queen Elizabeth, who had seen a play by him and wanted him in her theatrical company.

The friends to whom Richard sent copies of the printed play—Austin Dobson, Edward Dowden, Edmund Gosse, Thomas Hardy, Sidney Lee, and E. W. B. Nicholson, among others—were unanimous in praise of its youthful verve and humor, while the American Shakespeare scholar Horace Howard Furness wrote enthusiastically of the "refined wit, the same merry twinkle of the demure eye that did and does so take me in the Twilight of the Gods."[16] Indeed, the two works are comparable in their approach to the subject matter andin their portrayals of human nature. From Lady Lucy's choice of banishment as Shakespeare's sentence, to Ann Shakespeare's choice of whipping, to Sir Thomas's decree of both, to Shakespeare's farewell to Ann, saying, "tend the babes" and "cherish the harmless necessary cat," the play exemplifies Richard's style at its best. Needless to say, it is written in blank verse.

By now Richard had become quite lame, more than ever stooped, and was prone to take cold. He had difficulty reading small print and his hand was not as steady as formerly; yet he continually assured Violet that there was no cause for concern. He simply stayed at home as much as possible and was cautious when he had to go out. His horoscope, interpreted for each day, showed his mid-heaven afflicted, shadowing his happiness with Violet with forebodings for the future; but he kept these to himself. He retained his optimistic view of all health problems, telling Dowden, "I have been troubled with lameness, which throws my work on the biography of Fox and other matters back, but I am getting better."[17] Olive served as his amanuensis when he needed help with his literary commitments, but he also had the service of a typist, as well as the constant attention of a doctor and a twice-daily nurse. He seemed frail to those who saw him, and he was plagued by minor afflictions in addition to his sore foot. The medical therapy was effective enough to allow him a few more months of activity, and he would never cease to exert himself to the limit of his endurance.

On 10 December 1904 Richard had written to Violet, "I did not expect to go back to Shelley," but he had received a copy of the Oxford edition of Shelley's poetry and he was pleased by the extensive use the editor, Thomas Hutchinson, had made of his work on the Shelley manuscripts. People still sought him out with mementoes of the poet and asked for information in the confidence that he would be able to obtain it. In May of 1905 he visited Boscombe Manor for the last time. He was received as an intimate by Lord Abinger, Sir Percy's grand-nephew, and was given a fine room overlooking the sea. He was allowed to go through papers, some of which were new to him—especially some very early writings of Mary Shelley. "The particular letters which I am supposed to have come to see have not turned up, though I hope they may," he told Violet on 10 May, "but I am lucky to take back with me a number of my own old letters, which will recall former times."

The chief event of the year 1905, however, was the publication of *De Flagello Myrteo*. In March Elkin Mathews delivered an estimate of the cost of printing five hundred copies—it was only £14.10.0 for the text, without binding or advertising, and Richard agreed to pay it. Mathews thought he might arrange for its distribution by a firm in the United States, but Richard felt "a little nervous" because Violet was sure his authorship would be detected. He was touched by her confidence in the success of the book, remarking on 18 April, "I have no doubt that it will, like everything else, gain in the long run exactly as much success as it deserves . . . though [its] fate is in a certain measure dependent upon that of the classics: some [of the thoughts] will be 'scarce intelligible without Greek,' as Byron said of Keats."

Meanwhile he was arranging for private publication of Violet's selections from Shelley's prose with the Hampstead printer, Mayle, who wanted to delete some of them. Richard told Violet in the same letter that he needed to talk to her about this, but he found himself "so pulled about by things to be done at home and from home that I scarcely see my way to an appointment." He was thinking of publishing his translations, and possibly a complete edition of his poetry, including "The Book," as he called *De Flagello Myrteo*. "I hope for this in three or four years; but it requires both life and money, things which one must not too confidently promise oneself." He took care that Violet was involved in some literary project, such as transcribing, to keep her spirits up, for she tended toward melancholia. She enthusiastically encouraged all his publishing plans.

Publication day for "The Book" was 1 June 1905, and Richard took Violet copies to send to Dowden, George Meredith, Swinburne, Symons, Yeats, and several others, as well as to reviewing journals. The reviews were complimentary, the mystery of the author's identity intriguing, and Richard became more and more confident about letting the world know of his responsibility for the book and his reason for writing it.

The epigrams in *De Flagello Myrteo* lasted a long time in public favor, being anthologized for many years in books of quotations.[18*] They have faded only with the fading of the classics from modern life. The book was originally subtitled "CCLII Thoughts and Fancies on Love," but the second edition, which was published on 26 March 1906 over Richard's name, contained 360 (CCCLX) thoughts, to conform to the degrees of the zodiac. The contents had been painstakingly selected over the preceding months from a much larger number, for Richard had continued to phrase his ideas on love, and had produced many that he discarded as not up to standard, as well as some that he considered too intimate for any eye but Violet's.

In June Olive visited some cousins in the West of England, and Richard and Violet were freer to meet than they had been, or would be again. Fortunately, Richard was better able to get about, now that mild weather had come.

On 10 August he declared himself to be "in a playful mood, as one is when one is happy," and told Violet to send a copy of *De Flagello Myrteo* to Thomas Hardy. "He is as likely as anyone to appreciate the book: but O! if he knew that any human being thought him an author of stories for boys, he would turn a great variety of colours, whether most black, red, or blue, or green I can not undertake to say. But what is my Violet's ignorance of Mr. Hardy to her ignorance of Sappho!" Violet had confused Thomas Hardy with the author of the popular juveniles, the Hardy Boys series, which her brother may have read. They were by the American Edward L. Stratemeyer. The reference to Sappho recalls Richard's No. XLIV in *Idylls and Epigrams*:

> My fair barbarian speaks no Greek, of course,
> Nor knows divinest Sappho from a horse;
> Yet all the charms that Grecian bards extol
> Are hers, save those pertaining to the soul.
> What then in this dilemma shall I do,
> Who have not, certes, Greek enough for two?
> I'll tolerate the fault I can't remove
> And deem that Beauty is the Greek of Love.

Richard ended the letter with an ancient Roman cure for sciatica, from which Violet was suffering, beginning "Toast a green lizard . . . ."

He had asked that a copy of "The Book" be sent to Michael Field, upon whom he now paid a call and noticed it upon a table. One of the ladies asked if Richard had seen it and if he knew the author. He replied that he might possibly have some "thoughts and fancies" on the subject, and soon confessed that he had written it. "You never heard such a scream as they jointly gave," he wrote to Violet on 25 August. "The information was evidently the greatest surprise to them: they assured me that the idea had never entered their minds. They had come to the conclusion, in fact, that it was the production of a woman! . . . I told them with perfect sincerity that they had in my opinion thus paid me the highest compliment in their power." After promising not to reveal his authorship, the ladies expressed curiosity about the handwriting on the package; but Richard, declining to reveal Violet's part in the mystery, said only that "it was not in the least like the writing of Mr. Elkin Mathews!" Then he told Violet the visit had another result: "I have found out more about my friends than I ever knew before, long as I have known them. I have never made out till now which was Miss Bradley and which was Miss Cooper."

In September Richard went to see an old friend in the country, probably Noble, and upon his return, on the ninth, he proposed that he and Violet meet soon, "for we shall have to live on letters for three or four weeks afterward." He was taking a westward journey, and Olive was to accompany him, which made Violet a little jealous. He was to stop at Lichfield for the celebration of Samuel Johnson's one hundred ninety-sixth birthday anniversary on 18 September, and would be the "principal guest"[19] and speaker. Going to Wales, he began a paper for the *Hampstead Annual* on "Shelley's Voyages, the Ideal Navigations Described in His Poems," which was published the following year. He also wrote to Arabella Buckley Fisher for her opinion of the London oculists, an indication that his visual problems continued. Yet he told

Violet that he considered *De Flagello Myrteo* the best thing he had ever done, and he seemed to be in high spirits. In October he traveled to Lancashire to stay with his cousin William Garnett for the first time in many years, and for the last time as well.

Another achievement of 1905 was the completion of the supplement to the printed General Catalogue of Books in the British Museum, bringing to an end the publication project in which Richard's role had been instrumental. The supplement contained entries for the accessions from 1880 to 1900, and Richard would have preferred that a whole new edition be begun to encompass these; but still he could only take satisfaction in the appearance of the last volume of the work he had been so deeply involved in during his career at the Museum. That he had lived to see this result was largely because of his determination to push the project through as fast as possible. If it lacked the minute accuracy Panizzi would have desired, it nevertheless was a catalogue of which even the great man could have been proud.

Chapter 22

Finale, 1906

Richard returned to the British Museum as often as he felt able, and early in 1906 he fell into conversation with some of his former colleagues about the printed catalogue of books. The working staff had some suggestions for "reforms," or beneficial changes in the cataloguing, and Richard rose to the defense of the entries as he had edited them, "with all the vivacity of youth and the wise experience of age."[1] It would have been politic for the younger men to have refrained from letting Richard know that they detected any room for improvement in his catalogue.

An assignment he relished was to write an article on astrology for the next edition of the *Encyclopaedia Britannica*. He had thought it out and retained it in mind, ready to put down on paper when he had finished his biography of W. J. Fox. However, various requests for information continued to distract him. In January of 1906 he had to turn to Rossetti for an answer to a question dealing tangentially with Shelley. Rossetti responded with what facts he had, and on 21 February Richard sent him his own reactions to the matter. This letter was docketed by Rossetti: "The last letter I received from this valued friend" [UBC].

Six days later Richard turned seventy-one, and he celebrated the occasion by writing to Violet. She had sent him as a present an edition of Keats's poetry that he did not have; and after attending a meeting to memorialize the death of Keats, in February of 1821, Richard was to meet her at the National Portrait Gallery. He was rejoicing in the great literary success of his son Robert, who had discovered William Makepeace Thackeray's anonymous reviews of French books for the *Foreign Quarterly Review* in the 1840s. These had just been published as *The New Sketch Book*, considered as a sequel to the *Paris Sketch Book* of 1840 and the *Irish Sketch Book* of 1843. Robert had provided an introduction and an appendix on the authors Thackeray had reviewed. The London dailies carried large headlines about the work, and the general reaction was complimentary. Richard, while very proud of Robert's achievement, confessed in his birthday letter to Violet that he found all the publicity slightly unnerving: "I am almost thankful for the sequestered tranquillity of our little Book."

On Sunday, 25 March, Richard wrote a letter of apology for having had to miss an appointment with Violet the day before, a circumstance that "grieved" him. He had had "a quite unexpected bilious attack on Friday night," but instead of sending her a note the next morning he had hoped to be able to get out, and had been dismayed to find that he could not. He said that he was better now and would try to meet her at the Baker Street Station next day—"the Museum *might* be too far for me. . . . This attack is no doubt to be connected with the transit of Saturn over the Sun's place, and we must look for other troubles. Love cannot head off trouble, but he can sweeten and purify it."

On Monday he sent her a telegram to call at Tanza Road at three in the afternoon. She did, and found him in the sitting room on a long chair Edward had sent him. He gave her a copy of the second edition of *De Flagello Myrteo*, delivered that day by Elkin Mathews. On the following day he saw an oculist, who gave him "a good account," according to Richard, "but I must keep quiet." This mixed diagnosis must have resulted either from the incompetence of the physician or from Richard's persistent optimism, for his sight was severely diminished.

Arthur Symons had written on 14 March to ask for Richard's interpretation of William Blake's horoscope, which he wanted to print in his biography of Blake. Instead of drawing up a chart himself, Richard had recommended one done by John Varley, an astrologer friend of Blake's; but Symons was unable to translate it "into intelligible language" and asked Richard, as the only "master of the stars" he knew, to provide a description of it for laymen. At the end of the letter he asked for the new edition of *De Flagello Myrteo* as soon as it was out, showing that he was one of the very few who knew who the author was.[2*] He may have received a copy from Richard's own hands, for he called at Tanza Road early in April and Richard, on the chaise lounge before the sitting-room fire, his eyes shaded, interpreted Blake's horoscope in detail. Richard felt a special affinity with Symons because their birthdays were on successive dates. On this occasion his parting—and his last—words to Symons were, "If I can help you in any way . . ."[3]

He did not talk of astrology to everyone: Dowden knew nothing of his interest in it until after Richard's death. Yet Richard was not ashamed of his hobby nor embarrassed to admit it to those he sensed would be sympathetic, or at least not judgmental. Between 1897 and 1903 he had contributed many articles to the astrological journals *Coming Events* and *Star Lore* under his pseudonym A. G. Trent.

One of the copies of the new edition of *De Flagello Myrteo* had gone to Dowden, along with a letter saying, "I am suffering from my eyes just now, and am obliged to use the services of a secretary."[4] Dowden replied on 6 April with sympathy for Richard's affliction but praise for "The Book." "I cry out against you, 'By what right do you know my secrets!'—Many of the things you say belong to me, and here they are told to the public!'"[5] He also praised Robert's book, another gift from Richard. This letter, with two others in response to *De Flagello Myrteo*, were handed to Violet on her last visit to Richard on 7 April, of which she recorded that "he seemed so much better, and Olive went downstairs and left us a bit."[6]

Olive had met Violet in March of 1905, so she was aware of her father's friendship with her and could not help but guess something of its depth, despite all his attempts to dissemble. Olive was devotedly caring for Richard, and on 26 March 1906 she entered in her diary his symptoms: "Papa's left eye clouded and dazzled. Could not read." The blood vessels in that eye had ruptured, almost blinding him. He had just finished dictating the sixth chapter of *The Life of W. J. Fox*, despite the fact that he had been "very poorly all day." He had developed nephritis, which was slowly draining his life force. Still, he insisted on continuing to answer letters and to work on Fox, and he had his Easter gifts all ready for Olive to deliver.

During the following week he grew steadily worse, and on the morning of Good Friday, 13 April 1906, he died peacefully and quickly. All six of his children were nearby, but Edward had sat with him all night. Despite his desire to be cremated, which he had communicated to Violet in 1905,[7]* Richard was interred at Highgate East Cemetery in the grave of Mrs. Singleton and little Richard Copley Garnett. There was a service in the chapel, in deference to May's and Lucy's religious feelings. Carriages were hired to convey the family and guests to the cemetery on 17 April and Robert invited William Rossetti, who had written a fine letter of condolence, to take "a seat in one of them" if he would like.[8]

The large attendance at the cemetery included five of Richard's children (Lucy was absent); his two daughters-in-law, Constance and Martha, and two sons-in-law, Guy and Harry; Major Edward Singleton; Tom and William Garnett, from Lancashire; a representative of the Wreaks family; Charles Cumberland; the widow of Richard Garnett Janion, son of the third daughter of Jeremiah Garnett of Manchester; and, from the British Museum, Fortescue, Graves, Arthur Miller, and W. R. Wilson (now superintendent of the Reading Room), "as well as several habitual readers and a number of attendants."[9] Among the latter group was John Parker Anderson. Maunde Thompson sent in his place an assistant in the principal librarian's office.

Also present were representatives of the British Museum (Natural History), of the Hampstead Antiquarian Society and the Hampstead Art Society, the Urban Club, the Library Association, the Bibliographical Society, the Carlyle and Goethe societies, and the Royal Colonial Institute, along with journalists Walter Jerrold, Clement Shorter, Richard Whiteing, and Frederick Greenwood. Richard's dear friends William Rossetti, Ernest Coleridge, and Sidney Lee were joined by six of his "literary ladies," one of them Clementina Black, another Rosalind Travers—perhaps the earliest and the latest of that group. Ford Hueffer was there, John Collier, and W. H. Hudson, whose writings Edward had been editing and with whom he had become very friendly. Conspicuous by their absence were William John and Ellen, both apparently too ill or disabled to travel.

Violet was at the cemetery for the interment. Olive had advised her of the time of the funeral, and though she did not offer her a ride, she promised to "take special care of the flowers you send" and added, "You may be sure that anything personal to you that I may come across will be safe in my keeping: and when I and my brothers and sisters come to consider these matters: we shall also consider any wishes you may express. You are quite right in feeling that being in sympathy with my father I naturally feel cordially toward you."[10] Among the floral wreaths was one of "appropriately simple and significant laurel,"[11] which probably came from Violet.

Late in June there was placed on the grave a horizontal stone shaped as a cross, on which were carved Richard's name, honors, dates, and age, along with his "An Epitaph," last in the volume of his *Poems*:

> Death's due demanded and Life's task achieved,
> > I greet the home I sought not nor did shun:
> Thankful for the great good I have received,
> > More thankful for the little I have done.

The obituaries were glowing: "Dr. Garnett's death is an irreparable loss to the world of letters";[12] "His death removes one of the most striking, interesting, and charming personalities in the literary life of the country";[13] "His death marked the passing of a librarian and bookman of the old type, and of a fine old type";[14] "He lived the ideal life of the scholar spirit. He gave as freely as he absorbed . . . and he will be greatly missed."[15] Even the *Athenaeum* unbent enough to say: "As a critic he was admirably catholic and judicious as a rule. . . . He ranks high as a translator . . . [and as a poet] in the sonnet form he showed a richly stored mind to advantage. . . . A host of friends regret one who was widely beloved for the sweet simplicity of his nature."[16]

Richard left no will. One would like to think that he had meant to draw one, but had postponed it, for, despite astrological warnings, he seems to have been quite unprepared to die. He had told an astrologer friend early in the year, "The directions and transits in my nativity towards the end of 1906 are certainly very serious, my doubt is whether they will influence health or affairs"; and upon receiving confirmation of his calculations, he replied, "If either luminary [sun or moon] were hyleg [in the position they held at birth], they would probably be fatal, but I think this is not the case."[17] His stubborn optimism made him ignore information he might have taken seriously if it had applied to someone else. But his affairs were in good order. His total estate was valued at £2734, all but £80 of it in personal property, and his children decided to divide it in equal shares. Robert and Edward gave their shares to Olive for life. Now Richard's effects had to be disposed of and the Tanza Road house evacuated.

Violet's letters were found, and she approached Olive about the copyright to *De Flagello Myrteo*, which Richard had given her unconditionally. Robert and Edward feared she would make a public declaration of Richard's love for her, or publish his letters to her, and saw scandal in the offing. They were both outraged at her seeming imposition on Richard and suspected her of unpleasant ambitions. Robert's attitude toward the problem was legalistic; Edward's, literary and emotional. Robert wrote to Violet about the copyright, and in order to avoid any publication of Richard's letters to her, stipulated that they be suppressed during her lifetime. An agreement was drawn up on 29 April releasing "The Book" for sale. Violet wished to claim only the royalties from the second edition, unless she might recoup from the first edition her legal expenses for the agreement.

Edward read through her letters and marked them with his apprehension about her motives. His harsh estimate of her character as "absolutely unscrupulous" seems to have been born of a kind of panic that his father might be made "a general laughing stock" if his letters to Violet were published. He went so far as to advise Robert never to let her have her letters to Richard. In any case, the Garnetts avoided controversy with Violet Neale, and she kept her part of the bargain. She waited until October of 1932, after Robert's death (in July), to deposit in the British Museum her two personal copies of *De Flagello Myrteo*, inscribed by Richard and illustrated with snapshots and letters. Not until 1950, presumably shortly before or after her death, were Richard's letters to her deposited there.

The second edition of "The Book" was sold out in May, partly, no doubt, because of a very complimentary review in the *Athenaeum*, which called it a "rare, intimate, and beautiful book [that] can never expect a wide audience," but will always appeal to those who are "in love with love." It sounded, the reviewer said, like "the work of a man who is no longer young, but of one by whom love has been apprehended as at once the cause, support, and final meaning of life."[18] After noting the similarity to Patmore's *Unknown Eros* of 1877, which had also been published anonymously, the reviewer surmised that Patmore would have liked this "book of wisdom." He then stated that the author's name was revealed in the "Literary Gossip" section of the paper, and there it was said that the review had been in type when the news of Richard's death had been received, "so we are at liberty to say the charming work is his."[19] Richard would have been deeply gratified by this praise.

Violet negotiated a third impression of "The Book" with Elkin Mathews, and it came out on 11 June with Richard's name on the title page. In October she allowed an American edition to be published by Thomas Bird Mosher of Portland, Maine, for which she provided a preface, including forty-two thoughts that Richard had rejected as not up to his standard, or as excess over the zodiacal count. She also gave his translation of the Greek quotation that had been printed at the beginning of the book, and opened the text with his dedicatory sonnet to her.

Sir Frank Marzials, Richard's old friend, wrote an appraisal of *De Flagello Myrteo* for the *Hampstead Annual* and sent it to Violet for her approval before submitting it for publication. He called the work "the quintessence" of Richard Garnett and praised the "serenity and hopefulness" of the thoughts contained in it, as contrasted with the "irony, doubt, and disdain" of *The Twilight of the Gods*.[20] Other friends were writing their memoirs of Richard for various publications, and among them was Robertson Nicoll, who, as "Claudius Clear" in the *British Weekly*, said:

> Though I had many dealings with Dr. Garnett, and though these extended over a long period, I never felt that I really knew him. Always accessible and courteous, eager to communicate his knowledge, the readiest of helpers, there was nevertheless about him a singular reserve. He very rarely opened his mind. He did not care to talk about ultimate things, and he shrank from discussing personalities. . . . However, I knew quite enough of him to rank him one of the greatest gentlemen I have ever known—perhaps the greatest.[21]

It was to women that Richard was able to unburden his heart and to discuss the deeper aspects of life, and he was fortunate in having had such sympathetic women to support him—especially Narney, his assistant in making their home "a friends' house-of-call for mental refreshment, cordial sympathy, and wise advice."[22]

That home would be missed by many, young and old. The vacating of 27 Tanza Road proceeded apace. Olive took a position indexing at Kew Gardens, where she could keep house for Arthur nearby. Robert, who now lived with Martha and their four children in Highgate, was during this period conferring with William Rossetti about the impending sale of Richard's library. The most valuable pieces were, of course, the three Shelley notebooks, and both Robert and Sotheby's auction house needed help with the catalogue entries for them. Rossetti drew up detailed notes of the contents of the notebooks and then, with Robert's concurrence, approached Thomas James Wise about a pre-auction purchase. Wise quickly offered to buy them, and Robert considered accepting the offer at a price Rossetti would set, plus a fee for Sotheby's, if required. He told Rossetti he was convinced that Richard had "intended us to sell them, and to do so *to the best possible advantage*."[23] Sotheby's, however, strongly opposed removing the notebooks from the sale, arguing that they were sure to bring unusual attention and wealthy purchasers. Therefore Robert felt compelled to decline, through Rossetti and with apologies and regret, Wise's offer of £1000. He hoped Wise would be the successful bidder at the auction, as did Olive, who thought either Wise or a representative of the Bodleian should secure the mementoes—"Lady Shelley and Papa would have preferred it."[24]

Sotheby's not only gratefully used Rossetti's notes, but reduced the fee from 12-1/2 to 10 percent in consequence; yet the firm failed to ask Rossetti's permission to print the notes in its catalogue of the sale, and although he was given credit, Robert took it upon himself to ask for his permission as well. Richard would have been touched by the trouble his good friend, who was not well, had taken about the Shelley notes and the Wise offer.

The sale was held on 6 December 1906, and Rossetti and his daughters Helen and Mary attended it. Robert was relieved when the notebooks brought £1000 apiece, justifying his refusal of Wise's tender. They were purchased, as Robert had suspected they might be, for a wealthy American collector, W. K. Bixby of St. Louis, Missouri.[25]* Robert told Rossetti: "The pleased expressions of yourself and daughters when the Note books were 'knocked down' gratified me at the moment as much as the price obtained for them and will be an abiding memory when the money has taken to itself wings and has flown away."[26]

There were 395 lots in the auction, among them a few rare items, such as a complete run of the Pre-Raphaelite periodical *The Germ*, with names of the writers added in Richard's hand, and numerous presentation copies of books by many of the era's best writers of prose and poetry, as well as some excellent Shelley items. The *Nation* published a singularly undiscerning notice about the catalogue, wondering why Richard had no incunabula, no Whitman, and few other American authors. Neither Richard's income nor his interests were appropriate to the collecting of incunabula; but he had had Whitman's works and a number of other books of American authorship. He was too traditional and too essentially British to find much appeal in Whitman, and indeed he had said to Mathilde Blind on 22 July 1871, "I have always felt that an infusion of the Whitman element of thought would do us all much good, but I tremble and kick at the idea of his becoming an example of style. All he can offer us must be received with limitations here simply because we have not so much elbow room as he has. In a new country like America the ground is clear for the larger developments, here our existence is interwoven with the past, which has become part of the very texture and tissue of our being." The *Nation* took note of this attitude in its comment: "In general, Garnett's concession to modernity seems to have been the minimum practicable for a titular critic."[27]

This auction represented only a small and choice portion of Richard's library, for not only had he himself disposed of a large number of books in 1899, and had Robert, Edward, and Olive retained a number of their father's books for themselves, but the family had sold a great many to a dealer named E. Menken, whose shop was in Great Russell Street across from the British Museum. Menken divided these into 741 lots, ranging from a dictionary of abbreviations to Zola's *Ladies' Paradise*, and offered them for sale by means of a catalogue. One item was *The Tempest* in the Arden Shakespeare series, inscribed to "Dr. R. Garnett, with the Author's best thanks," the editor having unwittingly usurped Shakespeare's role.

A few posthumous works appeared in the next few years to add to Richard's bibliography—four introductions and a co-edited collection of letters of Peacock—while the *Life of W. J. Fox, Public Teacher and Social Reformer, 1786–1864* was completed by Edward Garnett and published by John Lane at the Bodley Head and in New York in 1910.

In 1928 Thomas Earle Welby of the *Saturday Review*, writing under his pseudonym Stet, devoted one of his regular series of essays, called "Back Numbers" (which reviewed articles from earlier issues of *Saturday*), to a commentary on Richard's literary output. His starting point was a piece written upon Richard's death in 1906 which said, "he did not himself add any strikingly original work to English literature."[28*] "That," said Welby, "is exactly what Garnett did do . . . he produced one of the most individual and startling books of his period, 'The Twilight of the Gods.' . . . A very queer and potent literary Hyde lurked somewhere in the helpful Jekyll of the British Museum Reading Room. In 'The Twilight of the Gods' that other Garnett had a holiday, utterly unlike anyone else's."[29] The two aspects of this remarkable man were, indeed, so different that it is hard to reconcile them, and acquaintances tended to stress one or the other aspect of his personality. Arthur Symons agreed with Welby that *"The Twilight of the Gods* is a masterpiece of that laughing wisdom which some wise men have found for themselves after they have cracked the shell of knowledge and found the nut small and bitter," then added, "But *De Flagello Myrteo* is the last word of that deeper wisdom which has sought love rather than knowledge, and found much more than knowledge in love."[30]

Those, on the other hand, who remembered Richard Garnett as the most noted and admired librarian of his era, praise more highly his contributions to the British Museum library and its usefulness as an institution. Beatrice Harraden spoke for many when she wrote: "His chivalry and his generosity of mind were his own jewels of birthright with which he beautified his whole private and official life, and the influence of which will always be felt at the British Museum. . . . He has passed away, but the value of his life as scholar, critic, poet, and librarian will remain as an abiding force."[31] Another writer remarked, "He seemed the very Genius of the [institution]. He was a more intimate part of the Museum than the Elgin Marbles or the Portland Vase."[32]

Garnett epitomized the Victorian scholar-librarian, the person whose love of reading made a life of handling books the ideal profession. Such persons usually were writers as well, having derived a good style from reading the best authors and having a desire to express the learning they had accumulated from their acquaintance with books. They were also eager to expand the field of knowledge within librarianship, as well as in other disciplines. There were many self-educated librarians whose economic situation did not allow for study at a university, but who had access to a wide range of literature and were ambitious enough to use it in writing and in advising others. Not all of them had ingratiating personalities and not all of them were willing to serve a public that was less conversant with books than themselves. Of Richard Garnett it was said: "His astonishingly successful self-education had left him without a trace of arrogance which so marred the character of, say, Edward Edwards; it gave him, instead, a wide and genuine sympathy with the municipal library movement which was not widely shared by the librarian-scholars of his own and later times."[33]

Still, Richard was not a humble man. His intellectual generosity was based on a firm understanding of the scope of his knowledge, the value of his abilities, and the importance of his common sense. He came from a family of proud industrialists and added his literary distinction to the annals of the Garnetts. His descendants have carried on the tradition he began by sustaining a vigorous mental life, a responsible position in society, and a notable literary output, all of which continue to this day.

Thus we find a rich and varied legacy lingering after Richard Garnett: his work as arranger of the British Museum library and adviser to its patrons; his facilitating the printed catalogue of its holdings, the first listing of a national collection that was available outside its walls; his constructive role in the advance of libraries and librarianship; his unique creative contributions; and the foundation of a literary dynasty. His was a good life and a fruitful one, and the world is better for it.

As early as *Io in Egypt*, Garnett had published his philosophy of old age, which he lived out when his time came:

> I will not rail, or grieve when torpid eld
>   Frosts the slow-journeying blood, for I shall see
>   The lovelier leaves hang yellow on the tree,
> The nimbler brooks in icy fetters held.
> Methinks the aged eye that first beheld
>   The fitful ravage of December wild,
>   Then knew himself indeed dear Nature's child,
> Seeing the common doom, that all compelled.
> No kindred we to her beloved broods,
>   If, dying these, we drew a selfish breath;
> But one path travel all her multitudes,
>   And none dispute the solemn Voice that saith:
> "Sun to thy setting; to your autumn, woods;
>   Stream to thy sea; and man unto thy death!"

Notes

Preface

1. *Times*, 14 April 1906, p. 4.
2. Ernest A. Savage, *A Librarian's Memories: Portraits and Reflections* (London: Grafton, 1952), p.121.
3. *Library*, n.s. 1 (1899):1.
4. See my *Power, Politics, and Print: The Publication of the British Museum Catalogue, 1881–1900* (Hamden, Conn.: Linnet Books, 1981).
5. A selection from the diary for 1890 to 1900 is being edited in England by Barry C. Johnson of the British Library, who has been generous in sharing information with me.

1. Richard Garnett the Elder, 1789–1850

1. Carolyn Heilbrun, in *The Garnett Family* (London: George Allen and Unwin, 1961), pp. 19–21, gives a good, brief account of the earliest Garnetts in England.
2. Southey to John Rickman, 10 April 1826, enclosing a letter of introduction to a mutual friend for Garnett. This portion of the letter was first published in *Selections from the Letters of Robert Southey*, ed. John Wood Warter, 4 vols. (London, 1856), 3:540–41. It was reprinted in Richard Garnett the younger's "Memoir of the Late Rev. Richard Garnett" in *The Philological Essays of the Late Rev. Richard Garnett of the British Museum*, edited by his son (London: Williams and Norgate, 1859), p.iv; and was quoted in part in Richard the younger's entry for his father in the *Dictionary of National Biography*.
3. Richard Garnett the younger, "Memoir," p.xi.
4. Edward Miller, *Prince of Librarians: The Life and Times of Antonio Panizzi of the British Museum* (London: André Deutsch; Athens: Ohio Univ. Pr., 1967), p.127. Also in Miller, *That Noble Cabinet: A History of the British Museum* (same publishers, 1974), p.148.

5. See my "Whose Ninety-one Rules? A Revisionist View," in *Journal of Library History* 18 (1983):170–72.

6. *Report of the Royal Commissioners on the British Museum, 1850, Minutes of Evidence*, Answers 6294 and 9737. Quoted with the permission of the Controller of Her Britannic Majesty's Stationery Office.

7. Ibid., *Appendix*, p.220.

8. Richard Garnett the younger, "Memoir," p.xi.

9. Francis Espinasse, "The British Museum Fifty Years Ago," *Bookman* (London, June 1893), p.78.

10. R. G. Latham, ed., *On the Eastern Origin of the Celtic Nations*, by James Cowles Prichard (London: Hertford, 1857) [the work that was the subject, in an earlier edition, of Garnett's third article for the *Quarterly*], p.372; also in Richard Garnett the younger, "Memoir," p.xv.

11. J. W. Donaldson, *New Cratylus, or, Contributions Towards a More Accurate Knowledge of the Greek Language*, 2nd ed. (London: J. W. Parker, 1850), p.47; also in Richard Garnett the younger, "Memoir," p.xv. The *Cratylus* is a discourse of Plato's on the origin and nature of language.

12. Manuscript by Olive Garnett, "Anecdotes of my Father's Childhood, told to me by my Aunt Ellen . . ."[HH].

13. Unidentified newspaper obituary of Richard entitled "Funeral at Highgate," dated April 18, 1906 [HH].

14. William Jackson Brodribb (1829–1905) was ordained in 1860 and spent the rest of his life in Wiltshire. Frederick Farrar (1831–1903) had a distinguished career in the Church of England, beginning as a schoolmaster and ending as dean of Canterbury. He wrote poetry, novels, theological works, and books on philology. John Padmore Noble (1834–1904) was the son of a London banker. He took orders and served several country parishes. The Pollocks were the sixth and seventh sons of Sir Jonathan Frederick Pollock, Bart (1783–1870), lord chief baron of the Exchequer. Frederick (1827–1899) became a lawyer, Julius (1835–1890) a physician. Linley Sambourne (1844–1910) was a book illustrator and a cartoonist for *Punch*.

15. *Dictionary of National Biography*, s.v. "Garnett, Richard (1835–1906)."

2. Young Man in London, 1851–1854

1. A. W. Pollard, "Richard Garnett," *Library*, 2nd ser., 7 (July 1906):253.

2. William John Garnett, manuscript biographical sketch of his brother [HRHRC].

3. Richard's letters from 4 June 1851 to 4 January 1864 were sold by William John on 13 April 1907 to the British Museum, where they became ADD. MSS. 37489. They will be cited within the text only by date or the symbol BL. William John edited a number of the letters for publication after

his brother's death, but was unable to finance the printing. Richard's grandson, David Garnett, read the manuscript in 1932 and thought that it did not promise commercial success. Still, he said, "It is an astonishing production; the definiteness of all Grandpapa's views, the almost Johnsonian language in which he expresses himself, and his extreme youth, combined with his *sense*, make it very curious reading. One is tempted to laugh at this boy, laying down the law, but he is almost always right." [Letter to his Aunt Olive Garnett, 30 November 1932, ALM]. William John told his nephew, Robert Singleton Garnett, that after this "gift" to the Museum, some of the letters "to my great vexation and distress have been abstracted without a word being said to me, though they were my property" [undated note, HH]. It is not possible to guess which gaps in the correspondence might be explained by this strange accusation, if it is, indeed, correct.

4. Ellen became governess to Sir George Reresby Sitwell and his sister Florence. Sir George was the father of the literary Sitwell brothers and sister, Sir Osbert, Sir Sacheverell, and Dame Edith. Sir Osbert described Ellen in his *Scarlet Tree* (London: Macmillan; Boston: Little, Brown, 1946), p.265, note; and he is said to have satirized her as Miss Collier-Floodgate in *Before the Bombardment* (London: Gerald Duckworth, 1926). The Sitwells maintained a home in Scarborough in addition to their seat in Derbyshire.

5. "Recollections of Coventry Patmore," *Saturday Review*, 82 (5 December 1896):582–83. Also quoted in *Memoirs and Correspondence of Coventry Patmore*, ed. Basil Champneys, 2 vols. (London: George Bell, 1900), 1:69; and in Edward Miller, *That Noble Cabinet*, p.284.

6. Patmore's biographer, J. C. Reid, in *The Mind and Art of Coventry Patmore* (London: Macmillan, 1957), p.196, considers Richard's epigram, in his sketch for the *Dictionary of National Biography*, about Patmore as a critic ("He had no perception of the sublime in other men's writing, or of the ridiculous in his own") to have been "completely destructive," because it has often been repeated, but, in Reid's opinion, is neither fair nor accurate.

3. Journalist, 1855–1857

1. Pierre Jean Marie Flourens (1784–1867) was a French physiologist who wrote *De la Longévité Humaine et de la Quantité de Vie sur la Globe* (1854). I cannot identify the second book Richard reviewed.

2. The *National Review* had been founded by Unitarians, among them James Martineau, a divine whose writings had had a great influence on Richard, who once listed his best teachers at this period of his life as Shelley, Goethe, Carlyle, Emerson, and James Martineau. The latter, he said, had bolstered his disbelief in miracles without making him lose his reverence for Christianity. Martineau's son, Russell, a Hebrew and Slavic scholar, was a member of the Department of Printed Books and a good friend of Richard's.

3. John Edward Taylor was the son of the co-founder with Jeremiah of the *Guardian* and was now its proprietor.

4. Miller, *Prince of Librarians*, p.255, note 67.

5. Richard to Panizzi, 6 March 1856, BL ADD. MSS. 36717, f.356.

6. The notations of Richard's work at this time are taken from his "Day Book" in HRHRC.

7. *Literary Gazette*, 28 June 1856, p.419. Sir John Cutler, (1608?–1693) was a penurious, though wealthy and charitable, London merchant. The anecdote about his hose came from the wit Dr. John Arbuthnot (1667–1735), but in it the hose changed from worsted to silk.

8. David Ayerst, *The Manchester Guardian: Biography of a Newspaper* (Ithaca, N.Y.: Cornell Univ. Pr., 1971), p.126.

4. Author and Editor, 1858–1859

1. *Literary Gazette*, 27 March 1858, p.299.

2. *Times*, marked but undated clipping [HH].

3. The memoir "drawn up by Uncle" must have been the obituary of the Reverend Richard by Jeremiah Garnett now at Hilton Hall. It was apparently written for publication, and by request, for Jeremiah asked Rayne to have it stylized and completed by someone at the British Museum; but it seems to have remained unpublished.

4. *Critic*, 19 (2 July 1859):7.

5. Sir Percy Florence Shelley (1819–1889) inherited the baronetcy of his grandfather, Sir Timothy Shelley, in 1848 and married Jane Gibson St. John, a young widow who was friendly with the widowed Mary Shelley in London. The couple lived for a year at Field Place, Sir Timothy's seat near Horsham, Sussex, then bought a house and two hundred acres on the Hampshire coast, where Sir Percy could be near his great love, the sea. They expected Mary to join them, but she died before renovation of the house could be completed.

6. Sir Percy to Hogg, 12 May 1858 (a copy made by Richard), in "Letters about Shelley from the Richard Garnett Papers, University of Texas," ed. William R. Thurman, Jr., unpublished doctoral dissertation, University of Texas at Austin, 1972, p.29. This work contains texts or annotations of all the letters dealing with Shelley that came to the Harry Ransom Humanities Research Center at the University of Texas at Austin with the Richard Garnett Papers. I am deeply indebted to it for the information it contains and for the meticulous scholarship with which it was compiled. I will refer to it hereafter as Thurman, and will use it for the cited source because it is more easily available than the originals in HRHRC.

7. Lady Shelley to Leigh Hunt, 3 June 1858, in *Leigh Hunt's Letter on Hogg's Life of Shelley, With Other Papers* (Cedar Rapids, Ia.: Privately Printed,

1927), p.9. Lady Shelley was asking Hunt to aid her in restoring a proper memory of Percy Bysshe and Mary Shelley.

8. "Memoirs of Percy Bysshe Shelley," *Fraser's Magazine*, 57 (June 1858):643–59. The third book was called *Shelley and His Writings* by Charles S. Middleton.

9. William Godwin (1756–1836) was a radical philosopher and author who advocated drastic reform of politics, religion, family structure (he preached free love, but himself preferred to marry), and property rights. His *Political Justice* (1793) had a profound influence on Shelley. Godwin's first wife was Mary Wollstonecraft (1759–1797), author of the *Vindication of the Rights of Women* (1792), who died in giving birth to Mary. Godwin then married a woman with two children, Mrs. Clairmont.

10. Mrs. Robert Louis Stevenson, for instance, called Lady Shelley "delicious," and added that she was "suffering from the effects of a terrible accident that has left her a hopeless invalid; but with all the fire of youth, &. . . ready to plunge into any wild extravagance at a moment's notice." [Mrs. Stevenson to Sidney Colvin, 1885, quoted in E. V. Lucas, *The Colvins and Their Friends* (New York: Charles Scribner's Sons, 1928), p.167.] This seldom-mentioned disability explains much of the indisposition that marked Lady Shelley's life, preventing many planned meetings with Richard.

11. Richard to W. M. Rossetti, enclosure with a letter of 23 July 1903 [UBC]. Lady Shelley had acknowledged Ollier's help with the *Memorials* in her preface to the first edition (p.ix).

12. "The Occasional, XV," *Spectator*, 32 (13 August 1859):835. Reprinted in *Leigh Hunt's Letter*, p.32.

13. Richard to Lady Shelley, 17 August 1859, Thurman, pp.30–33.

14. Thurman, p.35. This friend must have been Edmund Ollier.

15. Richard to Violet Neale, 28 September 1904, BL ADD. MSS. 42861.

16. Today Boscombe is part of metropolitan Bournemouth, the entire area being built up. The manor house has been purchased by the University of Bournemouth and is used for educational purposes. The attached theater is still intact, as is a window let into the wall of Lady Shelley's bedroom to overlook the theater, so that she might watch the performances when too unwell to join the audience of friends below.

17. Lady Shelley to Richard, 19 November 1859, Thurman, p.37.

5. Shelley Scholar, 1860–1861

1. *Fraser's Magazine*, 61 (January 1860):92–109.

2. This is now considered untrue, although Harriet did have one lover, a soldier who left her pregnant when he was ordered to India, a second desertion that the young woman could not endure.

3. Richard to Lady Shelley, 20 February 1860, Thurman, p.50.

4. For a tally of the issues of *Stockdale's Budget of "All That Is Good, and Noble, and Amiable, in the Country"* that contain references to Shelley, see Clement Dunbar, *A Bibliography of Shelley Studies: 1823–1950* (Folkestone, Kent: Wm. Dawson; New York: Garland, 1976), pp.11–12.

5. Lady Shelley to Richard, 9 May 1860, Thurman, p.74.

6. Richard to Lady Shelley, 26 April 1860, Thurman, p.71.

7. Charles and Eliza Andrews Orme lived at Avenue Road, Regent's Park, and entertained a brilliant literary and artistic circle, including the Pre-Raphaelites. Mr. Orme was a distiller, and the couple had a large family, Emily Masson being their eldest daughter.

8. Thomas Hughes (1822–1896) was the anonymous author of *Tom Brown's School Days* (1857) and *Tom Brown at Oxford* (1861), the latter having run serially in the first volume of *Macmillan's Magazine*. In addition to writing these very popular boys' stories, Hughes was a founder of the Christian Socialist movement, along with Charles Kingsley (1819–1875), the novelist-clergyman, and Frederick Denison Maurice (1805–1872), professor of English history and literature, as well as theology, at King's College, London.

9. Sir Percy Shelley to Richard, 1 September 1878, Thurman, p.156. Richard, unable to swim, had another close call with the waves, recounted in Robert Singleton Garnett, *Some Book-Hunting Adventures: A Diversion* (London and Edinburgh: William Blackwood, 1931), p.211. An acquaintance, who was a good swimmer, drew Richard along a narrow beach, chattering about Byron, while the tide was coming in, and at last, in desperation at the man's refusal to see danger, and in order "to save his own life, [he] had fairly taken to his heels and raced the tide homewards under the unscaleable cliffs."

10. Basil Champneys, in *Memoirs and Correspondence of Coventry Patmore*, 2:432–45, quotes the letter. The book was *Faithful For Ever*, a quasi-epistolary poetic narrative. Richard's essay-review was entitled "Poetry, Prose, and Mr. Patmore," and appeared in *Macmillan's* for December 1860 [3:121–30]. On 29 November Richard gratefully acknowledged a check from Alexander Macmillan for "£9.10s. on account of my contribution to the current number of the Magazine," and commented on his difficulty with the writing and on Macmillan's good editorial advice. [Macmillan Papers, Vol.1, Berg Collection, New York Public Library.]

11. Charles Morgan, *The House of Macmillan 1843–1943* (New York: Macmillan, 1944), p.50.

12. John Westland Marston (1819–1890) was a dramatic poet, drama critic for the *Athenaeum*, a friend of Dickens and of most of the actors of the day. He had eschewed a more lucrative calling to devote himself to the theater, in which he had considerable success early in his career.

13. Henry Pelham Fiennes Pelham Clinton, fifth duke of Newcastle-under-Lyme (1811–1864), and Charles Shaw Lefevre, Viscount Eversley (1794–

1888), may have been on the selection committee. Eversley had been speaker of the House of Commons, and therefore one of the principal trustees of the British Museum who had signed Richard's appointment in 1851.

14. Manfred was the hero of Byron's dramatic poem of that name (1817). He lived in a castle in the Alps and spent much time alone in a tower. Percy Bysshe and Mary Shelley in 1821 rented the top floor of one of the four- or six-story houses that lined the Arno in Pisa, and Byron took a palazzo across the river.

6. Year of Fate, 1862

1. *Spectator*, 35 (1 February 1862):132.
2. Ibid. (22 February 1862):209.
3. All the information about Narney's family is taken from a typescript on the subject by her daughter Olive, in the Singleton-Marston Papers at Hilton Hall.
4. *Macmillan's Magazine*, 6 (June 1862):122.
5. Bessie Florence Gibson Scarlett died in 1934. She had married Captain Leopold Scarlett of the Fusilier Guards, descendant of the first baron Abinger, and their sons inherited the baronetcy. Richard was acquainted with them all.
6. Edward Ellerker Williams (1783–1822) had been an officer in the British army in India and had retired on half pay. Jane was a married woman who had left her husband. She and Williams lived together in Switzerland and Italy, until he was drowned with Shelley when their sailboat capsized off Lerici. Jane then returned to England and eventually married Thomas Jefferson Hogg.
7. *Cornhill Magazine*, 6 (July 1862):274.
8. *Spectator*, 35 (2 August 1862):859–60.
9. *Complete Poetical Works of Percy Bysshe Shelley*, ed. George Edward Woodberry, 4 vols. (Boston: Houghton Mifflin; London: Kegan Paul, Trench, Trübner, 1892), 1:xii.
10. *Complete Poetical Works of Percy Bysshe Shelley*, ed. Thomas Hutchinson (London, New York, Toronto: Henry Frowde, Oxford Univ. Pr., 1904), pp.v, vi.
11. "Literature: Causerie for the Week: Richard Garnett," *Speaker*, 14 (21 April 1906):59.
12. *Complete Poetical Works of Percy Bysshe Shelley*, ed. Neville Rogers, 2 vols. (Oxford: Clarendon, 1972), 1:xxiv.
13. "Stonewall" Jackson was conducting his Shenandoah Valley campaign at the time. John Pope, the Union general, had been relieved of his command after his defeat at Second Manassas in August.
14. *Journals of a Lancashire Weaver 1856–60, 1860–64, 1872–75*, ed. Mary Brigg, Record Society of Lancashire and Cheshire (Printed for the Society, 1982), 122:xxix.

7. Married Life, 1863–1867

1. The Garnetts owned the leasehold by 1890, when they sold it to Mrs.William Rossetti for £950. Mrs. Rossetti's father, the artist Ford Madox Brown, had moved into No. 1, St. Edmund's Terrace, in 1888.
2. *Reader*, 1 (11 April 1863):356–57.
3. Sir William Robertson Nicoll, founder of the monthly *Bookman*, in *A Bookman's Letters* (London: Hodder & Stoughton, n.d., but preface dated November 1913), 3rd ed., p.212. This obituary tribute to Richard was first published in the *British Weekly* for 19 April 1906, p.35, in the section called "The Correspondence of Claudius Clear," Nicoll's pseudonym.
4. Ernest Hartley Coleridge (1846–1920), grandson of Samuel Taylor Coleridge, was a writer. Sir John Duke Coleridge (1820–1894), first Baron Coleridge, was the son of Sir John Taylor Coleridge (1790–1876), nephew of the poet and justice of the Queen's Bench until 1858, hence "the Judge." The judge had known Shelley at Eton and despised him.
5. Patmore to Richard, 7 April [misdated March] 1864, in Champneys, *Memoirs... of Coventry Patmore*, 2:221. The flowers had been planted by the poet Alfred Austin in 1863. One violet and a leaf are still preserved in Narney's album at Hilton Hall.
6. Merle Mowbray Bevington, *The Saturday Review, 1855–68* (New York: Columbia Univ. Pr., 1941), p.266.
7. Richard to Mathilde Blind, fragment, October, n.y., BL ADD. MSS. 61,930.
8. Richard to Mathilde Blind, 17 February 1873, BL ADD. MSS. 61,927.
9. Robert S. Garnett in *Some Book-Hunting Adventures*, p.3, as well as Olive Garnett in manuscript notes [ALM], mentions the books in the bathtub, attributing their presence there to Narney's distrust of plumbers and the failure of the drains to function properly; but Olive told her niece, Anne Lee Michell, verbally, that only once was the tub used as a receptacle for books, during one spring cleaning. [Olive's diary "A Bloomsbury Girlhood," ed. Anne Lee Michell, Introduction, p.2, HRHRC.]
10. Edward Miller, *That Noble Cabinet*, p.269.
11. For a full account of Ralston's career, see my "W. R. S. Ralston (1828–89): Scholarship and Scandal at the British Museum" in *British Library Journal*, 14 (Autumn 1988):178–198.

8. New Family, New Friends, 1868–1870

1. Macmillan Papers, BL ADD. MSS. 55253, f. 153.
2. *Saturday Review*, 25 (18 January 1868):97.
3. *Letters of Dante Gabriel Rossetti to William Allingham, 1854–1870*, ed. George Birkbeck Hill (New York: Frederick Stokes, [1897]), p.288.
4. *Rossetti Papers, 1862–1870*, a compilation by William Michael Rossetti,

ed. Odette Bornand (Oxford: Clarendon, 1977), p.333. [Original edition by Charles Scribner's Sons of New York in 1903.] The editor has erred in stating, on p.xxiii, that Richard, rather than Robert Garnett, "observed in 1917...."

5. Ibid., p.382.

6. William Rossetti to Richard, 11 June 1869, *Letters About Shelley Interchanged by Three Friends—Edward Dowden, Richard Garnett, and William Michael Rossetti*, ed. with an introduction by R[obert] S[ingleton] Garnett (London: Hodder & Stoughton, 1917; New York: AMS Pr., 1971), p.22.

7. *Rossetti Papers*, p.400.

8. Richard to D. G. Rossetti, 10 January 1871 [HRHRC].

9. Tennyson to Richard, 15 July 1871 [HH].

10. W. B. Rye to Richard, 6 March 1897, quoted in Miller, *That Noble Cabinet*, p.288.

11. Thurman, p.108.

12. Käthe Freiligrath Kroeker, quoted in Richard Garnett, "Memoir of Mathilde Blind," in her *Poetical Works*, ed. Arthur Symons (London: T. Fisher Unwin, 1900), p.13.

13. Richard Garnett, "Memoir of Mathilde Blind," p.23.

14. Ford Madox Ford, *Ancient Lights and Certain New Reflections: Being the Memoirs of a Young Man* (London: Chapman & Hall, 1911), pp.51–52.

15. Richard Garnett, "Memoir of Mathilde Blind," p.23.

16. Lady Shelley to Richard, 28 January 1870, Thurman, p.108.

17. Richard to Mathilde, 29 January 1870, BL ADD. MSS. 61,927, "Correspondence of Mathilde Blind... and Dr. Richard Garnett... 1860–1873." Subsequently quoted letters from this archive are taken from ADD. MSS. 61,928 (1874–1884) and 61,929 (1885–1896), and will be cited simply by date.

18. *Westminster Review*, 94 or n.s. 38 (July 1870):79.

19. Ibid., p.75.

20. Ibid., p.88.

21. *Letters About Shelley*, p.35.

22. Dowden to Richard, 26 February 1870, Thurman, p.225.

23. Franz Hüffer, anglicized to Francis Hueffer (1845–1889), came to London in 1869 from Germany and wrote reviews of musical events for the *Academy*, and then for the *Times*. He also wrote for Grove's *Dictionary of Music and Musicians* (1878–89) and the ninth edition of the *Encyclopaedia Britannica*. His son, Ford Madox Hueffer (1873–1939), who later changed his name to Ford Madox Ford and wrote poetry, criticism, and novels, became a good friend of the Garnetts.

24. The Tennants were a distinguished family in Yorkshire, and later in London. Robert (1828–1900) was a second son and only inherited the family estates at Chapel House, Kilnsey-in-Craven, in 1894, on the death of his older

brother. He had, however, received a large inheritance from his uncle, John Hope Shaw, who had reared and educated him in Leeds. Robert became the member of Parliament for Leeds from 1874 to 1880, after which he traveled to Sardinia and South America and published two books of statistics and descriptions about them, in 1885 and 1895, respectively.

9. Much Ado about Shelley, 1871–1874

1. Richard to Narney, 24 January 1871, ALM. The bride was a daughter of John Frazer Corkran, one-time correspondent of the *Morning Herald* in Paris, where he and his wife knew the Brownings and Thackeray. When he lost his job and returned to London, Corkran and his family were supported by Thackeray. They were good friends of the Garnetts, probably through the Marstons. "Mr. Poole" may have been John Poole (1786–1872), playwright, who had lived for some years in Paris, was befriended by Dickens, and was undoubtedly known to Marston. Robert Wiedemann Barrett Browning, son of the poets Robert and Elizabeth Barrett Browning, was a painter and sculptor. "Miss Thackeray" was Anne, daughter of W. M. Thackeray. Julian Hawthorne was the son of the American novelist Nathaniel Hawthorne, who had been United States consul in Liverpool and had lived in England from 1853 to 1860. Julian was visiting in London in 1871 and would come to live there in 1874.

2. Richard to Mathilde, 22 July 1871 [BL]. Richard here writes as one slightly moonstruck—he seems to have been at least half in love with Mathilde. In 1904 he would tell his last love that she was his third, and, Narney being the primary one, there is no other obvious candidate for the second than Mathilde. Only one faint possibility for this second love can be construed from a remark of William Rossetti in his memoirs: "Through Patmore I also knew—towards 1855—my excellent friend Dr. Richard Garnett, very youthful when I first met him and his fiancée." [*Some Reminiscences of William Michael Rossetti*, 2 vols. (London: Brown, Langham, 1906), 1:86–87.] Even at such a distance in time as fifty years, Rossetti should not have placed Richard's engagement to Narney eight years too early; but evidence for Richard's life in the years 1851 and 1854 is almost non-existent, as though it had been deliberately destroyed, so there could conceivably have been a very early affair of the heart.

3. *Athenaeum*, 27 January 1872, p.114.

4. Ibid., 3 February 1872, p.147.

5. Ibid., 10 February 1872, p.178. In "Shelley in Pall Mall" Richard had admitted that he had not found out very much about the Stockdales, and, "Feeling . . . a very decided distaste to the minute investigation of unimportant matters," would not take the trouble to do so (*Macmillan's Magazine*, June 1860, p.100.)

6. Lady Shelley to Richard, 10 February 1872, Thurman, p.114.
7. *The Diary of W. M. Rossetti* (Rossetti Papers, 2nd series), ed. Odette Bornand (Oxford: Clarendon, 1977), 2 vols, 2:161.
8. Richard to Lady Shelley, 28 February 1872, Thurman, p.115.
9. Lady Shelley to Richard, 28 February 1872, Thurman, p.117.
10. Sir Percy Shelley to Richard, 29 February 1872, Thurman, p.118. What the libel was is not revealed in the correspondence.
11. Sir Percy Shelley to Richard, 10 April 1872, Thurman, p.122.
12. Miss Rumble to Richard, 25 July 1877, Thurman, p.367.
13. Frederick Startridge Ellis to Richard, 15 August 1879, Thurman, p.385.
14. Sir Percy Shelley to Richard, 19 February 1873, Thurman, p.126.
15. Lady Shelley to Richard, 9 February 1873, Thurman, p.126.
16. Richard to Lady Shelley, 17 May 1873, Thurman, p.128.
17. Lady Shelley to Richard, 29 January 1874, Thurman, p.130.
18. *Times*, 3 October 1874, p. 9.
19. Ibid., p.10.
20. Robert Singleton Garnett, *Odd Memories: More Book-Hunting Adventures* (Edinburgh and London: William Blackwood, 1937), p.14.
21. Lady Shelley to Richard, 31 January 1875, Thurman, p.133.

10. Portrait Interlude

1. Richard Rogers Bowker, quoted in E. McClung Fleming, *R. R. Bowker, Militant Liberal* (Norman: Univ. of Oklahoma Pr., 1952), p.170.
2. The Reverend Richard Garnett seems to have more resembled his brother Jeremiah of Manchester in having a narrow, upturned nose (see Heilbrun, *The Garnett Family*, plate 1, opp. p.32).
3. Sir William Robertson Nicoll, *A Bookman's Letters*, p.214.
4. Arthur Symons, "Dr. Richard Garnett," *Athenaeum*, 21 April 1906, p.481.
5. Nicoll, *A Bookman's Letters*, p.212.
6. Ford Madox Hueffer (Ford), "Dr. Garnett: In Memoriam, III," *Bookman*, June 1906, p.90.
7. "Modern Men: Dr. Richard Garnett," *National Observer*, 5 December 1891, p.60, unsigned.
8. Sir Sidney Colvin, *Memories and Notes of Persons and Places 1852–1912* (New York: Charles Scribner's Sons, 1921), pp.207–8. Richard's attendance at such occasions as the "tobacco parliaments" of the 1860s and "smoking concerts," one of which he went to in 1892, where pipes and tobacco were provided, indicate that he may have been a smoker.
9. Agnes A. Adams, "Dr. Richard Garnett: In Memoriam, V," *Bookman*, 30 (June 1906):92.
10. Ford Madox Hueffer (Ford), *Memories and Impressions: A Study in Atmospheres* (New York: Harper, 1911), p.76.

11. David Garnett, *The Golden Echo* (London: Chatto & Windus, 1954), p.41.
12. H. E. Bates, *Edward Garnett* (London: Max Parrish, 1950), p.23.
13. Arthur Symons, "Richard Garnett," *Speaker*, 14 (21 April 1906):59.
14. G. K. Fortescue, "Richard Garnett," *Library*, 7 (July 1906):232.
15. R. S. Garnett, *Letters About Shelley*, Introduction, p.5.
16. Ann Thwaite, *Edmund Gosse: A Literary Landscape 1849–1928* (London: Secker & Warburg, 1984), p.72, quoting Gosse's obituary of Richard in the *Author*.
17. Sidney Lee, *Dictionary of National Biography*, sv. "Garnett, Richard (1835–1906)."
18. A. W. Pollard, "Richard Garnett," *Library*, 7 (July 1906):252.
19. Ernest A. Savage, *A Librarian's Memories*, pp.150–51.
20. Beatrice Harraden, "Dr. Richard Garnett: In Memoriam, IV," *Bookman* 30 (June 1906):92. A good example of this trait is given in the story " 'Chipp on Stars' " by Robert S. Garnett, in *Some Book-Hunting Adventures*, pp.286–301.
21. Nicoll, *A Bookman's Letters*, pp.210–11.
22. Fortescue, "Richard Garnett," *Library*, 7 (July 1906):231.
23. Symons, "Richard Garnett," *Speaker*, 14 (21 April 1906):59.
24. Nicoll, *A Bookman's Letters*, p.214.
25. David Garnett, *The Golden Echo*, p.42.
26. Ibid., p.41.
27. Ford Madox Ford, *Return to Yesterday: Reminiscences 1894–1914* (London: Victor Gollancz, 1931, p.45; New York: Horace Liveright, 1932, p.52), says Richard "knew the contents of a hundred thousand books and must have stroked as many thousand pussies, pronouncing the *pus* to rhyme with *bus*." A. W. Pollard, in the *Library* for July 1906, p.252, uses as an example of this trait the word "butcher," the first syllable rhyming with "butt," in Richard's anecdote "of a butcher, who exclaimed when he had slain a refractory sheep, 'I've conciliated that one, anyway.' " It was the only story Pollard heard Richard tell twice. Arundell Esdaile, in *The British Museum Library* (London: George Allen and Unwin, 1946), p.367, note 8, calls the peculiarity a "native provincialism," as if it were a Yorkshire trait. Richard never lived in Yorkshire, but may have taken the pronunciation from his father and relatives.
28. Heilbrun, *The Garnett Family*, p.64.
29. David Garnett, *The Golden Echo*, pp.40–41.
30. David Garnett, note [HH].
31. David Garnett, note [ALM].
32. Richard to William John, 25 September 1866 [HRHRC]. The stick had "served this morning to demolish a snake" (on a waste-land walk), which he realized he should have let alone, "but for the ardour of the chase."

33. Robert S. Garnett, "Swinburne Reads His Poems," *Odd Memories*, pp.1–6. The other point of the story is that after the reading Swinburne disappeared and was found asleep on Mrs. Marston's bed. Richard and Marston carried him downstairs and put him in a cab for home without his wakening.

34. David Garnett, *The Golden Echo*, p.41.

11. Assistant Keeper of Printed Books, 1875–1878

1. *The Actual Condition of the British Museum*, p.18.

2. The British Library, Department of Printed Books, Archives, DH2, draft by Rye dated 30 June 1875.

3. All testimonials in HRHRC.

4. Sir Percy Shelley to Richard, 20 July 1875, Thurman, p.138.

5. The British Museum, Minutes of the Trustees' Meetings, P.13331.

6. G. K. Fortescue, "Richard Garnett," *Library*, 7 (July 1906): 228.

7. Alice Zimmern, "Dr. Richard Garnett: In Memoriam, VI," *Bookman*, 30 (June 1906):94.

8. Richard to Edward Bond, 14 November 1882, Department of Printed Books Archives, DH2.

9. Richard Garnett, "The Printing of the British Museum Catalogue," *Essays in Librarianship and Bibliography* (London: George Allen, 1899; New York: Burt Franklin, 1970), pp.72–73.

10. *Library Journal*, 1 (November-December 1877):194–200; also in Richard Garnett, *Essays in Librarianship and Bibliography*, pp.210–24.

11. " 'Shelley's Last Days,' (A Reply to R. Garnett's Article in the 'Fortnightly Review')," *Athenaeum*, 3 August 1878, p.144.

12. Lady Shelley to Trelawny, [12] August 1878, quoted in R. Glyn Grylls, *Mary Shelley* (Oxford: University Pr., 1941), pp.285–87. Lady Shelley knew that Trelawny had offered marriage to Mary after Shelley's death, and this made his present criticism puzzling. However, Mary had been known to Lady Shelley only as a matron in her fifties, when she had mellowed considerably. In her youth, when Peacock and Trelawny had known her, Mary had been more temperamental, and not everyone had admired her then.

12. Dr. Richard Garnett, 1879–1884

1. "Public Libraries and Their Catalogues," *Essays in Librarianship and Bibliography*, p.51. First published in *New Quarterly Magazine*, n.s., 1 (April 1879):303–23.

2. Ibid., pp.61, 53.

3. Thurman, p.161.

4. Sir Percy Shelley to Richard, 2 February 1880, Thurman, p.163.

5. G. M. Mathews, "Shelley and Jane Williams," *Review of English Literature*, n.s., 12 (February 1961):40–48.

6. Lady Shelley to Richard, 25 March 1880, Thurman, p.164.
7. Richard to W. M. Rossetti, 17 November 1880 [UBC].
8. E. W. B. Nicholson to Richard, 6 February 1882 [HRHRC].
9. Edmund Gosse to Richard, 12 February 1882 [HRHRC].
10. Note in Richard Garnett, *The Twilight of the Gods* (London: T. Fisher Unwin, 1888), p.345.
11. Robert S. Garnett, *Some Book-Hunting Adventures*, p.3.
12. Lady Shelley to Richard, 29 July 1883, Thurman, pp.181–82.
13. Richard to Dowden, 28 July 1883, *Letters About Shelley*, p.79.
14. *Essays in Librarianship and Bibliography*, p.252.
15. Richard to Ashton, 14 November 1884 (draft) [HRHRC].
16. *Library Chronicle*, 2 (July 1895):96–97.
17. *Letters About Shelley*, p.106.
18. John Ballinger, "Richard Garnett," *Library*, 2nd. ser., 7 (July 1906):233–34.
19. A. W. Pollard, "Richard Garnett," *English Illustrated Magazine*, 30 (February 1904):554.
20. William John Garnett, manuscript biographical sketch of his brother, 1910, p.4 [HRHRC].
21. David Syme (1827–1908) had married Annabella Johnson, granddaughter of the Reverend Richard Garnett's sister Martha, whose son, John William Johnson, had emigrated years before. Syme was one of the most influential men in the state of Victoria, and had an important role in the formation of the Australian federal system in 1901.

13. More Shelley, 1885–1887

1. Sir Percy Shelley to Richard, 6 May 1885, Thurman, p.187.
2. J. Cordy Jeaffreson, *The Real Shelley*, 2 vols. (London: Hurst & Blackett, 1885), 1:65.
3. Ibid., 1:277.
4. *Athenaeum*, 6 June 1885, p.721.
5. The poem is quoted entire in *Letters About Shelley*, pp.119–21; also in Robert Metcalf Smith, *The Shelley Legend* (Port Washington, N.Y.: Kennikat, 1967), pp.249–50.
6. Lady Shelley to Richard, 28 May 1885, Thurman, p.188.
7. Sir Percy Shelley to Richard, 14 June 1885, Thurman, p.190.
8. Memoranda for Sir Percy on Dowden's chapter, enclosed with a letter to Dowden of 29 June 1885, *Letters About Shelley*, p.134.
9. Richard to Dowden, 15 July 1886, *Letters About Shelley*, pp.136–37. The only Peacock paper published in the *National* was "The Last Day of Windsor Forest," with introductory note by Richard, 10 (September 1887):106–11.
10. The deceit was revealed during Wise's lifetime, entirely by innuendo,

rather than outright accusation, by John Carter and Graham Pollard in *An Enquiry into the Nature of Certain Nineteenth Century Pamphlets* (London: Constable; New York: Charles Scribner's Sons, 1934; 2nd ed., Berkeley, Calif.: Scolar, 1984).

11. Carter and Pollard (1934, pp. 143–45) give a list of the forged pamphlets in the British Museum library.

12. Thurman, pp.376–78.

13. Richard to Dowden, 29 November 1886, *Letters About Shelley*, p.151.

14. Richard to Dowden, 10 December 1886, Thurman, p.238.

15. Dowden to Richard, 2 July 1888, *Letters About Shelley*, p.167.

16. *Nineteenth Century*, 23 (January 1888):28. Arnold used quotation marks around, and italics within, the famous phrase because he had previously given the same description of Shelley in the introduction to his selections from Byron, published in 1881; but the effect was intensified in his article on Shelley.

17. William Cosmo Monkhouse in his introduction to selections from Richard's poetry, in A. H. Miles, ed., *The Poets and Poetry of the Nineteenth Century*, 12 vols. (London: Hutchinson, 1905; Routledge, 1905–1907; New York: AMS Pr., 1967), 6:168.

18. Rossetti to Richard, 16 June 1888, Thurman, p.281.

19. *Nation*, 50 (20 February 1890):164.

20. "The Printing of the British Museum Catalogue," *Essays in Librarianship and Bibliography*, pp.75–76.

21. For the complete story, see my "Nineteenth-Century 'Swingers': The Movable Press at the British Museum," *Library Review*, 25 (Autumn/Winter 1975–76):119–23. The library staff called the cases "swingers," for they were swung away from the adjoining cases on the wheel, a task requiring considerable strength.

22. Ernest A. Savage, *A Librarian's Memory*, p.122.

23. "The Sliding-Press at the British Museum," *Essays in Librarianship and Bibliography*, pp.262–71.

14. The Twilight of the Gods, 1888–1889

1. Richard to Dowden, 17 April 1888, *Letters About Shelley*, p.161.
2. Richard to Dowden, 27 October 1888, ibid., p.172.
3. Dowden to Richard, 23 October 1888, ibid., p.169.
4. Richard to Dowden, 27 October 1888, ibid., p.171.
5. George Jefferson, *Edward Garnett: A Life in Literature* (London: Jonathan Cape, 1982), p.16.
6. Richard to Rossetti, 17 December 1889 [UBC].
7. The first three quotations appear in an advertisement at the back of Richard's *Poems*, 1893. The *Academy* notice [34 (15 December 1888):380] was by William Sharp, a poet friend of Richard's.

8. Richard to Dowden, 27 October 1888, *Letters About Shelley*, p.172.
9. Written upon receipt of the augmented edition on 3 June 1903, ibid., p.239.
10. Gosse to Richard, 24 May 1903 [HRHRC].
11. Richard had this letter inserted in a pocket at the back of his specially bound copy of *The Twilight of the Gods*, and this copy was listed in the sale of his library in 1906 (lot 86). Yet two copies of the letter still exist in the family, both kept in copies of the book.
12. A. W. Pollard, *Library*, 18 (July 1906):249–50.
13. *Academy*, 52 (4 September 1897):183.
14. *Letters About Shelley*, pp.164–65. The Coleridge was published in the November 1887 issue of *Atalanta*; the Hawthorne in June 1889. These were numbers two and nine in the series "English Men and Women of Letters of the Nineteenth Century." Richard contributed articles on Herbert Spencer, Keats, Pope, and part of Shakespeare in issues for 1889 and 1890, and Edward Garnett wrote one on De Quincey for the August 1890 issue.
15. I. "Timon of Athens," *Scots Observer*, 23 March; II. "Napoleon's Sangaree," 30 March; III. "Concerning Daniel Defoe," 13 April; IV. "Cornelius the Ferryman," 18 May 1889.
16. Arthur Symons, *Library* 18 (July 1906):246.
17. For bibliographical descriptions of the English-language editions of *The Twilight of the Gods*, see Claude A. Prance, *The Laughing Philosopher: A Further Miscellany on Books, Booksellers, and Book Collecting* (London: Villiers [1976]), pp.252–58. Prance misses only the Knopf Blue Jade Library edition of 1926.
18. Introduction to *The Twilight of the Gods*, 1924 ed., p.xi.
19. "The Past, Present, and Future of the British Museum Catalogue," *Universal Review*, 2 (October 1888):241–53; also in *Essays in Librarianship and Bibliography*, pp.87–108.
20. *Universal Review*, 3 (April 1889):556–66. The argument was restated for his introduction to *The Tempest* in the Henry Irving Shakespeare, 1890; was translated for the *Jahrbuch* of the German Shakespeare Society, Vol.35, 1901; and was reprinted in *Essays of an Ex-Librarian*, pp.29–54.
21. *Universal Review*, 5 (15 September 1889):226–39.
22. Ibid., 8 (15 November 1890):366–72; also in the second edition of *The Twilight of the Gods*.

15. Keeper of Printed Books, 1890–1892

1. Richard to Rossetti, 24 January 1890 [UBC].
2. Richard to William John, 29 March 1888 [HRHRC].
3. F. J. Hill of the British Library, typescript prepared for a prospective biography of Richard [HRHRC].
4. Richard to Edward Dowden, 24 April 1890, *Letters About Shelley*, p.176.

5. Olive Garnett's diary, ed. Anne Lee Michell [HRHRC], entry for 24 February 1892.

6. Two Rossetti daughters, Helen and Mary, still occupied the house in June of 1944, when it was destroyed by a V2 rocket. It has since been rebuilt.

7. Ford Madox Ford, *Return to Yesterday*, London edition, p.11; New York edition, p.20.

8. Ibid., London edition, p.176; New York edition, p.173.

9. *Tales and Stories by Mary Wollstonecraft Shelley*, now first collected, with an introduction by Richard Garnett (London: William Paterson; Philadelphia: J. B. Lippincott, 1891; Folcroft, Pa.: Folcroft Library Editions, 1976). Richard gave Florence Marshall a copy for Christmas of 1891. Her *Life and Letters of Mary Wollstonecraft Shelley* had been published in 1889 and Richard had reviewed it for the *Scots Observer*.

10. *The House of Dent, 1888–1938* (London: J. M. Dent [1938]), p.96, note.

11. *The Works of Thomas Love Peacock*, edited with an introduction and notes by David Garnett (London: Rupert Hart-Davis, 1948), p.xix.

12. Carl Van Doren, *The Life of Thomas Love Peacock* (New York: Russell & Russell, 1966), pp.269–70.

13. Henry Festing Jones, *Samuel Butler: A Memoir*, 2 vols. (London: Macmillan, 1919), 2:123.

14. Ibid., 2:131.

15. *Athenaeum*, 18 December 1897, p.849.

16. Olive Garnett's diary, 24 March 1892.

17. Richard's report to the trustees, quoted in notes on his official reports, 1890–1899, in his own hand [HH].

18. *Library*, 5 (July 1893):93–94; *Essays in Librarianship and Bibliography*, pp.109–10.

19. Beatrice Harraden (1864–1936), feminist and novelist, was writing a novel that Olive described as "rather mad and at present without a plot, but true to life as seen through her eyes" [Diary, 23 March 1892]. Agnes Mary Clerke (1842–1907) was a historian of astronomy and had published "Familiar Studies in Homer" in the *Edinburgh Review* in 1892. She was almost certainly the subject of Robert Garnett's story " 'Chipp on Stars' " in *Some Book-Hunting Adventures*, although the biographical details may have been heightened for effect. Her sister Ellen (1840–1906) published original verse and translated Italian poetry. Richard would use some of her translations in his *History of Italian Literature* (1898).

20. Olive's manuscript notes for her niece, Narney Macdonald [HRHRC].

21. *Letters Between Samuel Butler and Miss E. M. A. Savage, 1871–1885*, ed. Geoffrey Keynes and Brian Hill (London: Jonathan Cape, 1935), p.196.

22. Olive's diary, 31 December 1892.

16. Poems and Problems, 1893–1894

1. *Essays in Librarianship and Bibliography*, p.30.
2. *Library*, 18 (July 1906):237.
3. Dr. Francis T. Barrett, librarian of the Mitchell Library, Glasgow, ibid.:241–42.
4. Sir John Ballinger, ibid.:235–36.
5. Joe W. Kraus, in *Messrs. Copeland and Day* (Philadelphia: George S. McManus, 1979), p.15, uses a letter of the American poet Imogen Guiney to Richard, dated 4 August 1893, to establish the date of the founding of the firm in Boston. Miss Guiney told Richard that she had informed Fred Holland Day, the co-founder of the company, of the projected publication of Richard's poems in London in the fall, and that Day wanted them for his list, sending by her letter "his affectionate remembrances" to Richard. [Quoted from her *Letters* (New York: Harper, 1926), 1:46–47.] Kraus's bibliography of the press has Richard's *Poems* as the seventh of their publications.
6. Olive's diary, 30 July 1894.
7. All are described in my "Richard Garnett as Censor," *British Library Journal*, 12 (Spring 1986):64–75.
8. Sir Charles Edward Pollock (1823–1897) was a son of Sir Jonathan Frederick Pollock, and, like him, was baron of the Exchequer. For a full account of the case see my "Victoria Woodhull Sues the British Museum for Libel," *Library Quarterly*, 45 (October 1975):355–72.
9. Olive's diary, 23 and 26 February 1894.
10. Sir Frederick Pollock, third baronet (1845–1937), was a nephew of Sir Charles Edward Pollock, and therefore a cousin of Julius Pollock. He was a professor of law and author of text books and a history of English law.
11. Richard to Rossetti, 5 March 1894 [UBC].
12. The best account of this affair may be found in Thomas C. Moser, *The Life in the Fiction of Ford Madox Ford* (Princeton, N.J.: Princeton Univ. Pr. [1980]), pp.14–20. It is based on Olive's diary.
13. Mark Twain, "In Defense of Harriet Shelley," *North American Review*, 159 (July, August, September 1894):108–19, 240–51, 353–68.
14. Richard to Dowden, 9 August 1894, *Letters About Shelley* (where it is misdated 1892), p.184.
15. See "William Morris Makes an Exchange with the British Museum," note 391, *Book Collector*, 24 (Winter 1975):606–7.

17. Richard Garnett, C.B., LL.D., 1895

1. Olive's diary, 25 February 1895.
2. Ibid.
3. *Nation*, 60 (7 February 1895):105.

4. Notes on his reports to the trustees as keeper of printed books, in his own hand, 28 January 1895 [HH].

5. Harold Orel, *The Final Years of Thomas Hardy, 1912–1928* (Lawrence/Manhattan/Wichita, Kan.: Univ. Pr. of Kansas [1976]), p.28.

6. In the *Pall Mall Gazette* on the twelfth, the *New York World* on the thirteenth, and the *Athenaeum* on the twenty-third of November 1895.

7. *Illustrated London News*, 108 (11 January 1896):50.

8. Carl J. Weber, *"Dearest Emmie": Thomas Hardy's Letters to His First Wife* (New York: St. Martin's, 1963), p.29, note.

9. Ibid.

10. Ford Madox Ford, *Your Mirror to My Times*, pp.66–67; *Memories and Impressions*, Penguin edition, p.94. The triple dots are Ford's punctuation. Emma was really an archdeacon's niece, and Ford knew it. May and Lucy were the Anglicans, Edward probably the Agnostic, and Olive the Nihilist because that was the political philosophy of her Russian refugee friends.

11. Robert Gittings, *The Older Hardy* (London: Heinemann Educational Books [1978]), p.116.

12. Weber, p.29, note. Weber seems to have had more information than is contained in Ford's account, but he does not name his sources.

13. Alfred Sutro, *Celebrities and Simple Souls* (London: Gerald Duckworth, 1933), p.58.

14. Ford Madox Ford, *Your Mirror to My Times*, pp.50–51; *Memories and Impressions*, Penguin edition, pp.77–78; 1932 edition, pp.51–52. A variant of the story appears in the Harper, 1911, edition of *Memories and Impressions*, p.169, where Richard is quoted as saying, "The only poets we have are the Pre-Raphaelites, and this will cast so much odium upon them that the habit of reading poetry will die out in England." Ford proceeds to discourse on the difference between the earlier Pre-Raphaelites and Wilde's Aestheticism, as though Richard had been unaware that they were separate movements, an example of Ford's tendency to bend facts for effect. Another version is in *Return to Yesterday*, London edition, p.45; New York edition, pp.51–52. The lions have disappeared from the Museum railings and have reappeared on the main doors of the building.

15. Richard to Mathilde, 9 November 1895 [BL]. Richard occasionally misspelled a surname, and here he confused the similar names of Arthur Symons and John Addington Symonds.

16. British Library, Department of Printed Books Archives, DH2, 1895, 15 June committee. The *Times* account of the hearing [5 July 1895, p.6] gave Richard the proper title of "Mr." Nevertheless, Harry Furniss labeled his caricature of Richard in about 1905 as "Sir R. Garnett."

17. G. F. Barwick, *The Reading Room of the British Museum* (London: Ernest Benn, 1929), p.143. Barwick remembered the incident as occurring in September, but the suit was brought in June and heard in July. Chaffers was a

litigious man who had been ejected from the House of Lords lobby six months earlier and sued various people as a result, losing each case.

18. *Library*, 18 (July 1906):255.

18. The Old Order Changeth, 1896–1898

1. *Pageant*, 1896, pp.117–18.
2. Richard to Dowden, Christmas Day, 1900, *Letters About Shelley*, pp.224–25. Constance also had a family connection with Russia which her son David made into a novel, *Up She Rises* (1977).
3. "Living Critics, VI: Mr. Coventry Patmore," *Bookman* (London), 9 (March 1896):180–82; *Bookman* (New York), 3 (June 1896):325–29, where it is numbered VII.
4. "Death of Mr. Coventry Patmore," *Times*, 27 November 1896, p.10; "Recollections of Coventry Patmore," *Saturday Review*, 82 (5 December 1896):582–83.
5. The pictures were conveyed to Richard in February of 1897, but they are no longer in the family.
6. Richard to Olive, 18 September 1897 [HH].
7. Richard to Olive, 1 September, 1897 [HH].
8. *Essays in Librarianship and Bibliography*, pp.115–126.
9. Edward Miller, *That Noble Cabinet*, p.282.
10. *Bibliographica*, 3 (1897):29–45; *Library*, 9 (April 1897):133–36.
11. Gosse to Richard, n.d., but after 13 November 1897 [HRHRC].
12. A. M. Wakefield to Richard, 21 November 1898 [HRHRC].
13. *Times*, 22 June 1898, p.6, reporting the presentation. Thurman, pp.413–21, has correspondence between Richard and John Wheeler Williams, grandson of Edward Ellerker Williams, on this subject. A photograph of the guitar may be found in N. I. White, *Shelley*, vol. 2, opp. p.364.
14. Francis Burdett Money-Coutts (1852–1923), later fifth Baron Latymer, was the grandson of Sir Francis Burdett (1770–1844), the great reforming politician whom Shelley admired, and his wife, a daughter of Thomas Coutts, banker to George III. Money-Coutts had published two books of poetry and had also provided the financial backing for the Bodley Head firm.
15. Lady Shelley to Richard, 16 October 1898, Thurman, p.211.
16. Richard to Dowden, 4 January 1899, *Letters About Shelley*, p.202.
17. Wise to Wrenn, 25 March 1899, *Letters of Thomas James Wise to John Henry Wrenn: A Further Inquiry into the Guilt of Certain Nineteenth-Century Forgers*, ed. Fannie Ratchford (New York: Knopf, 1944), p.166. The Wrenn library is now at the University of Texas at Austin, and contains the only complete set of the Wise forgeries.

Notes 191

19. A New Century, 1899–1900

1. Richard to Dowden, 19 February 1899, *Letters About Shelley*, p.208.

2. Olive's diary, 12 February 1899. Sir John Lubbock, first Baron Avebury (1834–1913), was a banker and naturalist. Charles D. E. Fortnum (1820–1899), an art collector, was a benefactor as well as a trustee of the British Museum.

3. *Three Hundred Notable Books Added to the Library of the British Museum under the Keepership of Richard Garnett, 1890–1899* (printed by T. and A. Constable for the Editors and Subscribers, March MDCCCXCIX), pp.vii–viii.

4. "Dr. Garnett's Retirement: A Chat in the British Museum," *Academy*, 56 (18 February 1899):222.

5. "A Faithful Servant of the Queen . . .," *Sketch*, 15 March 1899, quotation from the caption beneath a full-page photograph of Richard.

6. Thompson to Richard, 14 March 1899, Department of Printed Books Archives, DH2.

7. Proctor's diary, 2 March and 14 April 1899, quoted in Barry C. Johnson, *Lost in the Alps: A Portrait of Robert Proctor, the "Great Bibliographer," and of His Career in the British Museum* (London: Privately Printed, 1985), p.22.

8. *Times*, 24 June 1899, p.12.

9. *Literature*, 4 (1 July 1899):674.

10. Richard to Unwin, 21 February 1899, Berg Collection, New York Public Library.

11. *Bookman* (London), 14 (June 1898):71–73.

12. Prothero to Richard, 21 June 1898 [HRHRC].

13. Richard to Herbert Jones, 27 February 1899, Berg Collection, New York Public Library.

14. Lady Shelley to Richard, 11 February 1899, Thurman, pp.213–14.

15. Lady Shelley to Richard, 7 April 1899, Thurman, p.208, where it is misdated "1898 (?)."

16. Shelley Scarlett to Richard, 27 June 1899, Thurman, p.221.

17. Florence Scarlett to Richard, 3 July 1899, Thurman, pp.218–19. Shelley Leopold Laurence Scarlett (1872–1917) became the fifth Baron Abinger; Robert Brooke Campbell Scarlett (1876–1927) became the sixth baron. "The Cottage" was a retreat of Lady Shelley's on the Boscombe grounds.

18. *Library Association Record*, 1 (September 1899):651–52.

19. Elgar to Richard, 6 November 1902 [HRHRC]. He set Richard's translation of Marcus Argentarius's "Feasting I watch with westward-looking eye/ The flashing constellations' pageantry. . . ." (No. XXIV in *Idylls and Epigrams*) as No. 5 in his Opus 45, a group of part-songs for male voices, with texts taken from the Greek Anthology. It was completed in November of 1902 and first sung at the Royal Albert Hall in London on 25 April 1904.

20. *Times*, 31 October 1900, p.6.

21. Léon Vallée was librarian of the Bibliothèque Nationale in Paris. Alois

Brandl was professor of literature at the Royal University of Berlin. Donald Grant Mitchell was an author under the pseudonyms "John Timon" and "Ik Marvel," as well as under his own name. Only the first edition of the *International Library* listed him as co-editor, followed by "Yale University." He was a trustee of Yale, which had awarded him an LL.D. degree.

22. The Westminster Edition of the *Universal Anthology* was published in London by the Clarke Company; in New York by Merrill & Baker; in Paris by Emile Terquem; in Berlin by the Bibliothek Verlag, 1899–1902, in 30, 32, or 33 volumes. It was copyrighted by Richard Garnett. The set was re-issued in 1922 and 1923 as *The Book of Literature* by the Grolier Society in New York, 33 volumes in 17. Under its original title it was made available in facsimile by Folcroft Library Editions in 1977.

23. *The Letters of D. H. Lawrence*, ed. James T. Boulton et al. (Cambridge and New York: Cambridge Univ. Pr., 1979–), 1:4–6.

24. Volney Streamer, *What Makes a Friend?* (London and New York: Truslove, Hanson & Comba, 1900). The book was originally published in Chicago in 1892.

25. *Times*, 31 October 1900, p.6.

20. Journeys and Publications, 1901–1902

1. *Essays of an Ex-Librarian*, Preface, p.viii, dated "April 20, 1901."

2. *The Collected Letters of Thomas Hardy*, ed. Richard Little Purdy and Michael Millgate (Oxford and New York: Clarendon, 1978–), 2:291.

3. Ibid., 2:290.

4. Ibid., 2:291.

5. Alfred Sutro, *Celebrities and Simple Souls*, pp.58–59.

6. Hardy to Richard, [13] September 1901, *Collected Letters*, 2:299. A direct sundial was erected on the gate of the house after Hardy's death.

7. Hardy to Richard, 8 September 1901, *Collected Letters*, 2:298.

8. Thomas Greenwood, *Edward Edwards* (London: Scott, Greenwood, 1902), pp.231–35.

9. London, Edinburgh, New York: Thomas Nelson & Sons; part 1, 1902, part 2, 1904. Arranged for use as Book 6 of the Royal Prince and Princess Readers. Richard's introduction covered pp.i–viii; his poem "The Mermaid of Padstow" was on pp.58–59 of vol. 1.

10. Rosalind Travers, later Hyndman (1874–1923), became one of Richard's literary ladies. She published two books of plays and poems, for one of which, *The Two Arcadias* (1905), Richard wrote an introduction. Not long afterward she suffered Percy Bysshe Shelley's fate in being banished by her parents for her activity in favor of women's suffrage.

11. Richard to Michael Field, 5 October 1902, BL ADD. MSS. 46,867, "Correspondence of Michael Field," vol. 8, fol. 24.

12. *The Journal of Edward Ellerker Williams*, p.12.

13. Frederick L. Jones, ed., *Maria Gisborne and Edward E. Williams, Shelley's Friends: Their Journals and Letters* (Norman: Univ. of Oklahoma Pr., 1951), pp.ix–x. Richard's edition is here called "shocking," as it omits 119 of 257 entries, printing 69 of the rest in incomplete form, and only 69 actually complete; with errors, substituted words, and wrong identifications making it "so inaccurate as to be unfit for scholarly purposes." It might be questioned whether Richard had a scholarly purpose in mind. Letters on the subject of the journal are in Thurman, pp.423–33.

14. *English Literature: An Illustrated Record*, 2 vols. (London: William Heinemann; New York: Macmillan, 1903, 1935; New York: Grosset & Dunlap, 1903–1904, 1906, 1908, 1910, etc.; New York: Somerset, 1980).

15. Richard to Dowden, 4 June 1903, *Letters About Shelley*, p.240. Volume 3 was published in January 1903; volume 1 in May 1903; and volumes 2 and 4 in 1904.

16. *Athenaeum*, 25 July 1903, p.133.

17. Dowden to Richard, 3 June 1903, *Letters About Shelley*, p.239.

21. An Ending and a Beginning, 1903–1905

1. *Speaker*, 8 (12 September 1903):553.

2. *Outlook*, quoted on an advertising page at the end of the 1924 edition of *The Twilight of the Gods*.

3. Richard to Dowden, 4 June 1903, *Letters About Shelley*, p.241.

4. Olive's diary for 16 July 1900.

5. Ibid., 20 July 1903. The following account is taken from Olive's diary entries for 21–27 June and Anne Lee Michell's commentary upon them.

6. Anne Lee Michell, note to Olive's diary of 27 June 1903.

7. Richard to Dowden, 4 May 1902, *Letters About Shelley*, p.235. Chesterton's *Robert Browning, the Napoleon of Notting Hill* was published by Macmillan in 1903 in the English Men of Letters series. *Tennyson* was published by Hodder and Stoughton as No. 6 of the Bookman Biographies, and Richard's essay occupied pp.13–34 of forty pages.

8. Violet Neale was born on 25 April 1873 and died about 1950. Her father, Melville Neale, was an artist from Bath, and she had a brother and sister in London. The letters she wrote to Richard are at Hilton Hall; Richard's to her are in the British Library, Department of Manuscripts, ADD. MSS. 42,861. Both collections have been culled and censored, but remain substantial. In the following section of the text, quotations from these letters will not be cited, as all of them will be Richard's [in BL].

9. Violet Neale, introduction to "Letters of Richard Garnett to Violet Neale," BL ADD. MSS. 42,861.

10. *Nation*, 77 (12 November 1903):380.

11. Ibid., 78 (21 January 1904):49.
12. *Yearbook of the Brontë Society*, 1904, pp.204–16.
13. *Dante Society Lectures*, vol.1, no.59 (London: Athenaeum, 1904).
14. Published later in the year by Elliot Stock in *At Shakespeare's Shrine: A Poetical Anthology*, ed. Charles F. Forshaw, pp.3–15.
15. The original bound manuscript copy that Richard made for Violet, BL ADD. MSS. 42,857, has an extended form of the epigraph from the *Pervigilium Veneris*:

> Amorum copulatrix inter umbras arborum
> Implicat casas virentes de flagello myrteo.

16. Furness to Richard, 4 December 1904 [HRHRC]. Richard dedicated the second edition of *The Twilight of the Gods* to Furness and to the Danish scholar Georg Brandes.
17. Richard to Dowden, 25 March 1905, *Letters About Shelley*, p.249.
18. John Bartlett's *Familiar Quotations*, 10th ed., 1926, had six quotations from *De Flagello Myrteo*, while the 11th, 1937, had fifteen. The 14th edition went down to five, and the 15th, 1980, had only two; but one of the "thoughts" was recently used on an American television show.
19. *Times*, 19 September 1905, p.4.

22. Finale, 1906

1. Note by F. J. Hill [HRHRC].
2. HRHRC. When he had received the first, anonymous edition of *De Flagello Myrteo*, on 7 June 1905, Symons had written to Elkin Mathews, calling the book beautiful, conjecturing that, as it reminded him of Coleridge, it might be by Ernest Hartley Coleridge, and asking if Mathews were free to tell him. [Mathews Papers, University of Reading Library].
3. Symons in the *Speaker*, 14 (21 April 1906):59.
4. Richard to Dowden, 4 April 1906, *Letters About Shelley*, p.261.
5. Dowden to Richard, 6 April 1906, BL ADD. MSS. 42860, "Letters from those who received copies of 'De Flagello Myrteo.' "
6. Ibid., note by Violet on the cover of Dowden's letter.
7. BL ADD. MSS. 42861, No. 36, fragment (1905): [Violet was shocked at the idea of cremation] "Why, if I have my own way I shall be cremated myself."
8. Robert to Rossetti, 14 April 1906 [UBC].
9. Unidentified newspaper report of the funeral [HH]. The *Times* of 18 April had basically the same list.
10. Olive to Violet, 14 April 1906, BL ADD. MSS. 42860.
11. Unidentified newspaper report of the funeral [HH].
12. *Illustrated London News*, 21 April 1906, p.552.
13. *Daily Mirror*, n.d., clipping [HH].

14. *Boston Transcript*, 8 August 1906.
15. *Nation*, 82 (19 April 1906):324.
16. *Athenaeum*, 21 April 1906, p.481.
17. "The Horoscope of Dr. Richard Garnett, with a delineation by the editor," *Modern Astrology*, July 1906, p.305, quoting Richard's letters.
18. *Athenaeum*, 21 April 1906, p.472.
19. Ibid., p.480.
20. *Hampstead Annual*, 1906–1907, pp.24–29.
21. *British Weekly*, 19 April 1906, p.35.
22. Aphra Wilson, "Dr. Richard Garnett, C.B.," *Hampstead Annual*, 1906–1907, p.20.
23. Robert to Rossetti, 6 September 1906 [UBC].
24. Olive to Rossetti, 21 September 1906 [UBC].
25. William Keeny Bixby (1857–1931) had made a fortune manufacturing railroad cars, and used it to acquire a collection of art, books, and manuscripts. His library was bought in 1918 by Henry E. Huntington (1850–1927), a fellow railroad magnate, for his great library and art gallery in San Marino, California. Included in the purchase were the Shelley notebooks, today known as the "Bixby-Huntington notebooks." They were edited for publication in 1911 by Harry Buxton Forman for the Bibliophile Society of Boston, of which Bixby was a member. A fourth notebook had been given by Richard to Violet Neale in 1904. It also was sold in the United States, and went from the collection of John A. Spoor, another railway capitalist, to the Library of Congress in 1939. With Silsbee's Harvard copybook, these make five Shelley notebooks in America, while twenty more are in the Bodleian.
26. Robert to Rossetti, 8 December 1906 [UBC].
27. *Nation*, 83 (29 November 1906):457.
28. *Saturday Review*, 101 (21 April 1906):480, "Notes of the Week." The quotation continued, "but wrote cultivated verse and a quantity of prose, critical and biographical, strong in knowledge and admirable in form."
29. "Back Numbers—LXXIV," *Saturday Review*, 144 (26 May 1928):664.
30. *Speaker*, 14 (21 April 1906):60.
31. *Bookman*, June 1906, p.92.
32. "Modern Men: Dr. Richard Garnett," *National Observer*, 5 December 1891, pp.60–61, unsigned, describing him as superintendent of the Reading Room.
33. W. A. Munford, *A History of the Library Association, 1877–1977* (London: Library Association, [1977]), p.38.

Appendix: Works of Richard Garnett

Listed below are works of Richard Garnett mentioned in the text, exclusive of reviews, introductions, etc. These are but a small sample of Garnett's writings. I have identified 754 poems as his, as well as 25 addresses, 18 of them subsequently printed, 120 articles and essays, 24 contributions to works, not including the *Encyclopaedia Britannica* (52) and the *Dictionary of National Biography* (117), 27 editions and 51 introductions to the work of others, 43 stories, 11 monographs, 3 verse dramas, and numerous reviews, translations, epigrams, memoirs, "notes," and letters to the editor. There are surely many more.

Books

The Age of Dryden (1895)
Coleridge (1904)
Dante, Petrarch, Camoëns: CCCIV Sonnets (1896)
De Flagello Myrteo (1905)
Edward Gibbon Wakefield: The Colonization of South Australia and New Zealand (1898)
English Literature: An Illustrated Record (with Gosse) (1899)
Essays in Librarianship and Bibliography (1899)
Essays of an Ex-Librarian (1901)
History of Italian Literature (1898)
Idylls and Epigrams, Chiefly from the Greek Anthology (1869)
Io in Egypt and Other Poems (1859)
Iphigenia in Delphi (1890)
Life of John Milton (1890)
Life of Ralph Waldo Emerson (1888)
Life of Thomas Carlyle (1887)
Life of W. J. Fox (1910)

The Philological Essays of the Late Rev. Richard Garnett of the British Museum (1859)
Poems (1893)
Poems from the German (1862)
Poems Selected from Percy Bysshe Shelley (1880)
Primula: A Book of Lyrics (1858)
The Queen and Other Poems (1901)
Relics of Shelley (1862)
Richmond on the Thames (1896)
Select Letters of Percy Bysshe Shelley (1882)
Tennyson [as an Intellectual Force] (with Chesterton) (1903)
The Twilight of the Gods (1888, 1903)
William Blake, Painter and Poet (1895)

Addresses

[Presidential] Address to the Library Association (1893)
"The British Museum Catalogue as the Basis of a Universal Catalogue" (1892)
"The Date and Occasion of 'The Tempest' " (1887, printed 1889)
"Note on the Printing of the British Museum Catalogue" (1885)
"On Some Colophons of the Early Printers" (1889, printed 1899)
"The Printing of the British Museum Catalogue" (1882)
"On the Provision of Additional Space in Libraries" (1894)
"On the System of Classifying Books on the Shelves Followed at the British Museum" (1877)
"Photography in Public Libraries" (1884)
"The Place of Charlotte Brontë in Nineteenth Century Fiction" (1904)
"Plays Partly Written by Shakespeare" (1904)
"Shelley and Lord Beaconsfield" (1887)
"Shelley's Views on Art" (1899)
"The Sliding Press at the British Museum" (1887)
"The Vicissitudes of Dante's Literary Reputation" (1904)

Essays and Articles

"Coleridge," in *Atalanta* (1888)
"De Quincey and Musset" (1885)
"The Early Italian Book Trade" (1897)
"Hawthorne," in *Atalanta* (1888)
"Living Critics: Mr. Coventry Patmore" (1896)
"The Manufacture of Fine Paper in England in the Eighteenth Century" (1897)
"Notes on Some Poets Connected with Hampstead" (1900)
"On the Protection of Libraries from Fire" (1899)
"On Translating Homer" (1889)

"Paraguayan and Argentine Bibliography" (1897)
"The Past, Present, and Future of the British Museum Catalogue" (1888)
"Portraits of Shelley in the National Portrait Gallery" (1901)
"Public Libraries and their Catalogues" (1879)
"Rome and the Temporal Power" (1902)
"Shelley, Harriet Shelley, and Mr. T. L. Peacock" (1862)
"Shelley in Italy" (1894)
"Shelley in Pall Mall" (1860)
"Shelley's Last Days" (1877)
"Shelley's Voyages, the Ideal Navigations Described in His Poems" (1906)
"The Soul and the Stars" (1880)
"The Telegraph in the Library" (1899)
"Tennyson as an Intellectual Force" (1903)

Editions
Browning, Robert. *Poems* (1897)
De Quincey, Thomas. *Confessions of an English Opium Eater* (1885)
Dickens, Charles. *Complete Works of* (1900)
International Library of Famous Literature, or *Universal Anthology* (1899)
Nelson's Literature Readers (1902)
Orations of American Orators (1900)
Orations of British Orators (1900)
Peacock, Thomas Love. *Novels* (1891)
Shelley, Mary Wollstonecraft. *Tales and Stories* (1891)
Shelley, Percy Bysshe and Elizabeth. *Original Poetry by Victor and Cazire* (1898)
Williams, Edward Ellerker. *Journal of* (1902)

Individual Poems
"An Epitaph" (1893)
"The Fair Circassian" (1859)
"Garibaldi's Retirement" (1860)
"Imitation of Leopardi" (1859)
"Io in Egypt" (1859)
"Lines at Boscombe" (1862)
"Mignon's Song" (1859)
"Miora" (1861)
"Nausicaa" (1893)
"Our Crocodile" (1859)
"The Pope's Daughter" (1859)
Sonnet "Age" (1859)
"The Queen" (1901)

Shelley birth room memorial verse (1871)
"Sir Isumbras: A Fragment" (1859)
"To One in Russia" (1894)
"To the Crimea" (1859)
"To the Memory of Shelley" (1859)
"Where Corals Lie" (1859)
"A Welcome" (1863)

Poetic Dramas
Iphigenia in Delphi (1890)
Michael Angelo (1862)
William Shakespeare: Pedagogue and Poacher (1904)

Stories
"Abdallah the Adite" (1888)
"Alexander the Ratcatcher" (1896)
"Ananda the Miracle Worker" (1872)
"The Autobiography of an Evil Spirit" (1862)
"Concerning Daniel Defoe" (1890)
"Cornelius the Ferryman" (1890)
"The Dumb Oracle" (1878)
"The Elixir of Life" (1881)
"The Firefly" (1870)
"A Handful of Dust" (1896)
"Napoleon's Sangaree" (1890)
"New Readings in Biography" (1890)
"A Page from the Book of Folly" (1871)
"The Philosopher and the Butterflies" (1886)
"The Poison Maid" (1903)
"The Potion of Lao-tsze" (1888)
"The Purple Head" (1877)
"A Real German Mystery" (1861)
"The Rewards of Industry" (1888)
"The Talismans" (1890)
"Timon of Athens" (1890)
"The Twilight of the Gods" (1888)
"The Wisdom of the Indians" (1889)

Index

Abinger, James Scarlett, 1st baron, 177 n.5
Abinger, Robert Scarlett, 6th baron, 144, 177 n.5, 191 n.17
Abinger, Shelley Scarlett, 5th baron, 144, 158, 177 n.5, 191 n.17
Academy, 65, 99, 110, 111
Acton, John Dahlberg-Acton, 1st baron, 143–49
Age, 97, 123
Alexander VI, pope, 135–36
Alexandra, Princess of Wales. See Wales, Alexandra, Princess of
Allen, George, 137
Allen, S. J., 3
American Library Association, 84, 100
Anderson, John Parker, 83, 102, 129, 133, 164
Anglo-Saxon Review, 143
Archaeologia, 7
Archbishop of Canterbury. See Canterbury, Archbishop of
Ariosto, Lodovico, 9
Arnold, Matthew, 101, 112, 185 n.16
Ashburnham, Bertram, 4th earl, 142
Ashley Library, 100
Ashton, John, 95
Atalanta, 112, 196 n.14
Athenaeum, 13, 20, 25, 28, 57, 60, 66, 85–86, 87, 89, 95, 99, 110, 118, 119, 138, 150, 165, 166, 176 n.12
Audiffredi, Giovanni Battista, 7
Austin, Alfred, 178 n.5

Baber, Rev. H. H., 5, 6
Ballinger, Sir John, 96

Balzac, Honoré de, 15
Baudelaire, Pierre Charles, 73
Baynes, Thomas Spencer, 80
Beaconsfield, 1st earl of. See Disraeli, Benjamin
Beanlands, Anne Garnett (aunt), 4, 7, 52
Beanlands, Benjamin (son of Anne), 7, 10, 14, 15
Bell, George, & Sons, 101, 133, 137, 156
Bell & Daldy, 28, 51, 101
Besant, Annie, 82
Biagi, Guido, 140
Bibliographica, 137
Bibliographical Society, 133, 137, 164
Bibliophile Society of Boston, 195 n.25
Biblioteca Mediceo-Laurenziana (Florence), 140
Bibliothèque Nationale (Paris), 191 n.21
Bismarck, Prince Otto von, 59
Bixby, William Keeney, 168, 195 n.25
Black, Clementina, 106, 164
Black, Constance. See Garnett, Constance Black
Blackmore, Mrs., 64, 65
Blake, William, 133, 163
Blanc, Louis, 59
Blind, Ferdinand (son of Mrs. Karl), 59
Blind, Karl, and Mrs., 59
Blind, Mathilde (daughter of Mrs. Karl), 59–62, 64–67, 69, 70, 81, 100, 117, 123, 131, 132, 136
Blomfield, Bishop Charles James. See London, Bishop of (C. J. Blomfield)
Bodleian Library, 91–92, 119, 122, 139, 167, 195 n.25
Bodley Head, 123, 135, 169, 190 n.14

201

Boiardo, M. M., 9
Bond, Sir Edward Augustus, 87, 89, 91, 94–95, 107
Bonner, Hypatia Bradlaugh, 124
Bookman (London), 136, 143, 154
Booth, Mary Anne Garnett (aunt), 53
Borgia family, 28, 136, 149
Bourke, Rev. John, 44, 45
Bourke, Louisa Potts (Mrs. John), 44, 45
Bradlaugh, Charles, 124
Bradley, Katherine Harris ("Michael Field"), 149, 160
Brandes, Georg, 194 n.16
Brandl, Alois, 145, 192 n.21
Bright, John, 23
British Museum: accessions, 80, 88, 116, 119, 142; catalogue (early English), 85, 95; catalogue (general), 4, 15, 20–21, 81, 83–85, 87–88, 91, 94– 96, 103, 113, 115, 120, 137, 145, 146, 161, 162, 170; catalogue (subject), 103, 137; changes at, 6, 20, 23, 24, 41, 54, 55, 58, 79–91, 95, 107, 115; litigation against, 123–25, 132–33; movable bookcases in, 104; Private Case in, 116; Reading Room, 23, 24, 78, 81–83, 85, 88, 92, 95–96, 125, 132–33, 154, 164, 169; scandal at, 78–79
British Weekly, 110, 167
Brodribb, William Jackson, 9, 27, 172 n.14
Brontë, Charlotte, 156
Brontë Society, 156
Brooke, Rev. Stopford A., 101
Brown, Catherine. *See* Hueffer, Catherine Brown (Mrs. Francis)
Brown, Ford Madox, 59, 62, 64, 117, 136, 178 n.1
Brown, Lucy. *See* Rossetti, Lucy Madox Brown (Mrs. William)
Browning, Elizabeth Barrett, 180 n.1
Browning, Robert, 94, 100, 137, 154, 180 n.1, 193 n.7
Browning, Robert Wiedemann Barrett (son of Robert and Elizabeth), 64, 180 n.1
Buchanan, Robert, 60
Buckley, Arabella (later Fisher), 120– 21, 160
Buckley, Elsie (sister of Arabella), 120, 187 n.19

Bullen, George, 54–55, 79–80, 83, 84, 95, 101, 115, 124–25
Burdett, Sir Francis, 190 n.14
Butler, Samuel (1835–1902), 119, 121, 123
Butt, Dame Clara, 145
Byron, George Gordon, 6th baron, 17, 30, 93, 98, 115, 139, 140, 143, 154, 159, 177 n.14, 185 n.16

Calderon, Pedro, 20
Cambridge Modern History, 149
Camoëns, Luis Vaz de, 135, 136, 146
Canterbury, Archbishop of (William Howley), 6; (John Bird Sumner) 11; (Edward White Benson) 116
Carlyle, Thomas, 102, 117, 128, 142, 173 n.2
Carlyle Society, 164
Carter, John, 185 n.10–11
Cary, Rev. Henry Francis, 6
Catullus, Gaius Valerius, 155
Caxton, William, 116, 142
Chaffers, Alexander, 132–33, 189– 90 n.17
Chapman, Dr. John, 59, 60
Chapman & Hall, 146
Chapple, Christiana Jane, 52, 65, 77, 116, 126, 150
Chaucer, Geoffrey, 100
Chesterton, G. K., 154, 193 n.7
Chiswick Press, 28, 90
Clairmont, Claire, 66–67, 85, 89–90, 97, 138, 143
Clairmont, Mrs. *See* Godwin, Mrs. Clairmont
Clairmont, Paola (niece of Claire), 67, 89–90
Clarke, Edith Nicolls, 99
Clay, Richard, & Sons, 104–105
Clerke, Agnes, 120, 187 n.19
Clerke, Ellen (sister of Agnes), 120, 187 n.19
Clowes, William & Sons, 95
Coleridge, Ernest Hartley (grandson of Samuel Taylor), 53, 143, 149, 164, 178 n.4, 194 n.2
Coleridge, Sir John Duke, 1st baron (son of Sir John Taylor), 53, 178 n.4
Coleridge, Sir John Taylor (nephew of Samuel Taylor), 53, 178 n.4

Coleridge, Samuel Taylor, 52, 112, 156, 178 n.4, 186 n.14, 194 n.2
Collier, Hon. John, 143, 165
Collier, John Payne, 7, 88
Colvin, Sir Sidney, 73
Coming Events, 163
Conference of librarians: 1st international, 84; 2nd international, 137
Conrad, Joseph, 117
Cooper, Edith Emma ("Michael Field"), 149, 160
Copeland and Day, 123, 135, 188 n.5
Copley, John Singleton, baron Lyndhurst, 45
Corkling, Robert, 53
Corkran, John Frazer, 180 n.1
Cornhill Magazine, 47
Coutts, Thomas, 190 n.14
Cowlishaw, Harry, 133, 136, 153, 164
Cowlishaw, Lucy Garnett. *See* Garnett, Lucy (later Cowlishaw)
Cowlishaw, Olivia Margaret (daughter of Harry and Lucy), 153
Cox, Edward William, 28
Crawford, James Ludovic Lindsay, 26th earl, 133, 144
Creighton, Mandell, Bishop of London. *See* London, Bishop of (Mandell Creighton)
Critic (London), 28, 29
Cumberland, Charles the elder, 14, 54
Cumberland, Charles the younger, 151, 153, 164
Cumberland, Eliza Garnett (Mrs. Charles the elder) (cousin), 14, 54
Curran, Amelia, 148
Cust, Sir Lionel, 155
Cutler, Sir John, 21, 174 n.7

Daily News (London), 59
Dante Alighieri, 13, 135, 156
Dante Society, 156
Darby Books, 113
Darwin, Charles, 100, 102
Day, Fred Holland, 188 n.5
De Morgan, Augustus, 52
De Quincey, Thomas, 98, 186 n.14
Dent, Hugh (son of Joseph Malaby), 117
Dent, Joseph Malaby, 117
Dickens, Charles, 28, 92, 146, 176 n.12, 180 n.1

Dictionary of National Biography, 16, 58, 97, 101, 137, 171 n.2 ch. 1
Diodorus Siculus, 9
Disraeli, Benjamin, 1st earl of Beaconsfield, 15, 104
Dixon, Hepworth, 52
Dobson, Austin, 157
Donaldson, John William, 8, 27
Dowden, Edward, 61, 93, 95, 99, 101–102, 106, 107, 110, 126–27, 146, 149, 150, 157, 159, 163
Dryden, John, 133
Dublin University Magazine. See *University Magazine* (formerly *Dublin University Magazine*)

Eccles, G. W., 85
Edinburgh Review, 8
Edinburgh University, 53, 93, 102
Edinburgh University Press, 142
Edwards, Edward, 148–49, 170
Egyptian Gazette, 123, 131
Elgar, Sir Edward, 29, 145, 191 n.19
Elizabeth I (Queen of England), 157
Ellis, E. J., 133
Ellis, Sir Henry, 11, 20
Emerson, Ralph Waldo, 102–103, 136, 142, 173 n.2
Emery, Florence Farr, 157
Encyclopaedia Britannica, 38, 70, 71, 80, 97, 118, 162
Encyclopaedia Metropolitana, 3
English Illustrated Magazine, 127
Esdaile, Arundell, 185 n.27
Esdaile, Ianthe Shelley, 36
Evans, Frederick H., 117
Eversley, Charles Shaw-Lefevre, 1st viscount, 41, 176–77 n.13
Examiner, 69

Fabian Society, 107, 133
Farrar, Frederick, 9, 38, 41, 54, 80, 146, 172 n.14
Fawcett, Henry, 40
Field, Michael, 149, 160
Fifth Avenue Press, 146
Fisher, Arabella Buckley. *See* Buckley, Arabella (later Fisher)
Flourens, Pierre Jean Marie, 18, 173 n.1
Ford, Edward Onslow, 119
Ford, Ford Madox (formerly Hueffer), 72,

Ford, Ford Maddux (cont.)
73, 117, 126, 129–31, 153, 165, 179 n.23, 182 n.27, 189 n.10, 14
Foreign Quarterly Review, 162
Forman, Harry Buxton, 89, 90, 98, 100–101, 139, 195 n.25
Fortescue, George Knottesford, 75, 81, 103, 125, 137, 164
Fortnightly Review, 85
Fortnum, Charles D. E., 141, 191 n.2
Fox, William Johnson, 156, 158, 162, 169
Fraser's Magazine, 35, 46, 69, 86
Freiligrath, Ferdinand, 43, 64
Freiligrath, Käthe (later Kroeker) (daughter of Ferdinand), 64, 179 n.12
Furness, Horace Howard, 158, 194 n.16
Furniss, Harry, 189 n.16
Furnivall, Frederick J., 51, 100, 132

Galton, Francis, 51
Garibaldi, Giuseppe, 40, 59
Garnett, Arthur (son), 91, 119, 130, 153
Garnett, Constance Black (Mrs. Edward), 106, 107, 114, 119, 125–26, 136, 153, 164, 190 n.2
Garnett, David (grandson), 77, 113, 118, 119, 125, 173 n.3, 190 n.2
Garnett, Edward (son), 56, 75, 93, 106–107, 114, 117, 119, 125, 126, 130, 136, 138, 153, 154, 163–66, 168, 169, 186 n.14, 189 n.10
Garnett, Ellen Rayne (sister), 7, 10, 11, 14, 15, 19, 22, 27, 42, 49, 62, 151, 165, 173 n.4
Garnett, Henrietta (of Low Moor) (daughter of great-uncle), 14, 28
Garnett, James (of Low Moor) (cousin), 2, 49, 72
Garnett, Jeremiah (of Low Moor) (great-uncle), 1, 3, 10
Garnett, Jeremiah (of Manchester) (uncle), 2, 3, 11, 13, 14, 15, 18–19, 22, 23, 25, 27, 40, 41, 62, 164, 174 n.3 ch. 4, 181 n.2
Garnett, Jeremiah (of Otley) (great-grandfather), 1, 2
Garnett, Jeremiah (of Otley) (cousin), 2, 137
Garnett, Lucy (later Cowlishaw) (daughter), 83, 116, 130, 133, 136, 152–53, 157, 164, 189 n.10
Garnett, Margaret Heathcote (Mrs. Rev. Richard), 3, 22
Garnett, Martha Roscoe (Mrs. Robert), 133, 135, 136, 153, 164, 167
Garnett, Mary Rhodes (Mrs. William) (grandmother), 2
Garnett, May (later Hall) (daughter), 53, 56, 75, 93, 99, 114, 121, 130, 150–51, 153, 164, 189 n.10
Garnett, Narney. *See* Garnett, Olivia Narney Singleton ("Narney") (Mrs. Richard)
Garnett, Olive. *See* Garnett, Olivia Rayne ("Olive") (daughter)
Garnett, Olivia Narney Singleton ("Narney") (Mrs. Richard), 44–45, 49, 51–53, 61, 65, 66–67, 70, 75–77, 81, 83, 91, 94, 96, 106, 116, 121, 126, 129, 135, 136, 141, 143, 144, 147–48, 150, 152–53, 154, 156, 157, 167
Garnett, Olivia Rayne ("Olive") (daughter), 65, 75, 116, 121, 123, 125, 126, 130, 135–36, 151–53, 156, 158, 159, 160, 164, 165, 166, 167, 168, 189 n.10
Garnett, Peter (uncle), 2, 10, 27
Garnett, Rayne Wreaks (Mrs. Rev. Richard) (mother), 4, 7, 10–11, 14, 15, 19, 27, 38, 54
Garnett, Rev. Richard (father), 2–12, 27, 41, 52, 53, 58, 156, 172 n.10, 181 n.2, 182 n.27, 184 n.21
Garnett, Richard (1835–1906): addresses by, 89, 94, 99, 104–105, 113, 120, 122–23, 125, 134, 143, 149, 156, 160; adventure on cliffs, 38–39, on beach, 176 n.9; and American Civil War, 25, 44, 49–50: appearance, 72–73; applies for another position, 41–42, 91; and astrology, 43–44, 52, 91, 98, 133, 146, 156–58, 162, 163, 165; born, 4; and cats, 45, 75–76, 158, 182 n.27; and censorship, 66, 123–25; courage, 38–39, 77; death, 164; duties at British Museum, 13, 15, 20–21, 23, 24–25, 27, 75, 80–83, 91–92, 95– 96, 115–16, 119, 124–25, 137; early years, 8–12; engagement, 44; and epigrams, 57–58, 157–60; failing health, 137, 141, 158, 160, 163, 164; gives literary help, 14, 32–33, 36– 38, 41, 46, 48, 57, 60, 61, 65, 67–68, 73–75, 80, 82, 89, 90, 94,

99, 100, 117, 118, 130–31, 143, 148, 149, 163; honors: LL. D. 93; C. B. 128; 136, 140, 144; joins British Museum, 12, 13; literary criticism by, 16, 18, 21–22, 24, 25, 28, 40, 46, 51–54, 56, 66, 85, 99, 119, 132, 136; literary criticism of, 20, 22, 26, 27, 29, 43, 47–48, 52, 56, 57, 66, 85, 90, 98, 102, 110–13, 118, 133, 138, 139, 146, 150, 152, 157–58, 159, 163–64, 165, 166, 167, 169, 195 n.28; and literary ladies, 120–21, 164; marriage, 52; personality, 73–76, 80–82, 121, 122–23, 133–34, 167, 169–70; and poetry, 13, 15, 16, 26, 28–29, 32, 38, 40, 41, 43, 46, 48, 51, 57–58, 68, 99, 113, 123, 125, 135, 145, 147, 165, 170; and printing of British Museum catalogue, 83–84, 87–89, 91, 95, 99, 103, 113, 115, 145, 161, 162; and Private Case, 116; promoted, 24, 58, 79–82, 115; promotion denied, 54, 58; publishes books, 26–29, 43, 46–48, 57–58, 102, 107–11, 113, 117–18, 123, 133, 135, 137–38, 145–46, 147, 149–50, 152, 154, 156, 157–59, 169, 187 n.9; retires from British Museum, 141–45; retires from Reading Room, 95; schooling, 8–10; and the Shelleys, 29–30, 32–34, 35–38, 45–48, 57, 58–60, 66–70, 71, 80, 85–86, 89–90, 93–94, 98–101, 115, 119, 135, 139, 143–44, 167, 175 n.10; and the sliding press, 104; social life, 14, 27–28, 38, 40–41, 51, 52, 57, 62, 64, 75, 77, 116, 181 n.8 ch.10; spokesman for British Museum, 87–89, 99; stories by, 61, 69, 86, 92, 102, 107–13, 135–36, 152, 169; tastes, 9, 13–14, 16–17, 19, 52, 62, 73, 121, 132, 168; theory of art, 16–17; and tobacco parliaments, 40, 181 n.8; translations by, 15, 20, 21, 28, 38, 41, 43, 46, 58, 113–14, 135, 145, 146, 157; writes for periodicals, 18–19, 21–22, 24, 25, 28, 36–38, 51–53, 56, 58, 69, 85, 91, 99, 112, 113, 127, 136, 137, 145, 146, 148, 160

Garnett, Richard Copley (son), 85, 164
Garnett, Robert Singleton (son), 54, 56, 75, 92, 93, 126, 130, 133, 135, 136, 153, 162, 164, 166, 167–68

Garnett, Sarah. *See* Horsfall, Sarah Garnett
Garnett, Thomas (of Low Moor) (uncle), 2, 10, 27
Garnett, Tom (of Low Moor) (James's son), 2, 164
Garnett, William (of Otley) (grandfather), 2, 52
Garnett, William (of Low Moor) (cousin), 2, 49–50, 72, 161, 164
Garnett, William John (brother), 4, 8–25, 44, 49, 53, 62–63, 77, 92–93, 97, 114, 123, 131, 151, 165, 172–73 n.3
Gaskell, Elizabeth Cleghorn, 51
George III (King of England), 190 n.14
Germ, 16, 29, 168
Gibson, Thomas Milner, 23
Gisborne, Maria, 68
Godwin, Mary Wollstonecraft (1759–1797), 33, 70, 175 n.9
Godwin, Mary Wollstonecraft (1797–1851). *See* Shelley, Mary Wollstonecraft Godwin (wife of Percy Bysshe)
Godwin, Mrs. Clairmont, 66, 175 n.9
Godwin, William, 30, 52–53, 66, 68, 69, 70, 175 n.9
Goethe, J. W. von, 13, 15, 19–20, 28, 43, 157, 173 n.2
Goethe Society, 106, 164
Gosse, Sir Edmund, 73, 92, 101–102, 110, 129, 131, 138, 146, 150, 157
Graves, R. E., 119, 164
Greek Anthology, 57, 145, 146, 191 n.19
Greenwood, Frederick, 164
Greenwood, Thomas, 148
Guiney, Imogen, 188 n.5

Hall, Guy, 93, 114, 121, 150, 151, 153, 164
Hall, May Garnett. *See* Garnett, May (later Hall) (daughter)
Hamerton, Philip, 51
Hampstead Annual, 146, 160, 167
Hardy, Emma Gifford (Mrs. Thomas), 129–31, 147–48, 189 n.10
Hardy, Thomas, 107, 129–31, 147–48, 157, 159–60, 192 n.6
Harper & Brothers, 148
Harper's New Monthly Magazine, 129, 132
Harraden, Beatrice, 120, 169, 187 n.19

Harte, Bret, 146
Harvard College, 90, 126, 136, 195 n.25
Harwood, Philip, 80
Hawthorne, Julian (son of Nathaniel), 64, 180 n.1
Hawthorne, Nathaniel, 112, 180 n.1, 186 n.14
Heathcote, Margaret. *See* Garnett, Margaret Heathcote
Heathcote, Rev. Godfrey, 3
Heathcote, Mrs., 22
Heine, Heinrich, 15, 43, 73, 138
Heinemann, William, 138, 147, 150
Henry VIII (King of England), 150
Henry Irving *Shakespeare*. See *Shakespeare*, Henry Irving
Herder, J. G. von, 22
Heredia, Ricardo, Comte de Benahavis, 119
Hodder & Stoughton, 154
Hodgson's auction house, 144
Hoffmann, E. T., 9
Hofland, Barbara, 8
Hogg, Jane Williams (Mrs. T. J.), 46, 53, 138, 143, 177 n.6
Hogg, Prudentia (Mrs. Lonsdale) (daughter of T. J. and Jane), 148
Hogg, Thomas Jefferson, 29–31, 36, 53, 65, 98, 126, 138, 139, 143, 148, 149, 177 n.6
Hölderlin, Friedrich, 43
Homer, 46, 88, 113, 118, 123
Horsfall, Alexandrine Mendelssohn (Mrs. John), 42, 51, 52
Horsfall, Anne. *See* Moxon, Anne Horsfall (Mrs. William)
Horsfall, Emmeline (later Mrs. Hudlestone) (daughter of Thomas), 10, 81
Horsfall, John (of Berlin), 42, 52
Horsfall, Sarah Garnett (Mrs. Timothy) (great–aunt), 1, 4, 45
Horsfall, Sophie (later Mrs. Gethin) (daughter of Thomas), 10
Horsfall, Thomas (son of Timothy), 4
Horsfall, Timothy, 1, 2, 4, 45
Horsfall, William (son of Timothy), 1, 2
Hotten, John Camden, 66
Housman, Laurence, 142
Hudson, William Henry, 165
Hueffer, Catherine Brown (Mrs. Francis), 62, 126

Hueffer, Elsie Martindale (Mrs. Ford), 126
Hueffer, Ford Madox. *See* Ford, Ford Madox
Hueffer, Dr. Francis, 62, 64, 117, 179 n.23
Hueffer, Juliet (daughter of Francis), 117
Hueffer, Oliver (son of Francis), 117
Hughes, Thomas ("Tom Brown"), 38, 51, 176 n.8
Hunt, Holman, 14, 38, 40
Hunt, Leigh, 18, 19, 31, 66, 174–75 n.7 ch.4
Huntington, Henry E., 195 n.25
Hutchinson, Thomas, 48, 158
Huth, Alfred Henry, 143
Hutton, Richard Holt, 33, 48
Huxley, Thomas Henry, 40

Illustrated London News, 22, 52, 58, 65, 129
Institut Internationale de Bibliographie, 120
International conference of librarians. *See* Conference of librarians
Irving, Sir Henry, 115, 137, see also *Shakespeare*, Henry Irving

Jackson, Gen. Thomas Jonathan ("Stonewall"), 49, 177 n.13
James I (King of England), 113
James, Henry, 90, 146
Janion, Mrs. Richard Garnett, 164
Jeaffreson, John Cordy, 93, 98–99, 100
Jenner, Rev. Henry, 104
Jerrold, Walter, 164
Johnson, Annabella (daughter of John William), 184 n.21
Johnson, John William (son of Martha), 184 n.21
Johnson, Martha Garnett (sister of Rev. Richard), 184 n.21
Johnson, Dr. Samuel, 4, 16, 160, 173 n.3
Jones, John Winter, 21, 27, 54, 55, 58, 78, 81, 83, 84, 86

Kay, J. Illingworth, 123, 135
Keats, John, 13, 53, 61, 158, 162, 186 n.14
Keen, Henry, 113
Kelmscott Press, 127
Kemble, John Mitchell, 4
Kingsley, Charles, 15, 40, 176 n.8

Lamartine, Alphonse de, 21
Lane, John, 112–13, 123, 139, 147, 152, 157, 169
Lang, Andrew, 146
Latham, Robert Gordon, 8, 27
Lawrence, D. H., 146
Lawrence, T. E., 113
Ledru-Rollin, A. A., 59
Lee, Sir Sidney, 143, 157, 164
Leighton, Frederick, baron, 143
Lewis, Matthew Gregory ("Monk"), 32
Liberal Association, 119
Library, 89, 137, 141, 146
Library Association of the United Kingdom, 83, 89, 94, 104, 120, 122, 125, 138, 144–45, 148, 164
Library Association Record, 144–45
Library Journal, 87, 100
Library of Congress, 145, 195 n.25
Library Series, 137–38
Lichfield, Bishop of (John Lonsdale), 6
Lichfield, Dean of (Dr. Woodhouse), 3
Literary Gazette, 21, 22, 24, 26, 28
Locker, Frederick (later Locker-Lampson), 58, 80
Lockhart, John Gibson, 4, 6
London, Bishop of (C. J. Blomfield), 3, 4, 11; (Mandell Creighton), 141, 143
Longmans, Green & Co., 138
Lubbock, Sir John, 141, 191 n.2
Lucas, E. V., 111
Lucy, Sir Thomas, and Lady, 157–58
Lytton, E. R. Bulwer, 1st earl of ("Owen Meredith"), 29, 111, 186 n.11

MacAlister, Sir J. Y. W., 141
McCaul, Rev. Joseph B., and Mrs., 19, 44
Macmillan, Alexander, 36, 38, 40, 56
Macmillan Company, 40, 49, 57
Macmillan's Magazine, 36–38, 40, 41, 45, 48, 53, 66
Madden, Sir Frederic, 4, 5, 6, 87
Maeterlinck, Count Maurice, 146
Magazine of Art, 148
Major, R. H., 55
Manchester Examiner, 25
Manchester Guardian, 2, 13, 18–19, 21, 23, 25, 40, 106
Marcus, Rev. C. M., 9, 15, 27
Marshall, Florence A. (Mrs. Julian), 93, 187 n.9

Marston, Eleanor Potts (Mrs. Westland), 40, 45, 52, 54, 58, 62, 180 n.1, 183 n.33
Marston, John Westland, 40, 44–45, 52, 54, 58, 62, 115, 176 n.12, 183 n.33
Martin, Victoria Woodhull, 124–25
Martindale, Elsie. *See* Hueffer, Elsie Martindale
Martindale, William (father of Elsie), 126
Martineau, James, 173 n.2
Martineau, Russell (son of James), 52, 173 n.2
Marx, Karl, 56, 59
Marzials, Sir Frank, 102, 167
Marzials, Théophile (brother of Frank), 102
Massachusetts Historical Society, 136
Masson, David, 28, 36–38, 51, 52, 53, 80, 93, 103, 128
Masson, Emily Orme (Mrs. David), 28, 52, 176 n.7
Mathews, Charles Elkin, 123, 149–50, 154, 157, 158, 160, 163, 166, 194 n.2
Matthews, G. M., 90
Maurice, Frederick Denison, 38, 40, 176 n.8
Mayle, Sydney, 154, 159
Mazzini, Giuseppe, 59
Mediceo-Laurenziana library. *See* Biblioteca Mediceo-Laurenziana
Mendelssohn, Alexandrine. *See* Horsfall, Alexandrine Mendelssohn
Mendelssohn, Felix (grandson of Moses), 42
Mendelssohn, Moses, 51
Menken, E., 168
Meredith, George, 159
Meredith, Owen. *See* Lytton, E. R. Bulwer, 1st earl of
Michelangelo, 41
Mickiewicz, Adam, 21, 26, 28
Miles, Alfred H., 117
Millais, Sir John Everett, 9, 14, 16, 28
Miller, Arthur William Kaye, 103, 115, 164
Milnes, Richard Monckton, 1st baron Houghton, 16
Milton, John, 13, 17, 102–103, 150
Mitchell, Donald Grant, 145, 192 n.2
Moir, Mr. and Mrs., 153
Monach, Mr., 14, 22, 52
Monach, Mrs., 14, 52

Money–Coutts, Francis Burdett,
  5th baron Latymer, 139, 190 n.14
Monkhouse, William Cosmo, 102
Morison, Alfred, 93
Morley, John, 85, 141
Morris, William, 62, 101, 127
Mosher, Thomas Bird, 166
Moxon, Anne Horsfall (Mrs. William), 45
Moxon, Edward (publisher), 24, 29–30, 32, 45
Moxon, William (brother of Edward), 45
Moxon firm, 24, 32, 45–46, 57, 60, 90, 142
Mudie, Charles Edward, 40, 76
Mulock, Dinah Maria (later Craik), 40
Murray, John, 143
Musset, Alfred de, 98

Nation, 103, 128, 155, 168
National Portrait Gallery, 155, 162
National Review, 19, 99, 173 n.2, 184 n.9
Neale, Ethel (sister of Violet), 154
Neale, Melville (father of Violet), 193 n.8
Neale, Violet Eveleen, 154–61, 162–67, 193 n.8, 194 n.7, 195 n.25
Nettleship, J. T., 62
New Quarterly Magazine, 87
New Shakespeare Society, 113, 156
Newcastle–under–Lyme, Henry Pelham Fiennes Pelham Clinton, 5th duke of, 41, 176 n.13
Newnham College, Cambridge, 106, 136
Newton, Sir Charles Thomas, 84
Nicholson, E. W. B., 84, 91, 139, 157
Nicoll, Sir William Robertson ("Claudius Clear"), 72, 74, 154, 167
Nineteenth Century, 93
Noble, Rev. John Padmore, 9, 15, 16, 19, 21, 51, 54, 76, 160, 172 n.14
Norton, Charles Eliot, 128, 135

Ollier, Charles, 31
Ollier, Edmund (son of Charles), 31–32, 59, 174 n.11, 14
Orme, Charles, 38, 40, 52, 176 n.7
Orme, Eliza Andrews (Mrs. Charles), 28, 38, 40, 52, 176 n.7
Osgood, McIlvaine & Co., 129, 130
Outlook, 152
Oxford University, 91–92, 119, 139, 158

Pageant, 135
Palgrave, Francis Turner, 40, 142
Palmerston, Henry John Temple, 3rd viscount, 20, 23
Palmerston, Lady, 20
Panizzi, Sir Anthony, 6, 7, 10–12, 20– 21, 23, 41, 54–55, 58, 78, 79, 83, 84, 87–88, 96, 119, 133, 161
Parker, John, 6, 10
Patmore, Coventry, 16, 24, 26, 28, 40, 49, 51, 53, 64, 76, 80, 93, 102, 117, 136, 166, 173 n.6, 180 n.2
Patmore, Emily Andrews (Mrs. Coventry), 16, 28, 49
Patmore, Marianne Byles (Mrs. Coventry), 53, 64
Patmore, Milnes (son of Coventry and Emily), 93
Patten, Col. Wilson, 41
Paul, Charles Kegan, 66–67, 69, 87, 90, 91, 93, 98, 101
Payne, J. Bertrand, 57
Peacock, Thomas Love, 30, 35–38, 45–48, 54, 60, 98, 99, 117–18, 150, 169, 183 n.12, 184 n.9 c.13
Pearson, Emily Wreaks, 12, 14
Penny Magazine, 9
Petrarch, 135, 136
Philological Society, 8, 27
Poles, Stefan, 78–79
Pollard, Alfred W., 111, 115, 134, 141–42, 182 n.27
Pollard, Graham, 185 n.10, 11
Pollock, Sir Charles Edward (son of Sir Jonathan), 124, 188 n.8, 10
Pollock, Frederick (son of Sir Jonathan), 9, 172 n.14
Pollock, Sir Frederick (nephew of Sir Charles), 125, 188 n.10
Pollock, Sir Jonathan Frederick (baron of Exchequer), 172 n.14, 188 n.8
Pollock, Julius (son of Sir Jonathan), 9, 15, 172 n.14, 188 n.10
Poole, John, 64, 180 n.1
Pope, Alexander, 186 n.14
Pope, Gen. John, 49, 177 n.13
Portfolio, 133, 135
Potts, Eleanor. *See* Marston, Eleanor Potts
Potts, Elizabeth Narney (Mrs. J. D.), 44
Potts, James David (grandfather of Narney Garnett), 44

Potts, Louisa. *See* Bourke, Louisa Potts
Potts, Olivia. *See* Singleton, Olivia Potts
Prance, Claude A., 186 n.17
Pre-Raphaelite Brotherhood, 14, 16, 29, 168, 189 n.14
Proctor, Robert G. C., 141–42, 191 n.7
Protestant Guardian, 3
Prothero, Rowland E., baron Ernle, 143, 149
Pynson, Richard, 142

Quarterly Review, 4–7, 93
Queensberry, John Sholto Douglas, 8th marquis of, 131

Ralston, William Ralston Shedden, 55, 58, 78–79
Reader, 51–52
Revue Britannique, 69
Richardson, Charles, 4
Robertson, Eric S., 102
Rogers, Neville, 48
Roscoe, Martha. *See* Garnett, Martha Roscoe
Roscoe, Richard (father of Martha), 133
Roscoe, William (great-grandfather of Martha), 133
Rosebery, Archibald Primrose, 5th earl of, 128, 142
Rossetti, Arthur (son of William), 54
Rossetti, Christina (sister of William), 52, 76
Rossetti, Dante Gabriel (brother of William), 14, 28, 29, 38, 52, 58, 62
Rossetti, Mrs. Gabriele (mother of William, Christina, Dante Gabriel, and Maria), 52, 100
Rossetti, Helen (later Angeli) (daughter of William), 168, 187 n.6
Rossetti, Lucy Madox Brown (Mrs. William), 51, 62, 70, 116–17, 136, 178 n.1
Rossetti, Maria (sister of William), 52
Rossetti, Mary (daughter of William), 168, 187 n.6
Rossetti, William Michael, 29, 38, 51, 52, 54, 57–62, 66–67, 68, 70, 76, 86, 98–99, 100, 103, 115, 117, 138, 154, 162, 164, 167–68
Roy, Eugene Armand, 54
Royal Colonial Institute, 151, 164

Royal Society of Literature, 156
Rumble, Elizabeth, 68
Ruskin, John, 17
Rye, William Brenchley, 24, 58, 79–80

St. James's Gazette, 102
Sambourne, Linley, 9, 172 n.14
Sand, George, 15
Sappho, 160
Saturday Review, 54, 56, 57, 80, 136, 169
Savage, Elizabeth Mary Anne, 121
Savoy, 132, 135
Scarlett, Bessie Florence Gibson ("Florence") (Mrs. Leopold), 46, 90, 98, 144, 177 n.5
Scarlett, Capt. Leopold (father of Robert and Shelley), 90, 177 n.5
Scarlett, Robert. *See* Abinger, 6th baron
Scarlett, Shelley. *See* Abinger, 5th baron
Scots Observer, 112, 186 n.15, 187 n.9
Scott, Walter (publisher), 102
Scottish Leader, 110
Shakespeare, Ann (Mrs. William), 157–58
Shakespeare, William, 73, 88, 100, 132, 156–58, 168, 186 n.14
Shakespeare, Henry Irving, 132, 186 n.20
Sharp, Evelyn, 110
Sharp, William, 185 n.7
Shaw, John Hope, 180 n.24
Shelley, Sir Bysshe (grandfather of Percy Bysshe), 32
Shelley, Elizabeth (sister of Percy Bysshe), 33, 139
Shelley, Harriet Westbrook (wife of Percy Bysshe), 30–31, 36–37, 47, 59, 64, 85, 99, 126, 154, 175 n.2
Shelley, Jane, Lady (daughter-in-law of Percy Bysshe), 29–36, 39, 42, 45–48, 52–54, 57–60, 66–71, 85–86, 90, 93–94, 98–100, 119, 126, 135, 139, 143–44, 148, 167, 174 n.5 ch. 4, 174–75 n.7 ch. 4, 175 n.10, 11, 16; 183 n.12
Shelley, Sir John (brother of Percy Bysshe), 149
Shelley, Mary Wollstonecraft Godwin (wife of Percy Bysshe), 29–33, 36, 46, 48, 53, 66–70, 85–86, 89, 90, 93, 97, 100, 117, 127, 137, 143, 155, 158, 175

Shelley, Mary Wollstonecraft (cont.)
  n.5 ch. 4, 175 n.9, 177 n.14, 183 n.12.
Shelley, Percy Bysshe, 13, 17, 29–33, 36–37, 39, 42, 45–47, 53, 57–59, 64–71, 89–91, 93–94, 97–102, 104–105, 107, 115, 119, 126–27, 133, 137–40, 143, 147–50, 154–55, 158–59, 173 n.2, 174 n.6 ch. 4, 177 n.14 ch. 5, 178 n.4, 185 n.16, 190 n.14; works: *Adonais*, 115; *Defence of Poetry*, 17; *Epipsychidion*, 102; *Essay on Christianity*, 29; "Lines Written in the Bay of Lerici," 45, 90; *Necessity of Atheism*, 30, 37; *Original Poetry by Victor and Cazire*, 32, 37, 139; *Posthumous Poems*, 48; "Prologue to Hellas," 48, 100; *Queen Mab*, 66, 100; *Refutation of Deism*, 33; *Relics of Shelley*, 24, 46–48, 60, 99, 100, 118, 119; *St. Irvine, or the Rosicrucian*, 37; "To Constantia, Singing," 138; *Zastrozzi*, 107
Shelley, Sir Percy Florence (son of Percy Bysshe), 29–36, 39, 42, 45–48, 54, 57, 58, 60, 66–71, 80, 86, 90, 93, 98–101, 115
Shelley, Sir Timothy (father of Percy Bysshe), 30, 37, 98, 174 n.5 ch. 4
Shelley legend, 31
Shelley Memorials, 29, 31–33, 35, 61, 65, 93
Shelley notebooks, 33, 48, 119, 167–68, 195 n.25
Shelley Society, 100, 104
Shepherd, Richard Herne, 66
Shorter, Clement, 164
Silsbee, Edward Augustus, 89–90, 138–39, 195 n.25
Singleton, Major Edward James (brother of Narney Garnett), 44–45, 49, 51, 52, 77, 115, 153, 164
Singleton, Edward John (father of Narney Garnett), 44, 45
Singleton, Olivia Potts (mother of Narney Garnett), 44–45, 49, 51, 52, 77, 83, 85, 164
Sitwell, Dame Edith (daughter of Sir George), 173 n.4
Sitwell, Florence (sister of Sir George), 173 n.4
Sitwell, Sir George Reresby, 15, 173 n.4
Sitwell, Sir Osbert (son of Sir George), 173 n.4
Sitwell, Sir Sacheverell (son of Sir George), 173 n.4
Sketch, 142
Smithers, Leonard, 132
Società Bibliografica Italiana, 140
Society of Arts, 143
Sotheby and Company, 167–68
Southey, Robert, 3, 94
Speaker, 152
Speaker of the House of Commons (William Gully), 141
Spectator, 32, 33, 43, 47–48
Spencer, Herbert, 186 n.14
Spoor, John A., 195 n.25
Standard (London), 146
Star Lore, 163
Stephen, Sir Leslie, 51, 97, 128, 143
Stevens, Henry, of Vermont, 122
Stevenson, Mrs. Robert Louis, 175 n.10
Stockdale, John, 32, 37, 139, 180 n.5
Stockdale, John Joseph (son of John), 32, 37, 180 n.5
Stockdale's Budget, 32–33, 37, 66
Strang, William, 141–42
Stratemeyer, Edward L., 160
Sutro, Alfred, 131, 147
Swift, Jonathan, 38
Swinburne, Algernon Charles, 67, 77, 99, 159, 183 n.33
Syme, David, 97, 123, 184 n.21
Symons, Arthur, 48, 72, 75, 112, 132, 135, 136, 146, 159, 163, 169, 194 n.2

Tasso, Torquato, 9
Tauchnitz, Bernhard, 59, 65
Taylor, Sir Henry (friend of the Shelleys), 93
Taylor, John (of the British Museum), 125
Taylor, John Edward (of the *Manchester Guardian*), 19, 21, 174 n.3
Tedder, Henry R., 122
Temple Bar, 41, 61
Tennant, Cecil (son of Robert), 63, 151
Tennant, Frederick (son of Robert), 63
Tennant, Gilbert (son of Robert), 63
Tennant, Harriette Garnett (Mrs. Robert) (cousin), 62–63
Tennant, Robert, 62–63, 92, 179 n.24
Tennyson, Alfred, Lord, 13, 16, 23–24, 28, 40, 58, 142, 154

Tennyson sisters, 28
Terry, Ellen, 137
Thackeray, Anne (daughter of William), 64, 180 n.1
Thackeray, William Makepeace, 162
Thompson, Sir Edward Maunde, 107, 116, 124–25, 129, 132, 141–42, 164
Thurman, William R., Jr., 174 n.6 ch. 4, 190 n.13, 193 n.13
Tieck, Ludwig, 9
Times (London), 8, 26, 41, 60, 136, 145, 146, 156
Times Literary Supplement, 112
Titian, 52, 155
Tolstoy, Count Lev Nikolaevich, 125
Tomson, Mrs. Arthur ("Graham R. Tomson"), 114
Touchet, John, 31
Toussaint l'Ouverture, Pierre, 25
Travers, Major and Mrs., 149
Travers, Rosalind (later Hyndman), 149, 165, 192 n.10
Trelawny, Edward John, 30, 33, 57, 65, 66–67, 85–86, 97, 119, 143, 154, 183 n.12
"Trent, A. G." (Richard Garnett's pseudonym), 91, 163
Twain, Mark, 126, 188 n.13

Universal Review, 113, 186 n.19–21
University Magazine (formerly *Dublin University Magazine*), 86, 91, 113
Unwin, Thomas Fisher, 106–107, 111, 113, 114, 138, 140, 143, 146, 154
Urban Club, 164

Vallée, Léon, 145, 191–92 n.21
Van Doren, Carl, 118
Vaughan Williams, Ralph, 110
Victoria (Queen of England), 10, 86, 128, 145, 147
Virgil, 13, 79
Vizetelly, Henry, 130

Wakefield, Edward Gibbon, 138, 144
Wales, Albert Edward, Prince of (later King Edward VII), 51, 62, 132, 141

Wales, Alexandra, Princess of (later Queen Alexandra), 51
Watts, C. A., & Co., 113
Watts, Thomas, 24, 27, 54, 58
Webster, Noah, 4
Wedgwood, Hensleigh, 4, 27
Weekes, Henry, 33
Welby, Thomas Earle, 169
Westminster Review, 57, 59
Whitefriars Club, 129, 147
Whiteing, Richard, 164
Whitman, Walt, 73, 168
Whittingham, Charles, 28
Wilberforce, Rev. Wilfrid J., 116
Wilde, Oscar, 131, 132, 189 n.14
Williams, Edward Ellerker, 46, 68, 143, 149, 154, 177 n.6, 190 n.13
Williams, Jane. *See* Hogg, Jane Williams
Williams, John Wheeler (grandson of Edward Ellerker Williams), 68, 149–50, 190 n.13
Williams & Norgate, 27, 56
Wilson, William Robert, 164
Winchester, Bishop of, 141
Winsor, Justin, 136
Wise, Thomas James, 100–101, 139–40, 167–68, 184 n.10, 190 n.17
Wollstonecraft, Mary. *See* Godwin, Mary Wollstonecraft
Woodberry, George Edward, 48, 90
Woodhouse, Rev. Dr. *See* Lichfield, Dean of (Dr. Woodhouse)
Woodhull, Victoria. *See* Martin, Victoria Woodhull
Worde, Wynkyn de, 142
Wreaks, Jane Rayne. *See* Garnett, Rayne Wreaks
Wreaks, John (father of Rayne), 4
Wreaks family, 164
Wrenn, John Henry, 140, 190 n.17
Wycliffe, John, 100

Yeats, William Butler, 133, 159
Yellow Book, 125–26, 132, 136

Zaehnsdorf, Joseph William, 142, 143
Zola, Emile, 130, 146, 168

Barbara McCrimmon has enjoyed a varied career in librarianship, including posts as assistant librarian of the Illinois Natural History Survey, librarian of the American Meteorological Society in Boston, and acting managing editor of the *Journal of Library History*. She is the author of *Power, Politics, and Print: The Publication of the British Museum Catalog, 1881-1890* (Shoe String Press and Clive Bingley, 1981).